BATTLES
OF THE MEDIEVAL WORLD
1000 ~ 1500

BATTLES
OF THE MEDIEVAL WORLD
1000 ~ 1500

FROM HASTINGS TO CONSTANTINOPLE

KELLY DEVRIES MARTIN DOUGHERTY IAIN DICKIE PHYLLIS G. JESTICE CHRISTER JORGENSEN

amber
BOOKS

First published in 2006 by Amber Books Ltd
Bradley's Close
74–77 White Lion Street
London N1 9PF
United Kingdom
www.amberbooks.co.uk

ISBN 1-904687-64-4

Produced by
Amber Books Ltd
Bradley's Close
74–77 White Lion Street
London N1 9PF
United Kingdom
www.amberbooks.co.uk

Project Editor: Michael Spilling
Design: Jerry Williams
Illustrations: JB Illustrations
Picture Reseach: Terry Forshaw

All map and linework illustrations © Amber Books Ltd.

Printed in United Arab Emirates

CONTENTS

INTRODUCTION

FROM THE BEGINNING OF THE FALL OF ROME UNTIL THE END OF THE FIFTEENTH CENTURY, WARFARE WAS A DOMINANT FEATURE OF MEDIEVAL LIFE. THE CROSSING OF THE VISIGOTHS INTO THE ROMAN EMPIRE IN 376 AD AND THEIR DEFEAT OF ROMAN TROOPS AT THE BATTLE OF ADRIANOPLE IN AD 378 MARKED THE END OF BARBARIAN EXCLUSION FROM WESTERN EUROPE. THE VISIGOTHS WOULD BE FOLLOWED BY THE OSTROGOTHS, VANDALS, BURGUNDIANS, ALANS, ALEMANNI, FRANKS, ANGLES, SAXONS, AND EVENTUALLY THE HUNS, THE TRIBE THAT HAD FORCED THEIR PREDECESSORS WEST. THE WESTERN PORTION OF THE ROMAN EMPIRE DISAPPEARED, REPLACED BY NUMEROUS TRIBAL ENTITIES WHOSE BOUNDARIES CONSTANTLY FLUCTUATED.

And so, it has generally been written, began the Middle Ages. However, historical understanding of an era, of few original sources has of course changed over the years. Certainly, the Visigothic invasions played their role in the end of the Roman Empire, and the defeat and death of Valens at Adrianople effectively divided the empire into two halves. The fall of Rome was not accomplished by a single event; actually, it took quite a long time to complete. Barbarian armies also seem not to have differed from their Roman counterparts by being less strictly disciplined, less bureaucratically organized, and less well armed and armoured, as was once also believed. Most instead learned their skills from serving with Roman armies, sometimes against other barbarians and sometimes against other Romans.

They also initially seem to have used Roman arms and armour, although before too long they had replaced the Roman bronze scale armour with iron mail and the Roman short sword and javelin with a longer sword for slashing, spear for thrusting, and axe for swinging or throwing.

They also had several of their own bellicose characteristics, holding an almost Homeric sense of heroism and revering martial skills, as reflected in their tales and their names, both male and female. Warriors were also recognized as the élite of society. They were placed at the top of the *wergeld* system of compensation and were buried with their arms and booty. Barbarian tribal chieftains and kings were also their military leaders.

THE FRANKS

By the sixth and seventh centuries AD, tribal organization and secure occupation of lands

The Byzantine foulkon, *an infantry formation formed of spearmen with interlocking shields, was designed to hold enemy cavalry at bay. As the thwarted enemy withdrew, the Byzantine cavalry charged through gaps in the infantry line to scatter the retreating horsemen.*

led to a strengthening of barbarian society and government in Western Europe. The most secure of these were the Franks. The Franks had crossed over the Rhine into northern Gaul peacefully to colonize Roman towns and serve in Roman armies even before most of these latter troops had been withdrawn to fight in more southern theatres of war. In their absence, the Franks began to assume positions of military and governmental leadership.

By 491, Clovis had united the various Frankish tribes, and by 507 he had defeated the Alemanni and the Visigoths and established the first Merovingian kingdom of the Franks covering most of the former Roman provinces of Gaul and Provence. Clovis was aided by the Frankish military and governmental organization, the disunity of other barbarian tribes, and their distance from the Eastern Roman (now Byzantine) Empire. As such, the Franks were able to develop and become stronger in a period when the rest of Europe was in flux. The Merovingian army was primarily an infantry force in which every free man was obligated to perform military service. They were armed with shield, spear and sword, and most were also outfitted in mail armour and helmet. However, their special weapon was a throwing axe known as the *francisca*. They seem also to have built earth-and-wood fortifications when unable to re-use Roman walls.

CHARLEMAGNE AND FEUDALISM

With the usurpation of the Merovingian kingdom in the eighth century by Charles Martel (the Hammer) and its replacement with the Carolingian kingdom of his son Pepin III (the Short) and Pepin's son, Charlemagne, military changes were enacted. Carolingian security necessitated the defence of the Frankish borders, especially against the Muslims of Spain – highlighted by the Hammer's victory at the Battle of Poitiers (sometimes called the Battle of Tours) in 732. A special system of military obligation, formerly termed 'feudalism' or 'feudo-vassalism' by medieval sociologists and historians, was instituted, possibly as early as the reign of Charles Martel. There is little doubt that this system was meant to provide a better-trained, more professional army. It was based strictly on the ownership of lands and the taking of profits from these lands.

Benefices in the form of lands were given to Carolingian soldiers and they, in turn, promised full-time military service and the provision of other soldiers to the king. These benefices, or fiefs, supported them in a lifestyle that paid for the expensive military equipment needed for combat, and enabled them to train for warfare and to respond with a retinue when called by the king for military service.

Standardization in equipment and weaponry also began to take place prominently and effectively, especially under Charlemagne who ordered that all benefice and office holders, titled 'nobles', in the Carolingian realm possess coats of mail armour, known to the Carolingians as *byrnies*, and shields as well as offensive weaponry. At about the same time, stirrups began to be added to the saddles of

horsemen, and with other changes to the technology – a high-pommel-and-cantle saddle, better-bred horses and stronger lances (and the eventual couching of these lances under the arm to carry the impetus of the horse with the attack) – led to the establishment of a cavalry-based army, horsemen that became the archetypal 'knights in shining armour'.

Charlemagne's military force of cavalry, which must be defined as a professional standing army, was mustered for action in nearly every year of his reign. By all evidence, his soldiers were well trained, well armed and armoured, highly organized, and very loyal to him. There is some dispute as to exactly how large this force was, but there is no dispute as to how successful it was. Once in battle the Carolingian army was almost invulnerable. Their overwhelming power was wisely utilized by a tactical system of advances which allowed the heavy cavalry troops to be used to the full extent of their capability, even against lighter, swifter armies. Sieges were also well planned and executed. At the sieges of Pavia in 773 and Barcelona in 802, Charlemagne's army was provided with heavy siege equipment and massive baggage trains for supplies. Under Charlemagne's leadership, Carolingian armies conquered the Avars, the Saxons, the Bretons and the Lombards, and they pushed the Muslims beyond the Pyrenees to Spain.

But Charlemagne also knew the value of a wise defence. He built several large fortifications along the borders of his kingdom, and he established an effective signalling system to call for reinforcements throughout the large empire. He also bribed certain enemy chieftains, most notably those of the Danes, to remain at peace with his empire. (The Danes themselves seem to have feared

The primary equipment of a Hun cavalry soldier was the bow, which he could fire effectively from his saddle at full gallop. Hun cavalry rode 'steppe ponies'. They were small horses, but were very strong and fast. Huns did not use stirrups, but this should not suggest an instability while fighting on horseback.

No army since the fall of Rome was as large, strong or successful as that put together by Charlemagne. Although his horse troops were never as numerous as his infantry, Charlemagne built his forces around a core of heavy cavalry, whose strategic and tactical mobility and power gave the Carolingians victory in nearly every military engagement they fought.

Pyrenees, while other Muslim forces began to attack Sicily and southern Italy. They were joined by new and more determined threats from the Vikings in the north and west and the Magyars in the east.

THE VIKINGS
Of these, the Vikings were the greatest threat. No historian has yet been able to offer a satisfactory reason for the sudden outburst of Viking raiders from Scandinavia in the late eighth century, although it has been suggested that the destruction of the Frisian fleet by Charlemagne at about the same time left no effective deterrents to their sea travel and may have been a factor in the launching of their invasions.

Still, this alone cannot be sufficient cause to explain the large number of voyages which were launched from Sweden, Norway, and Denmark between 789 and 1066 and extended along the coasts of continental Europe, England, Ireland, the

the Carolingians, as they constructed their own large and extensive fortification, the *Danewerk*, to wall off their kingdoms from that of Charlemagne.)

It was this successful army of Charlemagne's on which all later medieval armies would be based. But the empire which he built using it would not survive his grandsons. For although only one of Charlemagne's three sons, Louis the Pious, outlived his father, in 840 Louis' own sons, Lothar I, Louis the German, and Charles the Bald, followed the traditions of partible

inheritance. Their division of the empire would form the geographical basis of modern Germany, France, the Low Countries and Italy, but it also ushered in the eventual end of the Carolingian dynasty. Even if they had not practised partible inheritance, however, Charlemagne's grandsons and their descendants would have probably found it extremely difficult to put up an effective defence against all the raiders on all of the sides of the empire. Spanish Muslim armies continued to harass the borders of the empire across the

A cavalry formation favoured by the Carolingians consisted of several lines of horsemen that all charged their opponents at once. When a charge was stopped, the cavalry would break off, wheel towards their flanks and regroup behind other cavalry lines to be replaced by the next charging line. In this way an attritional effect could be achieved against a stationary enemy.

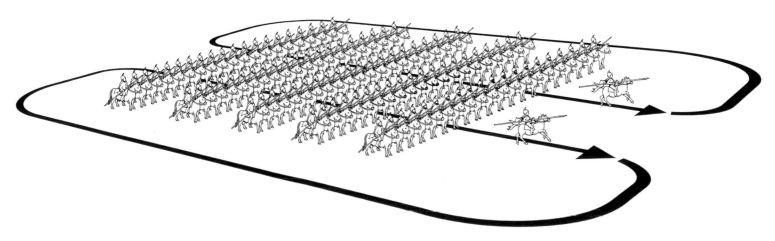

Baltic region, east to Russia, south to Byzantium, Italy and North Africa, and west to the Faroe and Shetland Islands, Iceland, Greenland and North America.

The first recorded attack of the Vikings was made in 789 on the southeastern coast of England, and in 793 they struck at Lindisfarne Abbey. For the next two and a half centuries, their dragon-prowed ships carried them onto the English, Irish, and northern European shores, especially to feast on the easy monastic and small urban pickings which were spread throughout the countryside. Early on, Ireland, Scotland, and northern England provided the richest targets; attacking lands filled with monasteries but without many fortifications or militias meant there was little opposition to the violent raids of the Vikings.

But by around 834, the ancient Irish civilization had been virtually destroyed and the countryside of Scotland, northern England and Ireland had been almost completely despoiled of its ecclesiastical targets. The Vikings were forced to turn elsewhere for their booty, towards the Continent. Their targets, too, had become larger. By 840, the Vikings had raided the towns of Noirmoutier, Rhé, Duurstede (sacked no fewer than four times), Utrecht and Antwerp in the Low Countries. In 843, they wintered for the first time in Gaul, capturing Nantes, ravaging the

valleys of the Loire and Garonne, and even, on their way home to Scandinavia, threatening the Muslim cities of Lisbon and Cadiz. Furthermore, in 845, a Viking force of more than 120 ships sailed up the Seine and sacked Paris. There was little to stop these raids. With no unified defence against them, no effective army, and the lack of good military leadership provided by later Carolingian kings, the Vikings were left to ravage the European countryside.

The many rivers on the Continent also provided them with conduits to a large number of inland sites, and in the following 30 years, the Vikings raided up the Rhine, Meuse, Scheldt, Somme, Seine, Marne, Loire, Charente, Dordogne, Lot and Garonne Rivers. No town, village or monastery close to a waterway was immune from attack. Nor were any coastal European

sites seemingly too far from Scandinavia to warrant their attention, for as the century progressed the Vikings became bolder. One expedition, from 859–62, even sailed through the Strait of Gibraltar and raided Nekur in Morocco, the Murcian coast of Spain, the Balearic Islands and Roussillon. After wintering on the Rhone delta, the expedition raided upstream to Valence, sacked Pisa and then Luna – which the Vikings apparently thought was Rome – before sailing back past Gibraltar and north to their base in Brittany. Only in a few battles – Englefield and Ashdown in 871 and Edington in 878 against King Alfred the Great of England; and the Dyle in 891 against King Arnulf of the East Franks – were the Vikings faced by European armies, and in each engagement they were defeated.

THE NORMANS

After 911, Viking activity seems to have slowed. Colonization had been taking place for some time during the raids, and trading with these communities and others had become more of a practice than raiding, especially with the discovery of cheap Islamic silver which could be obtained and

A motte-and-bailey castle was an early form of castle built of earth and timber. The motte or mound was the strongest part, and was natural or constructed of earth. It was generally topped by a stockade and a wooden tower or keep. The bailey or courtyard was the lower enclosure used for storage and housing the lesser folk. The whole might be surrounded by a rampart, stockade and moat.

INTRODUCTION

Conditions on a Viking longboat were cramped and crowded. Nearly every man would operate an oar, and skilled pilots would take turns at the steering oar and conning the ship from the bows.

undertaken by a Norman adventurer, Robert Guiscard, and his brothers against Sicily and southern Italy. The second was carried out by Duke William, known at the time as 'the Bastard' because of his illegitimate birth and later as 'the Conqueror' for his invasion of England.

It was this second invasion that is the more famous, undoubtedly because William the Conqueror was able to fight a decisive battle against the English king, at Hastings, in 1066. There had of course been many battles fought earlier in the Middle Ages, and many had proven quite consequential to the history that had followed: for example, at Adrianople in 378, at Chalons in 451, at Poitiers in 732, at Edington in 878, and at the Dyle in 891. But sources for these battles are scarce and almost always one-sided. This is certainly not the case with the Battle of Hastings, or for many other battles that followed. What the Hastings sources describe is a battle of uncommon length, but one in which William's forces

taken back to Scandinavia for enormous profits. However, at the end of the tenth century, perhaps due to the drying-up of the Islamic silver market, Viking raids again started to take place, especially against England. From 991 on, a succession of Scandinavian leaders attacked England, and in 1014 one of them, Svein Forkbeard, conquered it and ruled for a short time as king, being succeeded by his son, Cnut. An English king, Edward the Confessor, regained the throne in 1042, but it was not until later invasions in 1066 and 1085 were turned back that the Viking threat to Europe finally ended.

In 911 the Carolingian King Charles the Simple gave the Viking chieftain Rollo the territory surrounding the lower Seine River as a means of keeping further Viking attacks from entering his kingdom through those lands. Within a relatively short time, these Vikings who settled in what had become known as Normandy adopted the French language and religion, and they began to intermarry with the local peasantry and nobility. Soon the dukes of Normandy, as

Rollo's descendants became known, were doing homage to the French king and fighting with him in his battles, obligated it seems by a similar code to that of the king's other nobles. But these new religious, linguistic and familial ties seem never to have removed their military instincts nor their desire for further conquests. All of this came to a head in the second half of the eleventh century when two successful Norman invasions took place. The first was

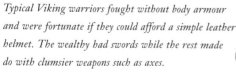

Typical Viking warriors fought without body armour and were fortunate if they could afford a simple leather helmet. The wealthy had swords while the rest made do with clumsier weapons such as axes.

prevailed, killing Harold, his brothers, and many of their soldiers. Although there would still be some limited resistance, with this victory William won England.

THE CRUSADES

Within 50 years of William's victory at Hastings a new struggle began, one that would characterize history for the rest of the Middle Ages: the Crusades. In the middle of the eleventh century a militarily powerful, united Muslim group, known as the Seljuk Turks, came south into the Middle East from an area that is today Afghanistan. In 1071, at the Battle of Manzikert, the Seljuk Turks defeated a large Byzantine army and advanced throughout Asia Minor until they stood on the very edge of the Bosporus. In response to this grave setback the Byzantine Emperor, Alexius I Comnenus, made an appeal to the Roman pope, Urban II, that he summon an army from the Western kingdoms to aid the Byzantines in regaining their lost territories. The First Crusade was launched.

By the beginning of 1097 the army of the First Crusade, probably numbering between 50,000 and 80,000, had reached Constantinople. The march across Asia Minor brought numerous difficulties. Although it began with a victory over the Turks outside the walls of Nicaea, it soon became apparent that the Crusaders had made a gross misjudgement regarding the distance of the march and their ability to live off the land. There was almost perpetual famine and lack of water. Many of the more prominent nobles gave up and returned home. But most kept on marching, and every time they encountered a Muslim force they defeated it, which brought them great confidence in their endeavour despite its hardships.

Finally, early in 1098 they reached the first large Muslim city, Antioch. Antioch was a strongly built walled city with a large citadel towering above it. But despite the Crusaders being weakened by starvation, they did not falter and, after gaining access to the city by bribery, and buoyed by religious visions and signs, they sallied out of the city and defeated a much larger and extremely surprised Muslim force. A year later, the Crusaders, by then possibly

numbering no more than 10,000–20,000, had reached their primary target, Jerusalem, which held out until 15 July 1099 when a major assault of the walls using siege towers and catapults finally enabled the Christians to capture it.

SALADIN

After the fall of Jerusalem the Crusaders began to extend their control over the various lands and cities that they had captured. Then in 1144 the Crusader city and kingdom of Edessa fell to a new Seljuk Turkish army, under the leadership of a young general named Nur ad-Din. Although Nur ad-Din would direct his army around the remaining Crusader kingdoms towards Egypt, the Crusaders had no means of knowing that this was his plan, and they immediately put out a call for a Second Crusade to travel to the Holy Land. But this turned out to be one of the worst campaigns in military history. Arguing

Charlemagne and his knights leaving Aix-la-Chapelle on pilgrimage to Santiago de Compostela. This piece dates from the twelfth century and so the details are contemporary to the artist.

against the plans of the resident Crusaders, on 24 June 1148 the leaders of the recently-arrived force in Jerusalem decided to advance on Damascus, a town whose leader opposed Nur ad-Din. Their attack failed and the Second Crusade was over.

Nur ad-Din began to extend his power in the region. Damascus, weakened by the Crusaders' attack, fell in 1154, and Egypt fell in 1168. Nur ad-Din died in 1174, but he was succeeded by an even greater general, Saladin. Saladin was a remarkable man. Fervent in *jihad* zeal, while at the same time patient and chivalrous, when he succeeded to Nur ad-Din's throne, he controlled all of the territory surrounding the Crusader kingdoms. His attack on them

INTRODUCTION

came shortly thereafter. Saladin then laid siege to the Crusader city of Tiberias. The Crusaders tried to relieve the city, but were surrounded by Saladin's force at the Battle of Hattin in July 1187, where they were defeated. Following this victory, Saladin moved against the now largely undefended city of Jerusalem, which he took on 2 October 1187.

THE END OF THE CRUSADES

The loss of Jerusalem came as a shock to all Christians in Europe, and immediately a Third Crusade was called. This Crusade attracted not only a large army, but also three kings: Frederick I Barbarossa of Germany, Philip II Augustus of France, and Richard I the Lionheart of England. Frederick left in 1189 via an overland route, but his force, decimated by disease, never reached the Holy Land; the aged Frederick himself died when he fell off his horse into the Saleph River in Asia Minor and drowned. The other two kings travelled by ship and arrived safely, but having arrived, they began to quarrel over their respective roles in the fighting.

Although they did succeed in retaking Acre and Jaffa in 1191, and Richard defeated Saladin's forces at the Battle of Arsuf on 7 September 1191, the Crusaders never could achieve the unified attack that was necessary to recapture Jerusalem. Finally, in October 1191, Philip returned to France and began attacking Richard's territory there. A year later, in October 1192, Richard also returned to Europe, but on his route home he was captured and held for ransom by Leopold, the Duke of Austria, whose banners he had insulted at the siege of Acre.

Knights clad in mail hack down unarmed Cathars during the Albigensian Crusade. This is a good illustration of the medieval riding style, despite the naive perspective. The leg is nearly straight to give stability for a downward cut.

The Third Crusade failed to accomplish almost everything it set out to do, although it included the best and brightest that the warrior class of Europe could provide. But Jerusalem could not be in Muslim hands, and before another decade had passed, a new pope, Innocent III, had called a Fourth Crusade. The Fourth Crusade was doomed from the start. Although again a large army assembled, it never seemed to matter what their goals were, for they were destined not even to reach the Holy Land. Trying to arrange passage by sea from the Venetians, they were first compelled by them to attack a Hungarian city, Zara, which despite being Christian threatened the Adriatic trading monopolies of Venice.

Then they proceeded to Constantinople where in both 1203 and 1204 they were compelled to besiege that city because it had recently signed a trading pact with the Genoese, Italian rivals to the Venetians. In the end, the Crusaders took the Byzantine capital by storm. The Latin Kingdom of Constantinople, which they established there, lasted until 1261 when an attack from the exiled Byzantine Emperor, Michael VIII Palaeologus, acting in concert with the Genoese, restored the capital city to the rest of the Byzantine Empire.

Descendants of the ancient cataphracti, heavy Byzantine cavalrymen of c.1100 had the defining characteristic that they, and their horses, were completely covered by armour. From contemporary artistic works it can be determined that these suits probably consisted of scale armour for the torso, a chain covering for the face, metal or hardened leather bands for lower arm and leg protection, a helmet and a small shield.

With the embarrassment of the Fourth Crusade, all remaining Crusading fervour seems to have left European warriors. The few thirteenth-century Crusades were almost all embarrassments to their participants. That is not to say, however,

that those who strove to fight in the Holy Land during that century were not earnest in their endeavours, such as the Crusaders who went with Andrew II, the King of Hungary, and Leopold VI, the Duke of Austria, in 1217–19, or with Emperor Frederick II in 1227 or 1228, or with Louis IX in 1248–50 and 1254. However, these Crusades were almost always poorly planned and even more poorly executed. By the end of the thirteenth century the

Muslim cavalry from the invasion of Spain in the eighth century through to the Battle of Nicopolis in 1396 were generally less heavily armoured than their Christian counterparts and relied more on skirmishing than the full frontal charge.

13

remaining Crusader kingdoms began to fall: in 1265 Caesarea, Haifa and Arsuf were taken; in 1268 Antioch fell; in 1289 Tripoli was captured; and, finally, in 1291 the last vestige of the Crusader kingdoms vanished when Acre fell to the Egyptians.

Castles often held the key to political control of an area, and siege warfare became increasingly common as commanders sought to avoid the potential costliness of a defeat in the field. Scaling walls using ladders was an ancient method, still used in the fourteenth century.

WAR IN EUROPE

Mounted soldiers continued to form the core of the armies. Outfitted in the finest arms and armour and mounted on expensive warhorses, these horsemen usually decided the course of battles by charging their opponents with couched lances. Most of these mounted troops were knights or their retinue, paid for by noble land-holdings.

However, by the thirteenth century, additional mounted troops, most of whom had few ties to the landed nobility but were instead paid for their services, were being

used to supplement the obligated 'feudo-vassalic' horsemen. Usually, the cavalry was supported by a larger number of infantry, some wielding spears, swords, or axes and some armed with missile weapons, generally bows and crossbows.

These forces were often levied from the general populace by the nobles who were required to provide infantry as well as cavalry, but eventually they, too, began to be paid. Throughout the Middle Ages, mercenaries could be hired to provide all types of military service.

Fighting the Crusades between 1099 and 1291 seems not to have disrupted warfare between and among Christian principalities to any major extent. With the division of the Carolingian Empire by Charlemagne's grandsons, Europe in its medieval sense was born. So, too, it seems, were jealousies between the princes – kings, dukes, counts, earls, etc – who inherited those lands and the lands into which those were further divided. Based on the system of obligation that sustained the nobility, strong and weak medieval rulers were almost always so because of their relatively strong and weak military leadership.

As such, strong rulership was deemed so because of its aggressive military actions, defence from domestic threats and offence against foreign targets; and weak rulership brought not only attacks from outside, but also, and sometimes more importantly, attacks from inside – civil war.

Strong princes generally crushed weak princes or principalities, although every once in a while a David did bring down a Goliath. Such was certainly the case at Legnano, on 29 May 1176, when Holy Roman Emperor Frederick I Barbarossa and his army, made up almost exclusively of cavalry, were defeated by an army of Milanese and other northern Italian cavalry and infantry drawn from towns' militias.

Still, it must be asserted, these instances proved to be few and far between during the period from the eleventh to the thirteenth century. More often, stronger leaders crushed their weaker opponents, and, at times, strong leaders faced equally strong opponents. It was often these occasions that produced the most interesting military engagements, at least for historians to study.

French knights in battle, from an illuminated initial found on a manuscript of Lancelot of the Lake, *c.1330. Depicting a scene from the Arthurian romance, it accurately portrays the arms and armour of the period, including great helms, triangular shields and metal-plate leg and arm guards.*

The successful siege of Château Gaillard by the French King Philip II Augustus in 1203–04 is an example of this. Even though this siege occurred after the death of King Richard the Lionheart, that it needed to occur at all is due to the construction of such a spectacular castle as Château Gaillard by that English sovereign in 1197–8. It was during the reign of John, Richard's brother, that Château Gaillard was lost. John, who acquired the nickname 'Lackland', was clearly not the military equal of his brother. The name was appropriate because at the Battle of Bouvines, on 27 July 1214, Philip Augustus

defeated an allied army (that included representatives of virtually every major principality in Western Europe), of which English soldiers were a main part.

The naval battle at Malta, on 8 June 1283, and the Battle of Bannockburn, in June 1314, provide two further examples of strong military leaders – at least numerically strong – facing each other. At Malta, an Aragonese galley fleet commanded by Roger of Lauria defeated a fleet of Angevin-Sicilian galleys commanded by William Cornut and Bartholomew Bonvin, ending an attempt by the Sicilians to capture the strategic island.

At Bannockburn, King Edward II led his English soldiers against a Scottish army seeking independence from the rule that had been imposed on them by Edward II's father, Edward I. They were ably commanded by Robert the Bruce, who after thoroughly defeating the English was crowned as Robert I, King of Scotland.

THE HUNDRED YEARS WAR

The largest amount of inter-European warfare was in the final two centuries of the period, however, and without a doubt the longest of these conflicts was the Hundred Years War – which was actually fought for 116 years, from 1337–1453. The chief combatants in this conflict were England and France, but it also included at various times the Holy Roman Empire, Burgundy, Scotland, Aragon, Castile, Portugal and the various principalities of the Low Countries.

The Hundred Years War could be described as a war of sieges, with the capture and loss of towns and fortifications the most important military actions. But it is the war's four large-scale battles that are most famous: Sluys (1340), Crécy (1346), Poitiers (1356) and Agincourt (1415). Strangely, all were won by the English, and yet they ultimately lost the war.

Sluys was a naval battle fought on 24 June 1340. The French fleet, assisted by

15

INTRODUCTION

some Genoese vessels, was anchored next to the Flemish town of Sluys in an attempt to prohibit the English army, under the leadership of King Edward III, from joining its allies from the southern Low Countries in a campaign against France. But it was the English ships, far more manoeuvrable than the French ships that had been chained together, which won the battle.

Six years later, at Crécy, on 26 August 1346, Edward III won his greatest victory, when his outnumbered men-at-arms, infantry, and longbow archers defeated a much larger army of French heavy cavalry and mercenary Genoese crossbowmen. On 18 September 1356, Edward's son, Edward the Black Prince, duplicated his father's feat by defeating a superior number of French soldiers and capturing their king, John II, at Poitiers, thus provoking the Treaty of Brétigny in 1360, which restored virtually all of the English lands in France lost after the Battle of Bouvines.

Finally, at the Battle of Agincourt, on 25 October 1415, the English King Henry V, using an especially large number of longbowmen to supplement his few men-at-arms, had surprisingly little difficulty in defeating his mounted French enemies.

Far less famous than those four battles, although it deserves to be more so, the Battle of Najera in 1367, fought in northern Spain, may best be described as a draw between the two sides – the English, led by Edward the Black Prince, in support of Pedro the Cruel in his fight for the Castilian kingdom against his half-brother, Henry of Trastamara, whose forces were supported by the French, led by their very capable general, Bertrand du Guesclin. However, it was during this campaign that the Black Prince caught the disease that would lead to his ineffectiveness in continuing the Hundred Years War and finally to his death in 1376 before he could ascend to the throne of England.

An English footsoldier takes a French nobleman captive at the Battle of Agincourt in 1415. This image symbolizes the superiority that infantrymen could exercise over their social betters.

EASTERN AND NORTHERN BORDERS

But wars between Christians and Muslims and between Christians and Christians were not the only later medieval conflicts. There was also frequent warfare along European frontiers which seemed to intensify between the thirteenth and fifteenth centuries. Attempting to defend their borders, European armies tried to halt the progress of invading foreigners by fighting and often losing extremely brutal and bloody battles.

There are a number of examples, such as the encounter at Leignitz on 9 April 1241 fought between forces from Poland and Hungary and the invading Mongols. In it the Mongol mounted archers quickly fatigued their opponents with their quick battlefield manoeuvres, and routed the eastern Europeans.

In what became one of the longest of medieval battles, the Battle of Peipus, fought on the frozen Lake Peipus, a year to the day after Leignitz, pitted the Teutonic Knights, a monastic military order sent on Crusade against the pagans of northeastern Europe, against an army of Novgorodian Russians and Estonians, led by the famous Alexandre Nevskii. There the Russians and Estonians eventually caused the Teutonic Knights to flee.

At the Battle of Nicopolis, on 25 September 1396, in an attempt to stem the advances into southeastern Europe of a relatively new threat, the Ottoman Turks, an army of Hungarians and Western Europeans, largely drawn from France and Burgundy, foolishly tried to use heavy cavalry charges against the lightly armoured, but very experienced Ottoman infantry. Ultimately, the Western European cavalry – the Hungarian infantry having not yet entered the battle – lost their impetus and were defeated.

At the Battle of Tannenberg, on 15 July 1410, another force of Teutonic Knights met their end at the hands of a northeastern European army, made up of Poles, Lithuanians, and others, in a fight largely between heavy cavalry on both sides. On Vitkov Hill, outside of Prague, on 14 July 1420, a one-eyed veteran of the victorious side at Tannenberg, Jan Zizka, led the followers of the executed heretic Jan Hus in an attempt to raise the siege of Prague by Bohemian and allied 'Crusading' soldiers. Zizka's soldiers were seemingly less well armed and armoured, carrying only staff weapons and hand-held guns, but they nevertheless defeated their more heavily armed and armoured enemies.

After laying siege to the strong defences of Constantinople from 5 April to 29 May 1453, the Ottoman Turks finally breached the walls of the city and conquered it, decisively ending a Byzantine Empire that they had been eroding with their warfare for more than a century.

Finally, at the Battle of Brunkeberg, on 10 October 1471, a large Swedish army led by an upstart, Sten Sture, defeated a Danish army sent against them by King Christian I, giving Sweden its independence and eventual control over much of Scandinavia.

* * *

Armies fighting at the end of the fifteenth century no longer looked like they had throughout most of the Middle Ages. Cavalry superiority on the battlefield had given way to infantry dominance. All these troops were paid for their military service rather than obligated by feudo-vassalic relationships. Chain mail armour had been replaced by heavy plate armour that completely covered the body, while those who could afford less turned to brigandines and other armours made up of smaller plates sewn onto fabric coverings. Some of the infantry carried halberds and other staff weapons, while others carried hand-held gunpowder weapons. Larger versions of these guns formed artillery trains, too expensive to be purchased by lesser nobles. Larger political entities now fought between themselves for land and dominance. The early modern era had arrived.

Flemish pikemen and handgunners, c.1500. This illustration comes from a late medieval manuscript depiction of the legendary exploits of the Persian King Cyrus. He was believed to be a great military innovator, so it is fitting that the system of 'pike and shot' represented here was the shape of things to come.

HASTINGS
1066

MEDIEVAL WARFARE HAD VERY FEW DECISIVE MILITARY ENGAGEMENTS, BUT ONE CERTAINLY WAS THE BATTLE OF HASTINGS, FOUGHT BETWEEN DUKE WILLIAM THE CONQUEROR'S INVADING NORMAN TROOPS AND KING HAROLD II GODWINSON'S ANGLO-SAXON ARMY. THE BATTLE WOULD LEAD TO A NEW ERA IN ENGLISH HISTORY.

WHY DID IT HAPPEN?

WHO A Norman army under William the Conqueror (1028–87) invaded England and fought a battle against an Anglo-Saxon force led by King Harold II Godwinson (c.1022–66).

WHAT The battle was fought largely between Norman cavalry who charged several times up a hill into a shield wall formed by Anglo-Saxon infantry.

WHERE At Senlac Hill, 11.2km (7 miles) north of Hastings, now called Battle.

WHEN 14 October 1066.

WHY William the Conqueror fought the battle in an effort to press his claim to the throne of England.

OUTCOME In a lengthy battle, after numerous Norman cavalry charges up Senlac Hill against the Anglo-Saxon shield wall, and two feigned retreats, many of the Anglo-Saxon infantry broke from their formation and ran down the hill into defeat.

It would still take Duke William time to complete his conquest of the rest of England; however, his victory gave him almost decisive control over the country, especially as not only Harold Godwinson, but also his two brothers, Gyrth and Leofwine, were slain. Duke William of Normandy's conquest of England in 1066 was instigated by the political chaos of the kingdom of the previous 50 years. After fending off more than two centuries of Viking invasions, in 1013 England finally fell to the Danish king, Svein Forkbeard, who defeated and slew King Ethelred II. Ethelred's reign had never been secure, and in order to preserve power in his kingdom, in 1002 he married Emma, daughter of Duke Richard I of Normandy. This move

A romantic portrayal of William the Conqueror from a nineteenth-century illustration. Born an illegitimate son of Duke Robert of Normandy, he became one of the greatest military leaders in history, not only fighting off rebels in his own duchy, but also conquering Maine, parts of Brittany, and England.

had not worked, as Svein Forkbeard's conquest proved. Yet, Emma's marriage to Ethelred, and then to Svein's successor, Cnut, introduced Normandy in a significant way into the political future of England.

Cnut ruled England until 1035, but once he died a succession crisis beset the kingdom. Two of Cnut's sons claimed the English throne: one, Harold I Harefoot, although an illegitimate son by Cnut's mistress, Ælfgifu, was in England at the time of the death of his father and thus became king. The other claimant, Harthacnut, was Cnut's legitimate son, by Emma, but he was ruling Denmark. However, in 1039 or 1040, Harold died, and Harthacnut returned to England and ascended the throne. However, his reign also was short, and he died in 1042.

EDWARD THE CONFESSOR

Neither of these kings had children, and with Cnut's line ended, the throne passed to Ethelred's remaining son, Edward the Confessor, who had been living in exile in Normandy. Edward's succession was welcomed. He further shored up his rule by marrying Edith, the only daughter of Godwin, the most powerful earl in England, and appointing two of her brothers to earldoms. The second of these, Harold, would succeed his father as Earl of Wessex in 1053, serving for the remaining years of Edward's reign as the chief counsellor to the king. This was when William the Conqueror appeared on the scene. He had become Duke of Normandy in 1035, but he was the illegitimate son of Duke Robert of Normandy, who had died on pilgrimage to the Holy Land. He was also young and was met immediately by rebellions among his nobles, but these were put down rather quickly, at first by barons loyal to William and later by the duke himself. William the Conqueror began to gain military experience and to develop expertise in generalship, especially when it came to waging cavalry warfare. By 1066, he had won not only Normandy, but also the county of Maine and parts of the counties of Brittany and Ponthieu.

Before 1052, William had little interaction with England. During that year, while Earl Godwin and his family were in

ENGLISH HUSCARL (C.1066)

The huscarls were an oath-sworn bodyguard of the Anglo-Danish aristocracy, which ruled England prior to the Norman Conquest of 1066. Although men of high status who rode to battle, huscarls dismounted to fight in the traditional Scandinavian manner. He wields a long-handled axe which could decapitate a horse at a blow, as the Bayeux Tapestry depicts. He has slung his kite-shaped shield, popular with both infantry and cavalry of his era, on his back to allow him a double-handed grip for extra weight in the blow. Axemen such as these were usually paired with a spearman, who also wielded a shield to cover both of them, so making a dangerous offensive and defensive team. Archaeological investigation in the River Thames produced several examples of such axes, probably connected with the Danish siege of London in 1012. They are known as 'bearded' axes because they are asymmetric, with the lower cutting edge being much longer, reminding observers of the long beards which the Vikings wore.

exile, he visited the island. It is this visit that most historians link to the promise of his inheritance of the throne, although when the Godwin family returned shortly thereafter – and despite Godwin's death the following year – it was Harold, not the Duke of Normandy, who became the obvious heir to Edward the Confessor's throne. But sometime in 1063–64 Harold is purported to have visited Normandy, either being driven off course while at sea or for a diplomatic meeting with William. Most importantly, Norman sources claim that while in Normandy Harold swore his allegiance to the Norman duke and his willingness to aid him in acquiring the English throne after Edward died.

CONTESTED SUCCESSION

However, even if this made William the rightful heir to the throne of England, on his deathbed, on 5 January 1066, Edward the Confessor recognized Harold Godwinson as the new King of England.

However, three claimants to the English crown disputed Harold's coronation. Svein

LOCATION

- Stamford Bridge
- ENGLAND
- London
- Hastings
- NORMANDY

Landing on England's southern coast near Hastings, William quickly built five motte-and-bailey castles, establishing a foothold. Harold's march to counter this incursion met the invader at Senlac Hill.

William the Conqueror's campaign to gain the English throne is depicted here in the Bayeux Tapestry. In the top sequence, after being shipwrecked in France, the chief English earl, Harold Godwinson, is rescued from a Breton lord by William and his Norman cavalry. In the second panel, a grateful Harold promises to support William's claim by making an oath on two relics. He then returns by Norman ship to England. And in the third panel an ailing King Edward the Confessor dies. He is carried for burial to Westminster Abbey, whereupon Harold Godwinson, breaking his oath to the Duke of Normandy, takes the English throne and thereby provokes William's conquest.

Estrithson, King of Denmark, whose claim was based on his kinship to Cnut, decided not to do anything about it. The other two, King Harald Hardrada of Norway and Duke William of Normandy, planned to immediately invade England. Harald Hardrada's claim to the English throne was weak and distant; mostly he believed that England had been weakened by the succession of Harold Godwinson, a belief seemingly confirmed by Harold's estranged brother, Tostig Godwinson, who had fled to Norway after being outlawed in 1065. Tostig was also willing to accompany Harald's Norwegian army on their invasion of England.

THE CAMPAIGN

Harald Hardrada and William the Conqueror were ready to launch their invasions by the summer of 1066. Harold

Godwinson certainly knew that the latter was planning an attack on his kingdom; he may also have thought that William was the greater of the two threats, or he may not have known of Harald Hardrada's plans, or even of Tostig's flight to him. Whatever the reason, his army remained waiting for William's invasion along the southern coast of England until 8 September.

However, because of poor weather in the English Channel, William had been unable to launch his invasion. Harald Hardrada was able to set sail, however, and in September 1066 he went first to the Orkney Islands and then to Scotland, where a few allied troops – although not many – joined his army. Finally, the Norwegians sailed along the northeastern coast of England to the Humber River. On 20 September, Harald landed his fleet in the Humber at Ricall and marched towards

York. In the way of his march, at Fulford Gate outside York, were the armies of two English earls, the brothers Morkere of Northumbria and Edwin of Mercia. Yet they proved no match for the much more numerous and skilled Norwegians, who quickly won the battle.

Harald Hardrada proceeded to York, where the town's leaders surrendered to him, and then he marched to Stamford Bridge, where he waited for the payment of promised tribute. His soldiers could relax in the knowledge that there was no one else in northern England to oppose him.

Or so they thought. It is not known when Harold learned of the Norwegian invasion nor when he began his army's march north to counter the threat. It is certain, however, that what he accomplished was an impressive feat – a swift march of his army to Tadcaster and then on to York, 306km (190 miles) north of London. It was achieved at an incredible pace of 32–40km (20–25 miles) per day.

Four days after Harald Hardrada landed at Ricall and no more than two days after he had arrived at Stamford Bridge, on 24 September, the English forces also arrived at the Humber River, in Tadcaster, and the next day they marched through York to Stamford Bridge. Their early morning approach completely surprised the Norwegians, some of whom were caught across the Derwent River away from their camp and their armour. The Battle of

Stamford Bridge was over quickly, with the Norwegians decidedly defeated, although how this was accomplished cannot be determined from contemporary sources. Both Harald Hardrada and Tostig Godwinson were slain.

Two days after Stamford Bridge, while Harold Godwinson and his men enjoyed

The Norman conquest of England remained of interest throughout the Middle Ages as evidenced in this illumination from a manuscript of miscellaneous chronicles painted between 1280 and 1300 and housed today in the British Library. Accuracy was clearly not an issue, as it shows both sides on horseback and William personally killing Harold.

English shield wall, mid-eleventh century. The troops are mainly spearmen, although some hold axes and swords. The formation depended upon the mutual support of the men within it for its strength.

THE OPPOSED FORCES

NORMANS (estimated)

Cavalry:	1–2000
Infantry:	5–6000
Total:	**6–8000**

ANGLO-SAXONS (estimated)

Huscarls:	1000
Infantry:	5–6000
Total:	**6–7000**

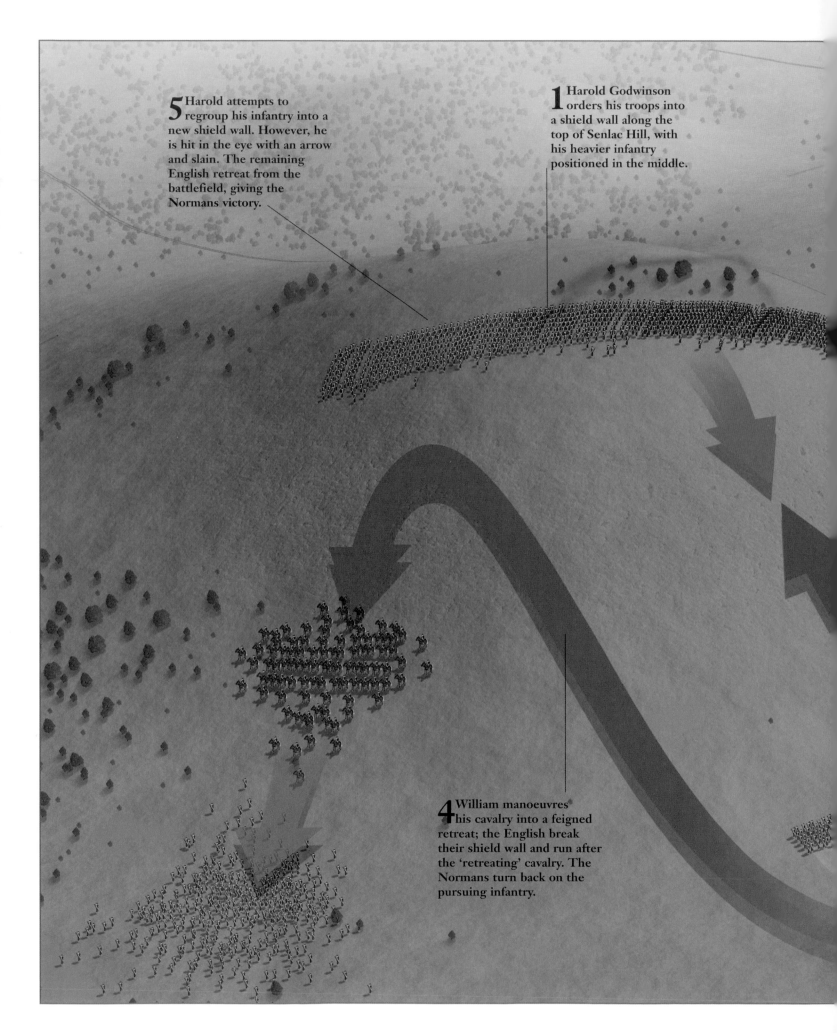

5 Harold attempts to regroup his infantry into a new shield wall. However, he is hit in the eye with an arrow and slain. The remaining English retreat from the battlefield, giving the Normans victory.

1 Harold Godwinson orders his troops into a shield wall along the top of Senlac Hill, with his heavier infantry positioned in the middle.

4 William manoeuvres his cavalry into a feigned retreat; the English break their shield wall and run after the 'retreating' cavalry. The Normans turn back on the pursuing infantry.

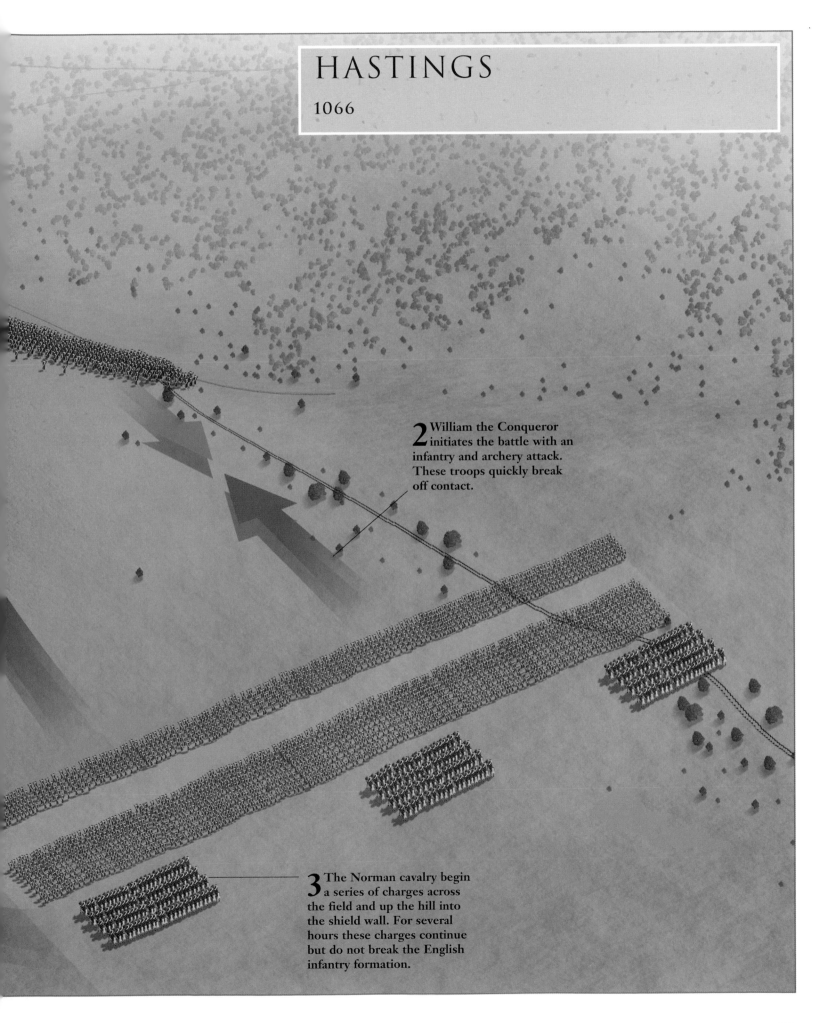

HASTINGS
1066

2 William the Conqueror initiates the battle with an infantry and archery attack. These troops quickly break off contact.

3 The Norman cavalry begin a series of charges across the field and up the hill into the shield wall. For several hours these charges continue but do not break the English infantry formation.

The Bayeux Tapestry, perhaps the most famous artistic depiction of medieval warfare, shows William the Conqueror's campaign to gain the English throne. This scene portrays the attack of Norman cavalry against the Anglo-Saxon infantry shield wall at the Battle of Hastings. Note that while one or two cavalry lances are shown to be couched, most are thrust down on the infantry, indicating that at this time there was no single preferred position.

their victory celebrations in York, William the Conqueror got his favourable weather and crossed the English Channel. His army landed without opposition at Pevensey on the south coast of England. They immediately erected an earth-and-wood motte-and-bailey castle, the first of five such constructions that William built in England before the Battle of Hastings. The castles were intended to provide the Normans with permanent bases from which they could operate and reinforce, in the

event that the conquest of England turned into a lengthy campaign. William's permanent positions would also have the effect of drawing Harold towards him and precipitating battle.

DISPOSITIONS

King Harold Godwinson learned of the Norman landing only a few days later, probably on or around 1 October. The king retraced his route. Repeating the speed of his earlier march, he passed through London and continued for another 80–96km (50–60 miles) to Senlac Hill. Here, some 600–800m (656–731 yards) along the crest, or slightly below it, facing south, he found terrain that he believed was favourable for a stand against the invading Normans. He estimated, correctly, that William wanted to fight a battle, and that this would keep the Duke of Normandy from avoiding his army, even if they occupied the better position.

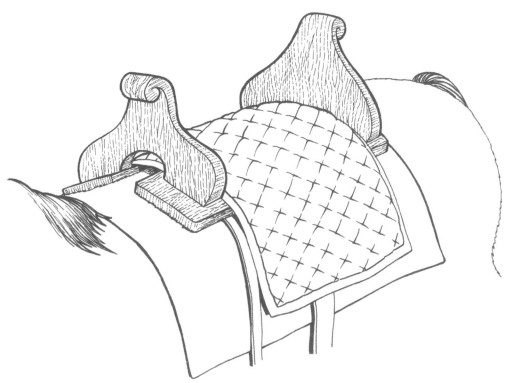

Technological improvements to the saddle, most notably the high cantle and pommel invented in the early twelfth century, increased the stability of a cavalry soldier. A high cantle, sitting against the rider's back, prevented him being thrown over the horse's rump. An equally high pommel protected the rider's genitals and lower stomach as well as preventing him being thrown over his horse's head.

Harold lined up his troops using a well-known tactic, the shield wall. His infantry and dismounted cavalry stood in a tightly packed formation, their shields overlapping one another in what was in effect a field fortification. If they could hold their position, it was almost impossible to break through this formation. The Anglo-Saxons were experienced warriors, many of whom had served with Harold in his victorious attacks on the Welsh in 1063 and all of whom had fought at the Battle of Stamford Bridge. In the centre of the shield wall fought the royal huscarls, Harold's most trusted and skilled troops, armoured in lengthy mail coats and able to fight with all weapons, but especially feared for their use of the two-handed battle-axe. On the wings of the shield wall were the fyrd, a well-trained and skilled militia, adept with the spear and sword. They, too, were well armed and well armoured. A few archers also fought with the English forces, although their numbers were likely small.

While his army was not entirely composed of cavalry, they were certainly

NORMAN CAVALRY

During the eleventh century, Norman horsemen dominated five military theatres: England, northern France, southern Italy, Sicily and the Holy Land. Their body armour, called a hauberk by this time, was mail, made in one piece. Most hauberks reached to the knees and were divided down the front and back by slits that allowed greater freedom of movement and comfort to a horseman. Some leaders and other more wealthy soldiers were also outfitted in mail leggings, or chausses. Other defensive equipment included the kite shield and helmet. A long lance was the chief weapon of the Norman horseman, while a sword could be used for close-combat situations.

the primary arm of William the Conqueror's force at Hastings. These horsemen were also very experienced warriors, with many having served the duke in his military adventures for many years. Most were from Normandy, but others had been recruited from the counties of Boulogne and Flanders. These, too, were quite experienced men. This was undoubtedly the most superb cavalry force in Europe since the time of Charlemagne.

William's tactics at the Battle of Hastings were simple, but also quite risky: his cavalry were to charge up the hill against the Anglo-Saxon shield wall. If stopped, they were to retreat, regroup, and charge again and again. It was hoped that this charge would break the line and send his opponents in rout from the field. William reasoned that under these continuous charges the English shield wall would eventually weaken, giving the Normans victory. There were also Norman archers and footsoldiers at the Battle of Hastings, but their roles, like their counterparts', seem to have been limited.

THE BATTLE BEGINS

William the Conqueror began the battle early in the morning by dividing his cavalry into three divisions, with most historians believing that these were then ordered across a single front. The Norman cavalry, led by William himself, were in the centre; on his left were Breton cavalry; and on his right were a mixture of other mounted soldiers, called 'French' by most Norman chroniclers, but probably Flemish and Boulognese cavalry. In front of the cavalry lines were the Norman archers and infantry.

These dismounted Norman troops began the battle by attacking the English infantry, but this turned out to be rather unimportant to the outcome. This may have been William's decision. He may have curtailed his infantry's attacks, as it was not honourable to his more noble cavalry to keep them out of the battle for too long. The cavalry charges soon began; 'those who were last became first', wrote the eyewitness William of Poitiers, referring to the reversal in the Norman formation.

Contemporary sources claim that the Norman cavalry was not as numerous as

their Anglo-Saxon infantry opponents. They delivered their initial charge with a heroism equalled by few other warriors in history, 'brave to the extreme', according to William of Malmesbury. But this charge was halted by the shield wall. So, too, was the next charge, and the next, and the next. No one, contemporary or modern, can agree on just how many cavalry charges were made by the Normans at the Battle of Hastings. But all were stopped by the extremely

King Harold II Godwinson was the son of the powerful Earl Godwin. Before ascending to the throne of England, Harold had served King Edward the Confessor as earl, first of East Anglia and then of Wessex, since 1044–45. His inheritance of the crown in January 1066 from the childless Edward was contested by the Kings of Denmark and Norway and the Duke of Normandy.

HAROLD.

Second Son of Godwin Earl of Kent, in 1065, seized the Crown Sep.3.1066. Will. Duke of Normandy made a descent upon the Coast of Sussex, with a great Army, to claim the Crown of England; came to an Engagement with Harold, 14 Oct. who was killed on the Spot, and his Army entirely defeated. He was bur.d at Waltham Abbey in Essex.

this Portrait is taken from one of his Coins. N.B. the Drapery is added.

disciplined English footsoldiers, who could not be moved from their strong defensive position. William of Poitiers describes the scene thus: 'this was a strange kind of battle, one side with all the mobility and initiative, and the other just resisting as though rooted to the soil.'

It was also quite a long battle. Most medieval battles were decided in a very short time, no more than an hour or even less. But not the Battle of Hastings. The

Norman cavalry delivered charge after charge. None broke the English infantry shield wall. Few were killed or wounded on either side, with the horses stopping their assaults on the infantry before actually clashing with them. However, at one time, well into the battle, a rumour passed through the Norman ranks that William the Conqueror had fallen. In an era before heraldry, such a mistake was excusable, as all Norman horsemen looked alike, as

The death of King Harold as recorded in the Bayeux Tapestry. In this panel he is shot in the eye with an arrow. In the following panel he is shown cut down by a sword. Other contemporary sources confirm these methods of death. They also indicate that his body was so mutilated following the battle that it could only be identified by his mistress, Edith Swan's Neck.

Since the time of the Battle of Hastings, the battlefield has been secured. On the crest of Senlac Hill, near the site of the Anglo-Saxon shield wall (and from where this photo was taken), William the Conqueror built an abbey, in part as penance for his participation in the battle.

confirmed by the contemporary Bayeux Tapestry. William is also shown in the tapestry to quash this rumour by lifting his helmet and showing his face. His cavalry immediately regrouped for another charge.

FEIGNED RETREAT

That William was still fighting with them seemed to re-energize the Norman cavalry, enough at least to pull off one of the most widely used but difficult cavalry tactics: the feigned retreat. Recorded in Vegetius' *De re militari* – the military manual read most frequently in the Middle Ages – the feigned

retreat demanded skill and discipline, for those 'retreating' had to look as though they were genuinely fleeing the battlefield, only to wheel and charge again in formation and unity. Such a tactic could not be performed too early in the battle, and rarely more than once – although at Hastings, the Normans attempted two feigned retreats, according to eyewitness testimony. Should a feigned retreat work, however, usually by drawing the opposing line into a celebratory pursuit, the battle would be over quickly. On the other hand, should it not work, military history had shown that, demoralized by

ET SAPIEN TEAR: AD PRE LIVM CONRA: AN

their failure, those who had attempted the tactic might actually flee the field in earnest.

At Hastings, the second feigned retreat worked well. Some Anglo-Saxon troops were able to remain in their lines, but many others broke and pursued the 'retreating' Normans, only to realize too late that the cavalry had turned around and returned to the attack. Very few of the English troops who had run down the hill after the Normans could escape the re-charging horsemen and they were ridden down and slain. Among these were Harold's two brothers, Gyrth and Leofwine, who had served as his lieutenants that day.

The battle had changed so quickly that Harold Godwinson could do little more than try to regroup those soldiers who had not fallen for the Normans' tactical trick. He attempted to form them again into a shield wall; however, this group proved to be too fatigued and disorganized to resist the Normans for long. They remained with their king until he was killed, the Bayeux Tapestry and William of Poitiers recording that this was by an arrow that struck him in the eye.

AFTERMATH

The last Anglo-Saxon/Anglo-Scandinavian army had been defeated, and it was a defeat from which the remaining military and governmental powers in England could not recover. William still had to face some opposition in the kingdom, primarily in the north from Earls Edwin and Morkere, who had been defeated at Fulford Gate and had not followed Harold Godwinson to Hastings. But they were defeated quite easily. William the Bastard, Duke of Normandy and Count of Maine, had become William the Conqueror, King of England, as well.

The Norman army as displayed in the Bayeux Tapestry consists of cavalry and archers. Other contemporary sources indicate that the cavalry greatly outnumbered the archers, but the latter's role in the death of King Harold Godwinson no doubt accounts for their exaggerated presence.

The most fearsome military tactic of the Middle Ages was perhaps the cavalry charge, as demonstrated here by Norman horse. At a time when success in battle often depended more on forcing one's enemies to flee the battlefield than on actually killing them, resisting such a charge depended on the discipline of much lower-class infantry troops and the leadership of their officers.

LEGNANO
1176

ON ONE OF HIS NUMEROUS CAMPAIGNS THROUGH THE ALPS INTO NORTHERN ITALY, THE HOLY ROMAN EMPEROR FREDERICK BARBAROSSA'S ARMY WAS DEFEATED BY NON-PROFESSIONAL SOLDIERS DRAWN MOSTLY FROM THE TOWN MILITIAS. THE BATTLE OF LEGNANO WAS A VICTORY OF INEXPERIENCED OVER PROFESSIONAL TROOPS.

WHY DID IT HAPPEN?

WHO A small German cavalry army, numbering no more than 2500, led by the Holy Roman Emperor Frederick Barbarossa (c.1123–90), was defeated by an equally small northern Italian army.

WHAT While Frederick Barbarossa's cavalry easily chased off their northern Italian counterparts, the Milanese, Veronese and Brescian infantry stood solidly against the Germans, allowing their own cavalry to regroup and defeat Barbarossa's army.

WHERE Legnano in northern Italy.

WHEN 29 May 1176.

WHY In an effort to stop an alliance between the Lombard League and Pope Alexander III (1159–81), Frederick Barbarossa marched through the Alps to restore his rule.

OUTCOME Having been defeated at Legnano, Frederick Barbarossa was forced to recognize Alexander III as pope and make peace with the Lombard League.

Throughout history, the Alps have stood as a geographical hindrance to any military force trying to cross over or through them. From Hannibal to Hitler, armies have been tormented by man and nature as they tried to travel through narrow and precipitous passes, making the journey long, gruelling and dangerous. Above all, this mountain range protected Italy. More than any strategy, army or weapon, the Alps saved Italy from numerous conquests. During the Middle Ages, the Italian people were politically and legally part of the Holy Roman Empire, but they almost always sought their own sovereignty, especially after the towns of northern and central Italy increased in population and

wealth during the High and Late Middle Ages. This meant that medieval Italians generally opposed being ruled from north of the Alps.

However, the Holy Roman Emperor often had other considerations that kept him from Italy. The difficulty of the Alpine passage, as well as the distance between there and his powerbase in Germany, allowed only an emperor who was completely secure at home to campaign in Italy. Such security was rare in medieval Germany, due to its custom of imperial election, which frequently fomented jealousy among imperial candidates and their adherents. When such security did reign, though, and the emperor came south,

This print shows the future Pope Alexander III at the Diet of Besançon in 1157, at which he claimed, in the presence of Frederick Barbarossa, that the Holy Roman Empire was a benefice of the papacy, thus incurring the emperor's antagonism. When Alexander was raised to the papal throne in 1159, Frederick opposed him, an opposition that led the emperor to undertake several campaigns into Italy, including that which ended at the Battle of Legnano.

the Italian towns were often unwilling to surrender their political independence without a fight. When these wars were fought, the Italians usually were defeated by the more professional, more experienced, more skilled, better-led, and better-armed and better-armoured German troops. But sometimes the Italians were victorious. One of the battles won by the Italians against the Germans was fought at Legnano on 29 May 1176 between the troops of the Holy Roman Emperor Frederick Barbarossa and the soldiers and militia of Milan and other allied Italian towns.

THE OPPOSING FORCES

Frederick Barbarossa was already an experienced military commander when he was designated the successor to Emperor Conrad III (1138–52) in 1152. In fact, it may well have been the generalship he exhibited when fighting Duke Conrad of Zähringen's rebellion on behalf of Emperor Conrad that led to his being recognized as his successor, despite having no familial ties to him. This same military leadership no doubt won him a unanimous election, a rarity in medieval German politics.

It had been a while since the Italians had seen a German army south of the Alps. Neither of the two emperors who preceded Frederick, Lothair II and Conrad III, were strong enough to pursue any more than a diplomatic connection with the inhabitants of Italy; in essence, the Italian towns were virtually independent for more than 50 years. Among other things, the Holy Roman Empire had been unable to collect taxes and other duties, while the Alpine passes were so filled with bands of thieves, that few traders, pilgrims, churchmen or other travellers could pass through them safely without paying for protection.

Two years after ascending to the throne, Frederick undertook his first campaign through the Alps, ostensibly to be crowned as emperor by the pope and to clear up the lawlessness of the roads and passes, but also, certainly, to bring Italy back into a political and economic union with the rest of the Holy Roman Empire. The latter aim brought an immediate response from the stronger northern and central Italian towns and their neighbours. But Frederick

Barbarossa realized little from this campaign, except for his coronation, necessitating his return again (and again).

That the townspeople of Milan led this first rebellion against Frederick is easy to understand since their wealth derived largely from being in control of many of the passes through the Alps. Any traveller who wished to journey along the shortest paths into Italy had to pass through Milan. This meant that the town was continually filled with pilgrims and traders, who spent large amounts on housing, transportation, guides, protection and victuals from the townspeople. As so often in medieval Europe, wealth translated into a longing for independence. Of course, this meant that the Milanese frequently opposed any control from the Holy Roman Empire or its lords. Perhaps also due their wealth, they were able to inspire the citizens of neighbouring towns to join their rebellions against the empire, even if neutrality might have served them better.

THE CAMPAIGN

When Frederick Barbarossa returned to Germany in 1155 without securing Italy's subjugation, his barons saw this as weakness, and the recently crowned Holy Roman Emperor had to quell dissent among them. Eventually, Frederick was able to placate or defeat all of his adversaries, through diplomacy as well as military power. His second campaign to Italy took place in 1158, and this one turned out to be quite a bit more successful than his first. His greatest victory was without a doubt the capture of Milan, which fell on 7 September 1158 to Frederick's forces after a short siege. Other rebellious Italian towns quickly surrendered.

But there was still no peace south of the Alps. Once Frederick returned to Germany, Milan and most of the rest of Italy again declared their independence, forcing the emperor's third expedition south of the Alps in 1163. On this occasion, his army faced a new alliance of earlier enemies, the

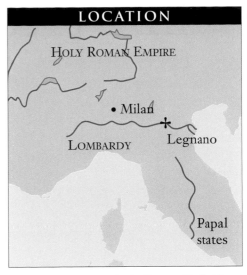

LOCATION

HOLY ROMAN EMPIRE

• Milan

Legnano

LOMBARDY

Papal states

As a German army, led by the Emperor Frederick Barbarossa, marched from Como to Pavia, it was surprised by the Milanese army outside of the town of Legnano.

GERMAN HERALD

Enemies have always needed to communicate with each other. This function in the medieval period was performed by the heralds. They also issued the king's proclamations to the army and kept the records of who was present with the army – nobles of course, not the peasants. These records were called 'Rolls of Arms' and recorded names and coats-of-arms.

31

LEGNANO

Emperor Frederick I Barbarossa's life ended in 1190 while participating in the Third Crusade, when he drowned in the River Saleph in present-day Turkey. Despite having taken the cross only two years before his death and never reaching the Holy Land, he nevertheless is remembered as a Crusader in this late twelfth-century portrait.

Frederick Barbarossa's military career has been celebrated since his death. His career included several marches through the Alps to put down northern Italian rebellions. Most of these were victories. Yet it is perhaps his defeat by the Milanese and other northern Italian militias at the Battle of Legnano (depicted in this nineteenth-century romantic painting by Amos Cassioli) that is most remembered.

Lombard League. The Lombard League had been formed initially by the smaller towns of Verona, Vicenza and Padua, but soon more substantial allies joined in: Venice, Byzantine Constantinople and the Kingdom of Sicily. In the beginning, Milan stayed out of the league, although probably

more out of fatigue than disagreement with its purpose. Facing the unity and military strength of the Lombard League, Frederick's 1163 campaign failed, as did another campaign, his fourth, in 1166. In this latter expedition, it was not only the Italians who defeated the invading Germans, but also disease, in particular fever, which almost annihilated them. Seeing their success, the Milanese joined the league.

Frederick Barbarossa did not campaign in Italy again until 1174, when he went there to prevent an alliance between the Lombard League and Pope Alexander III. Since being made pope in 1159, Alexander had remained neutral in more northerly Italian affairs, although never a friend or supporter of Frederick. Now he had begun to entertain the Lombard League's petitions for alliance, and with it, obviously, papal approval for their rebellion. Such an arrangement was not in Frederick's interest, and he was determined to stop it. When he was unable to do so diplomatically, he launched a new campaign. It was during this campaign, in 1176, that Frederick fought and lost the Battle of Legnano.

LEGNANO

DISPOSITIONS

The original sources for the Battle of Legnano do not provide adequate detail for all of the action on the battlefield. Surprisingly, despite its importance to his military career, the chroniclers and biographers of Frederick Barbarossa, generally quite descriptive about all facets of his life, are silent on the battle, while the few local Italian histories are quite short.

From 1174 to 1176 Frederick travelled around Italy, trying to bring the Lombard League to battle. By 1176 he had become frustrated at the lack of progress he had made: the Italians had not been pacified, nor had the pope backed down in his support of them. Early in the year, the emperor had called for reinforcements from

Germany, and in April, 2000 additional troops arrived from Swabia and the Rhineland. This force was led by Philip, the Archbishop of Cologne, Conrad, the Bishop-elector of Worms, and Berthold, Duke of Zähringen, a nephew of the empress. From the sources it appears that these soldiers were mounted men-at-arms – knights and sergeants – seemingly without any attendant infantry. Traditionally, the infantry should have been there, and why they were missing is not explained in the original sources.

There are several possibilities: perhaps it was because of the speed Frederick required of them; perhaps the Germans normally had their infantry supplied by local allied Italians or mercenaries; or perhaps

In this nineteenth-century painting by artist Albert Bauer, Frederick Barbarossa is shown receiving the praises of the citizens of Aachen. Aachen had been the capital of Charlemagne's empire, and Frederick regarded himself as the direct descendant of the great Carolingian emperor. He visited the town on numerous occasions and was responsible for transferring Charlemagne's bones to the famous golden reliquaries where they still lie.

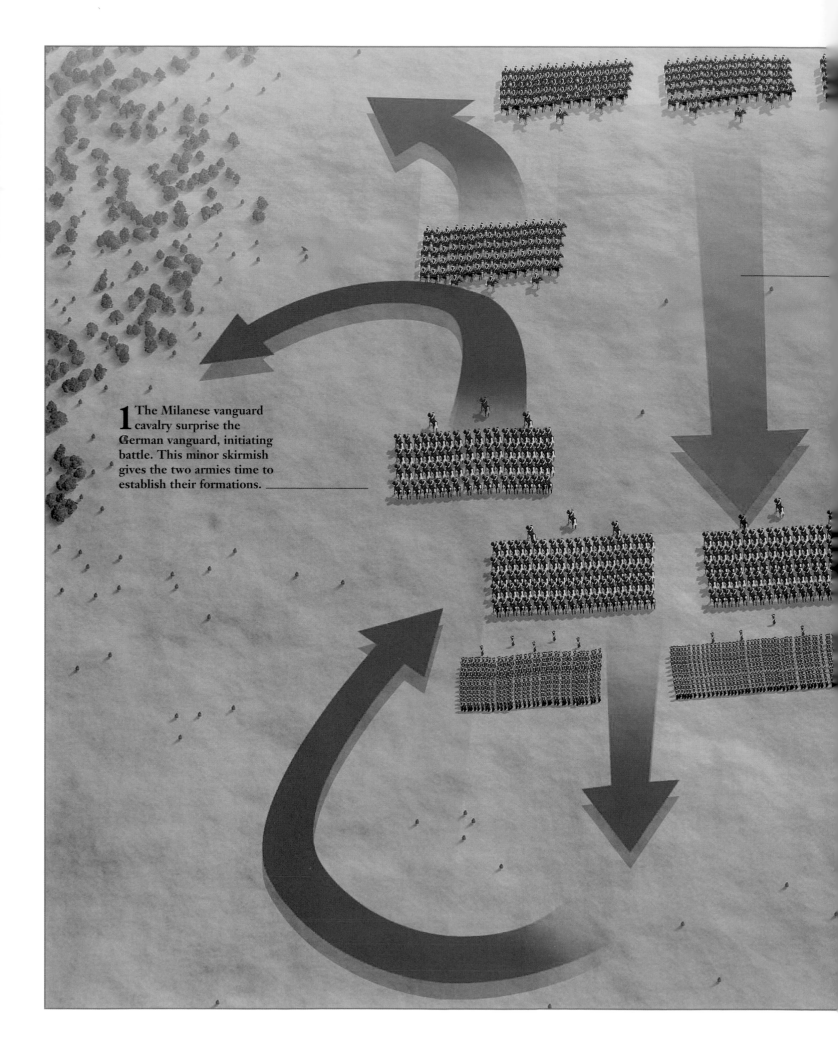

1 The Milanese vanguard cavalry surprise the German vanguard, initiating battle. This minor skirmish gives the two armies time to establish their formations. _____

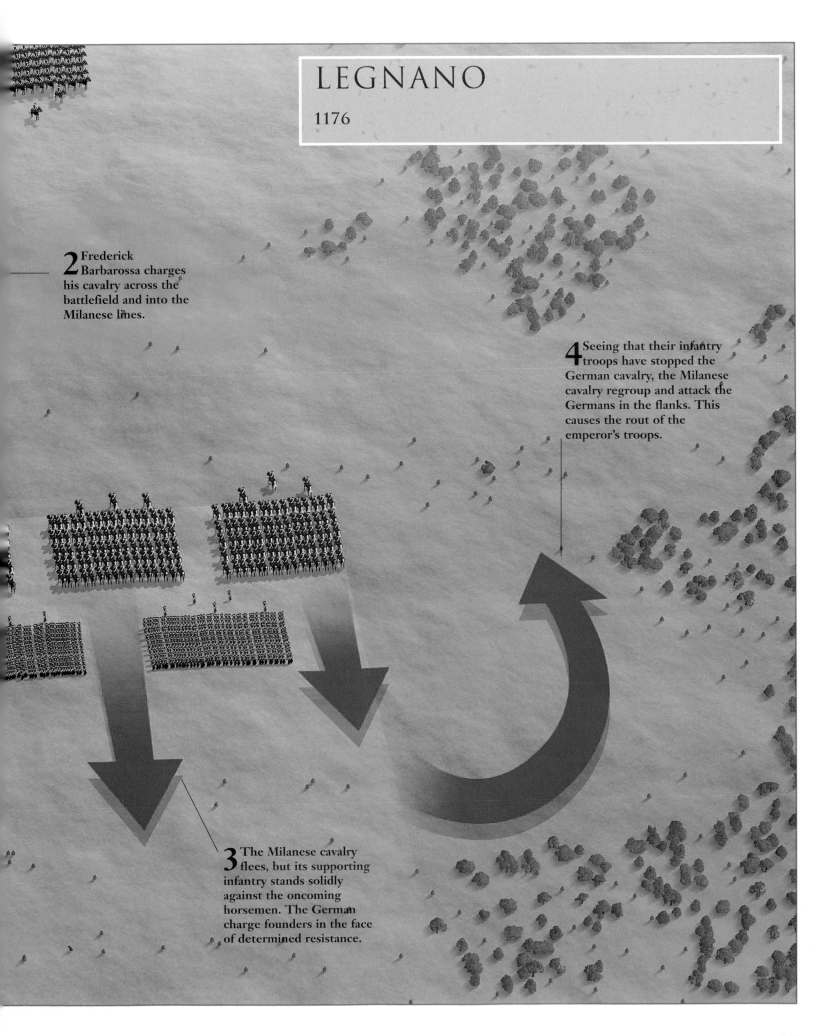

LEGNANO

1176

2 Frederick Barbarossa charges his cavalry across the battlefield and into the Milanese lines.

4 Seeing that their infantry troops have stopped the German cavalry, the Milanese cavalry regroup and attack the Germans in the flanks. This causes the rout of the emperor's troops.

3 The Milanese cavalry flees, but its supporting infantry stands solidly against the oncoming horsemen. The German charge founders in the face of determined resistance.

The Milanese carroccio was a ceremonial wagon built to reflect the town's pride and wealth. Taken with the town's militia to the Battle of Legnano, it was meant to encourage the more inexperienced soldiers when they faced Frederick Barbarossa's veteran forces, and did so successfully to judge by the result of the battle. Although never actually threatened during the battle, it is so portrayed in this painting, one of three created by Gaetano Previati (1852–1920) in 1916–17 depicting the carroccio at Legnano.

Frederick Barbarossa felt that cavalry reinforcements were what his army needed at the time.

Too little is known about Frederick's military organization or his needs on this campaign to determine the reason why there were no infantry among these reinforcements. But had they been present, the Battle of Legnano would probably have turned out differently.

MANOEUVRES

The emperor was at the head of his own 500 cavalry, and these joined the German reinforcements at Como early in May. This was certainly not the entire German army at Frederick's disposal in Italy at the time, and it may be that the 500 cavalry were only his bodyguard, who accompanied the Holy Roman Emperor to protect him on the journey to meet up with the Swabian and Rhenish reinforcements.

If this was the case, then Frederick likely wanted to add these to his army so that he might campaign more effectively against the Lombard League. He may even have felt that such a large cavalry army, all equipped in heavy armour on powerful, expensive horses, might intimidate the Italians into surrender without the need for military action – the most successful campaign is the one that brings its desired result without actual fighting.

But Frederick's main army was at Pavia at the time, putting the town of Milan between this force and those with him. Frederick hoped that he might be able to travel around Milan without meeting opposition from the Lombard League.

However, the Milanese knew exactly where the two German armies were, and they also recognized that Frederick's division of his forces offered them an extraordinary opportunity. The Milanese governors mustered the town's forces – probably any man who could bear arms – and also called in numerous neighbouring allies to join them. German narrative sources place these troops at 12,000 cavalry, with an even larger number of infantry, but

these tallies are surely exaggerated. Modern historians have suggested the number to be closer to 2000 Milanese cavalry, with no more than 500 infantry, the latter drawn from Milan, Verona, and Brescia. Present also was Milan's *carroccio*, a large ceremonial wagon that symbolized the wealth and independence of the city.

THE BATTLE

Not wanting the two German armies to unite, the Milanese moved to intercept them. This occurred outside Legnano on 29 May. From the original sources, it appears that the Italian army – which had effectively concealed their movement behind a forest – actually surprised Frederick Barbarossa. Before the emperor could organize his battlefield formation, the vanguard cavalry of the Milanese, numbering around 700, charged into the German vanguard cavalry, which numbered considerably fewer, probably no more than 300. The Germans

were quickly routed. But they had bought some time for their army to form up, which quickly took in those retreating and chased off their pursuers.

During this action, the Milanese had also moved onto the battlefield and formed their lines opposite the Germans. The cavalry was ordered in four divisions, with the infantry and *carroccio* behind these. How the German army was arrayed is not revealed in the contemporary sources. Frederick decided that it was to his benefit to go on the offensive, as he was in 'foreign' territory and could not count on his forces being relieved, while he feared that his opponents' numbers would only increase if he delayed for too long.

He also refused to retreat, although this may have been the wisest strategy at the time; the *Annals of Cologne* claims that the emperor counted 'it unworthy of his Imperial majesty to show his back to his enemies'. So, instead of taking a defensive

Another of the Carroccio Triptych *by Gaetano Previati, depicting the Milanese* carroccio *at the Battle of Legnano. Here the Milanese soldiers honour the wagon's presence on the battlefield.*

THE OPPOSED FORCES

ITALIANS (estimated)
Milanese cavalry:	2000
Milanese, Veronese and Brescian foot:	500
Total:	**2500**

GERMANS (estimated)
Frederick's bodyguard men-at-arms:	500
Swabian and Rhenish men-at-arms:	2000
Total:	**2500**

The wedge formation consisted of battle lines made up of a number of deep wedges of cavalry, followed by infantry. The more heavily armed knights would lead the wedge, while the more lightly armed men-at-arms would form the centres. The idea was to slice into the ranks of the enemy and disrupt their formation, after which the infantry could follow up to provide the final blow.

stance, the German cavalry charged 'strongly', and their attack quite easily broke through the Milanese cavalry.

INFANTRY STAND FAST

However, pushing through the cavalry, the Germans ran into the Italian infantry, who had held their positions despite the flight of the cavalry – an important and incredibly courageous stand. The German cavalry charge was halted. The Italian infantry – 'with shields set close and pikes held firm', states Archbishop Romuald of Salerno – caused the German horses to stop, unable to penetrate the massed infantry, and unwilling to run onto their long spears. This was not surprising, because such a result had happened before: if horses could not penetrate or go around an infantry line, they simply stopped. But it was a result that could only come about when the infantry was motivated to stand solidly and not flee, even when they faced soldiers whose armour and warhorses displayed a wealth and power attainable by very few, if any, footsoldiers. In the twelfth century, such a stand was rare.

The stubborn courage of the Milanese infantry allowed their fleeing cavalry to regroup and return to the battlefield, where they attacked the halted German cavalry in the flank. Frederick's horsemen, seeing that the charge that had so recently brought success against their cavalry counterparts had been stopped by lowly infantry, began to waver. They quickly turned from their

fight with the infantry and attempted to return to their former positions. But this retreat was very disordered and, lacking their own infantry to regroup behind, it quickly turned into a rout. Some time during this part of the battle, Frederick's banner was lost to the Milanese, and his horse was killed under him.

Frederick barely escaped – although how is not recorded in the original sources – and for several days, while he made his way secretly back to Pavia, it was feared that he had been killed at Legnano. Many Germans were captured, but the total number of either army slain on the battlefield seems not to have been large, undoubtedly a testimony to the protection given by the mail armour worn by the German and Milanese men-at-arms.

Few battles show the necessity of medieval armies to have both cavalry and infantry on the battlefield better that the Battle of Legnano. The Milanese had both infantry and cavalry in their army, and it was their infantry who were able to hold against the charge of the German cavalry. This gave them victory at Legnano. Frederick Barbarossa had not fielded a similarly organized army, leaving no relief for his cavalry when they began to flee, and this more than anything else decided his defeat.

AFTERMATH

Their victory at the Battle of Legnano brought immediate results for the Italians. By October, Frederick was forced to sign the Treaty of Anagni with Alexander III, recognizing him as pope and giving him numerous concessions. And the following

May, Frederick signed the Treaty of Venice, making a truce with the Lombard League and the Kingdom of Sicily.

Furthermore, over the following few years, Emperor Frederick Barbarossa was forced to become more involved in affairs in Germany. Another campaign across the Alps was, at least for the time being, unthinkable, and in June 1183 the emperor again made peace with the Lombard

League, under the Treaty of Constance, which granted nearly complete sovereignty to its members.

Although Frederick and his successors returned to Italy, they were never able to break the desire for independence among those towns in the north which had experienced this self-government. One might conclude then that at Legnano the Renaissance was born.

The victory of Milanese townspeople over the Holy Roman imperial army at the Battle of Legnano gave an early indication of the power and wealth of the northern Italian towns. This painting romanticizes the end of the battle as the double-headed imperial eagle banner is shown bowed and captured by those carrying the colours of Milan.

39

HATTIN
1187

THIS BATTLE MARKED THE TURNING POINT IN THE CRUSADES. THE MORE INTELLIGENT STRATEGY AND FLEXIBLE TACTICS OF THE ISLAMIC ARMY DELIVERED A CATASTROPHIC DEFEAT TO THE ARMY OF JERUSALEM. THE CHRISTIANS WOULD NEVER AGAIN HOLD AS MUCH TERRITORY AS THEY HAD PREVIOUSLY.

WHY DID IT HAPPEN?

WHO A Crusader army of 32,000 men under King Guy of Jerusalem (reigned 1186–92), opposed by 50,000 Seljuk Turks under Saladin (1138–93).

WHAT Thirsty, tired and dispirited Crusaders en route to relieve a castle could not catch the more nimble Turks until they were too exhausted to fight. Only then did the Turks surround and attack the remaining Crusaders.

WHERE The Horns of Hattin, near Tiberias on the Sea of Galilee in modern Israel.

WHEN June 1187.

WHY The Turks were responding to the Crusaders who had breached a truce by raiding a Turkish caravan.

OUTCOME Most of the Crusaders were killed or captured. The Turks went on to recapture Jerusalem.

The Crusades were an extraordinary phenomenon. Recruited by the clergy of a peace-professing religion, waves of invaders and their reinforcements were raised in Europe to conquer and convert both non-believers and heretics in Spain, the Pyrenees, Central Europe and the Baltic. For more than 1000 years the Romans and their successor state the Byzantines struggled to maintain their rule over Palestine and the holy sites of three great religions. Following the crushing defeat of the Byzantines by the Seljuk Turks at Manzikert in 1071 Pope Urban II

A thirteenth-century portrait of Salah ad-Din Yusuf Ibn Ayyub, known to us as 'Saladin', from a manuscript by an unknown Persian artist. This is a rare contemporary image of Saladin, who was Sultan of Egypt and Syria.

(c.1042–1099) called for a Crusade to occupy and hold the Christian sites in Turkish Syria. The Crusaders carried with them the social structures, attitudes and ambitions of the society they left, and met, when they arrived in Saracen lands, a completely different set of customs and outlooks and a different way of waging war. These strange Saracen lands were in fact the Seljuk Turkish Sultanates of Rum and Syria. They stretched from southern Turkey to the Persian Gulf and east to Afghanistan.

The Sultan Nur ad-Din incorporated Egypt into his empire and set Saladin to be its governor and thence sultan. The relatively tiny Crusader territories on the western edge of this vast empire ebbed and flowed like the tide as they struggled against their more numerous foes. This strange enemy did not seem to pin all on headlong rushes into combat but was content to shoot arrows from horseback, particularly at the horses which were too valuable in the West to be so targeted, and retire until he perceived it advantageous to close for hand-to-hand combat. By this time of course, if the Saracens had judged their moment right, the knights and footsoldiers of the Crusading armies were tired, desperately thirsty and disorganized.

Successive newly arrived and headstrong Crusader leaders did not always listen to the experiences of their predecessors and learnt the hard way, paying for their lessons with the lives of their own men. Their independent attitude also led to many feuds and disputes with their fellow Crusaders over land, precedence and women, but above all over power. They had no clear, accepted head of state to direct affairs and enforce unity. In such a long-drawn-out war, truces and periods of relative peace were inevitable, as were their breaches.

In the autumn of 1186 Reynald de Chatillon (c.1125–1187), Lord of Kerak and one of history's most brutal rulers, raided a Muslim caravan, breaking a long-standing truce. Both Saladin and King Guy of Jerusalem demanded the prisoners and stolen goods be returned but Reynald refused. Saladin declared war and summoned his own host from just a portion of his empire: northern Syria, Aleppo, Damascus and Egypt.

His first move in May 1187 was to send four of his *amirs* (troop commanders) and about 6500 men on a reconnaissance. Coincidentally the Grand Masters of the Knights of the Hospital and Temple were in the area to resolve a dispute between Count Raymond of Tripoli, who had negotiated the original truce, and King Guy of Jerusalem. The Grand Masters had little more than their immediate bodyguards.

They set off with just 140 knights and 350 infantry to intercept the Muslims. These they found watering their horses at the Spring of Cresson (also known as Kishon). The knights charged immediately, leaving their infantry behind. Not surprisingly they were almost all massacred – the odds were over 40:1. Only the Grand Master of the Temple, Gerard de Ridefort, and two of his brethren escaped. The Muslims' reconnaissance mission went on, via Tiberias on the Sea of Galilee, to massacre the Christian forces in Nazareth.

Through the deaths of their knights the Grand Masters had succeeded in their objective as Count Raymond and King Guy set aside their differences to deal with the new threat. By then King Guy had a mere 700 knights and men-at-arms left in his small kingdom.

THE CAMPAIGN

The city of Acre on the coast was chosen as the rendezvous of the Crusader host. It had a huge harbour and infrastructure to support the assembling troops before they set out. Here 2200 knights assembled. The feudal obligations of the component parts of the kingdom are recorded by various chroniclers at between 636 and 749 knights. The Temple had already lost two-thirds of its strength so could only provide about 40 true Templar knights.

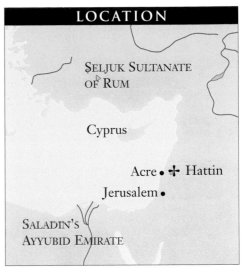

SELJUK SULTANATE OF RUM

Cyprus

Acre • ✝ Hattin
Jerusalem •

SALADIN'S AYYUBID EMIRATE

King Guy of Jerusalem set out to relieve the castle at Tiberias, but was cut off from his water supply by Saladin's larger Muslim army. The battle took place around two rocky outcrops – the Horns of Hattin.

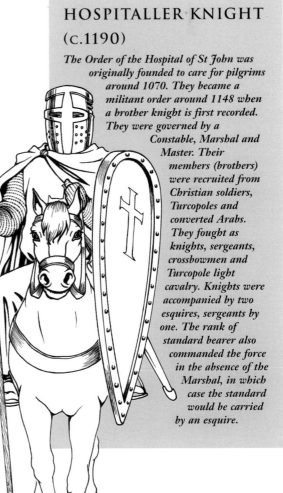

HOSPITALLER KNIGHT (c.1190)

The Order of the Hospital of St John was originally founded to care for pilgrims around 1070. They became a militant order around 1148 when a brother knight is first recorded. They were governed by a Constable, Marshal and Master. Their members (brothers) were recruited from Christian soldiers, Turcopoles and converted Arabs. They fought as knights, sergeants, crossbowmen and Turcopole light cavalry. Knights were accompanied by two esquires, sergeants by one. The rank of standard bearer also commanded the force in the absence of the Marshal, in which case the standard would be carried by an esquire.

HATTIN

Turcopole archers – whether on foot or mounted – were employed in large numbers by Crusader armies in the Kingdom of Jerusalem, since they added a valuable skirmishing element to match the enemy light cavalry. Most were recent converts to Christianity.

THE OPPOSED FORCES

MUSLIMS (estimated)
Askari:	12,000
Turcomans & other cavalry:	26,000
Infantry:	12,000
Total:	**50,000**

CRUSADERS (estimated)
Knights of the Holy Orders:	120
Feudal knights:	700
Mercenary men-at-arms:	1380
Turcopoles:	4000
Infantry:	32,000
Total:	**38,200**

The Hospitaller strength is generally estimated to be about the same; deducting their losses at Cresson gives around 80 true Hospitallers. This means that more than half the knights were secular and mercenary. Although they would fight well, they were less motivated by their pay than the Templar and Hospitaller knights were by their religious fervour. More lightly armoured and armed with sword, light lance and bow were 4000 Turcopole skirmishing cavalry. Local mercenaries who had converted to Christianity, they provided a vital skirmishing and scouting capability the Crusader armies otherwise lacked. The mass of the army was made up of 32,000 infantry – a motley crew, some veterans of earlier campaigns, some newly arrived pilgrims. Weapons would include spear and crossbow and many would have worn mail and a helmet for protection. Spearmen also carried a shield.

Saladin's host of perhaps 50,000 was reviewed and is recorded as including 12,000 regular Egyptian and Syrian cavalry (*Askari*) – five times the number of Crusader knights. These received regular pay and were fully equipped, mail-coated (some with plate reinforcement sewn on) cavalry, armed with bow as well as lance and shield. They were as well equipped as their Christian counterparts but less inclined to charge as ferociously and, more importantly, prepared to skirmish away if the moment was unfavourable. Some Muslim cavalry horses also wore barding, possibly concealing chain mail. An additional 12,000 unpaid and less well-equipped Kurdish, Bedouin and Turcoman cavalry fighting for loot and slaves seems likely. Finally, there was an unrecorded number of infantry: spear-and-shield- or bow-equipped volunteers from the locality as well as from the further corners of the Turkish Empire like Egypt. But not Saladin's Sudanese infantry who had been crushed after a revolt two years previously and had not yet been re-established.

This Turcoman auxiliary is typical of the numerous non-professional light infantry employed in Saladin's army. He is armed with a heavy axe and shield, but has little in the way of body armour.

A French woodcut from the nineteenth century depicts a romanticized death for the defeated Crusader knights at Hattin. Even 600 years after the event, the battle was capable of inpsiring sentimentality.

This Muslim host moved on the town and adjacent castle at Tiberias. The castle was ignored but the town was pillaged. This was very much an invitation to battle.

THE MARCH

The Crusaders obliged and marched out with the True Cross, the most potent symbol in Christendom, in their midst. They camped at Saffuriya, between Acre and Tiberias, a good site with both water and grazing for the horses. Between there and the Saracen camp 9.6km (6 miles) southwest of Tiberias lay the dry, baking-hot Plain of Toran. Raymond, an old hand, counselled against an advance. His castle at Tiberias, governed by his wife, would hold out; they should draw the Muslims on to

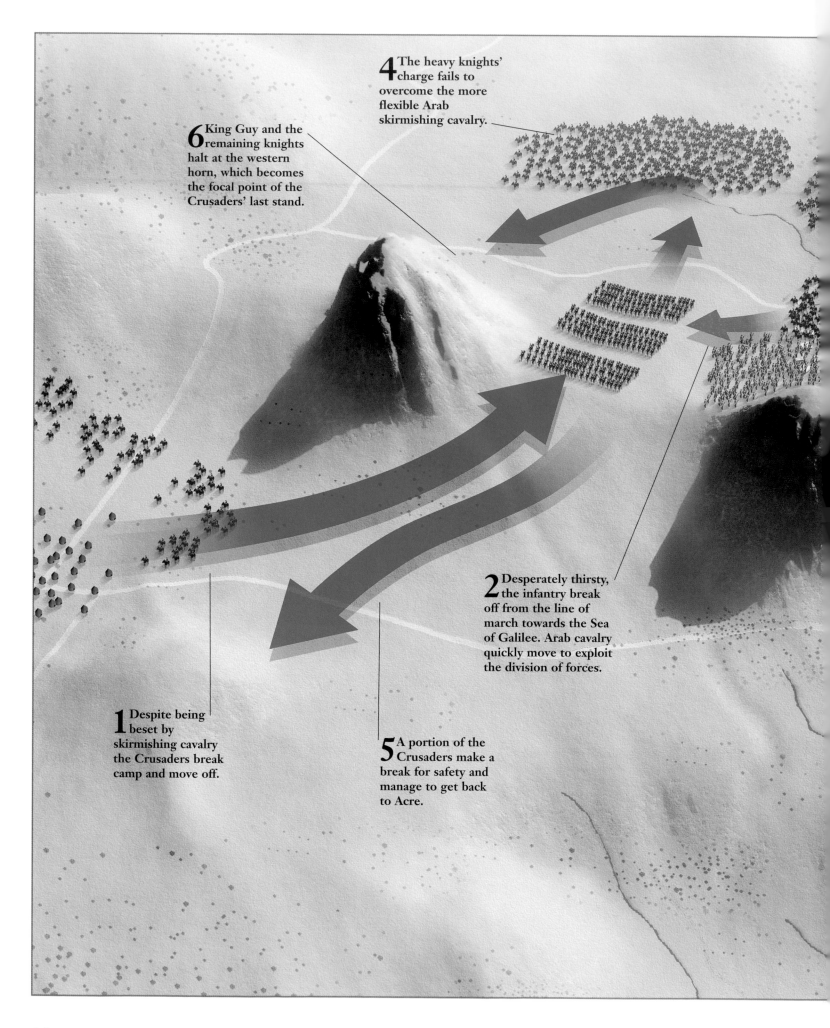

4 The heavy knights' charge fails to overcome the more flexible Arab skirmishing cavalry.

6 King Guy and the remaining knights halt at the western horn, which becomes the focal point of the Crusaders' last stand.

2 Desperately thirsty, the infantry break off from the line of march towards the Sea of Galilee. Arab cavalry quickly move to exploit the division of forces.

1 Despite being beset by skirmishing cavalry the Crusaders break camp and move off.

5 A portion of the Crusaders make a break for safety and manage to get back to Acre.

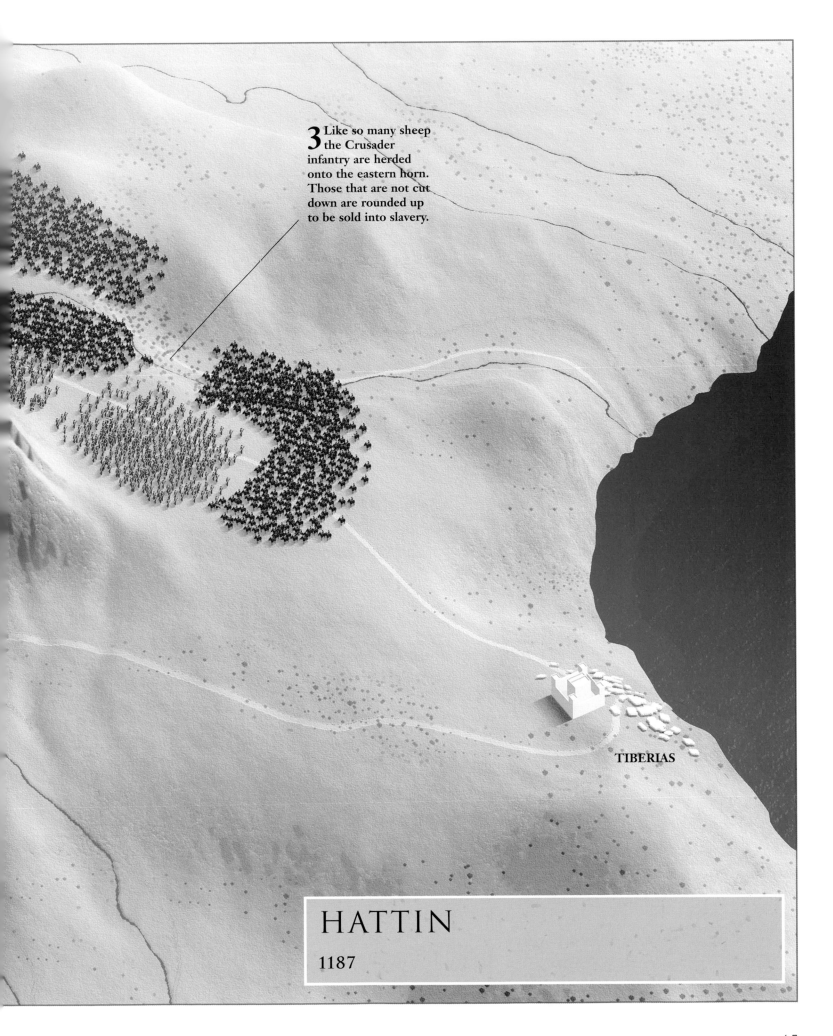

3 Like so many sheep
the Crusader
infantry are herded
onto the eastern horn.
Those that are not cut
down are rounded up
to be sold into slavery.

TIBERIAS

HATTIN

1187

HATTIN

their position, making them suffer the thirsty approach march. But Reynald de Chatillon and Gerard de Ridefort argued for a bold advance to strike the foe. King Guy vacillated but finally agreed to advance via Wadi Hamman, to the north of the direct route, where the Crusaders expected to find water. Saladin got news of this movement, probably from his scouts, and shifted his position northwards to block this route at the Horns of Hattin.

The Crusaders marched amidst continuous skirmishing from Muslim light cavalry who attacked both the van, under Raymond, and the rearguard of Hospitallers, Templars and Turcopoles. It was a sensible tactic: attack the rear and you will either split the column or make the whole formation slow down or even stop. The Muslims' primary target would have been the Turcopoles, the only ones with a realistic chance of catching the Muslim skirmishing cavalry. Once they were eliminated the Crusaders had little answer to the hit-and-run tactics of the enemy other than to use the plodding infantry as a

shield. Casualties were heavy at both ends of the column and the rearguard was nearly separated from the main column. After just 8km (5 miles) the whole army was forced to halt in the hot early afternoon and the order was given to make camp even though there was no water available. Only Raymond realized they must have water, but the infantry were exhausted and the rearguard was severely battered.

THE BATTLE

The Crusaders got but little respite during the night. The Muslims, however, were re-supplied by camels bringing 400 loads of arrows and 70 loads of water. Early the next morning the Crusaders made one more attempt to reach water at the village of Marescallia but were held back by the Muslims. Anyway the spring was dry. At about nine o'clock the main Muslim force advanced in a crescent formation. Arrows swept before them like rain before a storm. But this was not a charge to contact, merely an intensification of the arrow-storm and a further reduction in the Crusaders' morale.

Louis VII of France, the Emperor Conrad III of Germany and Baldwin III, King of Jerusalem, deliberate on the course of the Holy War, 1148. Baldwin III died without issue so the throne passed through his brother Amalric to Baldwin IV, thence, in 1186, to his brother-in-law Guy of Lusignan, after the short reign of Guy's stepson as Baldwin V.

The Crusaders could charge but all they would meet was another shower of deadly arrows. The Saracens would simply retire before them, keeping within bow range and targeting the Crusaders' horses to dismount the heavily armoured knights.

The tired, disorganized and above all thirsty Crusader infantry could see blue water ahead. They surged past the vanguard to push on to the Sea of Galilee which seemed so tantalizingly close, but they were instead herded onto the easternmost of two hills known as the Horns of Hattin. Halted by despair, frustration and Muslim arrows a mere 12.8km (8 miles) short of their destination, they were a spent force. Even

the king could not persuade them to take any further part in the battle and here those that weren't cut down were rounded up and later sold into slavery by the Saracens.

CAVALRY CLASH

Guy ordered Raymond and the remaining vanguard of about 200 knights to charge. The medieval knight was very much a one-shot weapon. You pointed him at the enemy and let him go. If he collided with the enemy it could be devastating. If not, his horse became blown and he was useless. A good commander might be able to halt the charge, rally the knights and make a second attempt, but it took an awful toll on the

Lower Galilee, Israel – the Horns of Hattin mountains. This photograph gives an excellent impression of the terrain: scrub with patches of rubble and rocky outcrops – sufficient to hinder free movement of the mounted Crusaders but not to impede the arrows of the Muslim horse archers.

horses' strength and exposed the knights to counter-attack from flank or rear when they were unprepared. Nothing saps a horse's strength like thirst. Instead of carefully husbanding his precious but powerful knights, Guy had frittered them away in topping and tailing his more numerous and now dispersed infantry. Richard the Lionheart at Arsuf four years later would use a better strategy.

The Muslims opened their ranks and Raymond's charge passed through, receiving more archery casualties on the way, in a classic response to the charge of Western knights and a tactic from the steppes with a pedigree of more than 1000 years. Raymond, thrice wounded in the charge, knew the day was lost and rode from the field into the steep-sided gorge of Wadi Hamman. The wadi was dry (some say Saladin had the stream diverted) and the Muslims closed behind him. Raymond knew he could not charge back up the slope, so he rode on to Tyre leaving behind at least

one son to be captured by the foe. He had been expected to follow a suicidal plan by people lacking his experience. Perhaps his efforts in securing the original truce persuaded Saladin to let him and his contingent escape.

The remaining knights made two or three more charges, but were still unable to come to grips with their highly mobile foes. Perhaps as many as 300 managed to escape back to Acre. Eventually the survivors were driven back onto the other Horn of Hattin where King Guy's red tent had been erected. The Muslims circled around the hill, cutting the Crusaders down. At some stage Saladin's men even set fire to the tinder-dry brush, sources differing as to exactly when. This was heaping misery upon misery for the parched Crusader soldiers. Finally, the tent was overrun and about 150 remaining knights surrendered. It is a testament to the armour they wore, which made them evidently so hard to kill, and the tenacious determination of the knights that they did not surrender earlier when all reasonable hope had passed. The last few surviving leaders were captured: King Guy, his brother Amalric, Constable of Acre, Reynald de Chatillon and Gerard de Ridefort along with so many others that the Muslims did not have enough rope to tie them all.

Muslim soldiers set upon a fallen Crusader cavalryman. Once a horseman had been brought down from his mount, his opponents generally had the advantage. Either he could be taken hostage and ransomed, or, as is most likely in the case of this Crusader at the Battle of Hattin, he would be killed by attacks through vulnerable openings in his armour – at the neck, armpit or groin.

AFTERMATH

The Battle of the Horns of Hattin was the high-water mark of all the seven Crusades to Palestine. Even the briefly combined armies of England and France failed to retake Jerusalem a few years later. Richard the Lionheart of England did learn from the mistakes of his predecessors, however. Four years later on the coast at Arsuf he inflicted a telling defeat on Saladin's warriors.

Saladin had the brutal Reynald de Chatillon executed along with all the surviving Knights Templar and Hospitaller, his most fervent and implacable foes, and the remaining Turcopoles. Raymond's wife, who had faithfully held their castle, was allowed to depart unharmed. The price of Frankish slaves in the Muslim markets tumbled because of the glut. It is recorded that one Frank was sold for a single shoe!

By the end of the year the Muslims had gone on to capture Ascalon and about 30 other Crusader castles; the city of Jerusalem surrendered in October. In addition, as ransom for King Guy and Gerard de Ridefort, Saladin received a further 11 cities. In another 100 years the Crusader presence in mainland Palestine would be eliminated. By then the Muslims were under attack from the east by the Mongols.

A romanticized version of the remaining Crusader leaders surrendering to Saladin after the battle (painting by S. Tahssin). Shortly after this the man who broke the truce, Reynald de Chatillon, and all the surviving Knights Templar and Hospitaller were executed by Saladin.

ARSUF
1191

THE BATTLE OF ARSUF PITTED A CRUSADER ARMY UNDER RICHARD THE LIONHEART AGAINST A SARACEN FORCE UNDER SALADIN. IT WAS A SEVERE TEST OF THE DISCIPLINE THAT RICHARD HOPED TO INSTIL IN THE CRUSADER ARMIES. ULTIMATELY, THE CRUSADER INFANTRY PROVED THEIR WORTH IN THE FACE OF CONSTANT HARASSMENT BY MUSLIM CAVALRY.

WHY DID IT HAPPEN?

WHO A Crusader army under King Richard I of England (1157–99) numbering about 12,000 men was attacked by a Saracen force approximately double in size, commanded by Saladin (1138–93).

WHAT The Crusaders, attempting to march along the Palestine coast, were attacked by the more mobile Saracens but were able to reach and occupy the town of Arsuf.

WHERE The town of Arsuf.

WHEN September 1191.

WHY Having taken Acre, Richard hoped to press on to Jerusalem. Saladin was determined to stop him.

OUTCOME The Crusaders were able to maintain formation and march under fire to Arsuf. A mounted counter-attack then drove off the Saracen force.

The Crusader armies tended to be an ill-assorted mix of troop types and fairly undisciplined. The backbone was provided by mounted men-at-arms and nobles from the Christian kingdoms of Europe. Armoured in chain mail and an open-faced metal helm, the man-at-arms was trained to war all his life. His sidearm was the long sword, but he might also carry an axe or mace as well as his shield and lance. Knights, noblemen and men-at-arms came to the Crusades from all across Europe. The most famous groups were the Knights Templar and the Order of St John (the Hospitallers).

WARRIOR MONKS

The Knights Templar, otherwise known as the Poor Fellows of Christ, were formed after the First Crusade (1096–99) in response to a need for fighting men to defend the conquered lands. Gaining papal approval in 1120, they were an order of warrior monks who took vows of poverty and chastity and lived according to a very strict code. They wore the white surcoat of their order over a plain and unadorned chain mail shirt called a hauberk, along with a mail coif (hood) and leggings. Their helm was plain and open-faced, similar to that worn by Norman knights at the Battle of Hastings. Under the mail hauberk was a padded jerkin to absorb the impact of blows.

The Templars have become the symbol of Christian knights. They were fearsome and unrelenting in combat against their Muslim foes, believing that death in battle against the enemies of Christendom was a direct route to heaven. The Templars had a fierce rivalry with the Hospitallers that did

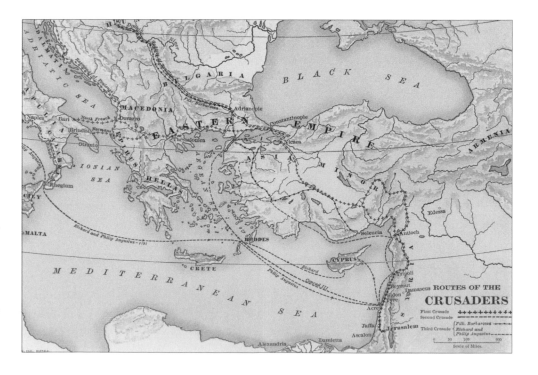

This map shows the routes of the three Crusader armies that gathered for the Third Crusade in 1190. While the forces of Richard I of England and Philip II of France chose to travel by sea, Frederick Barbarossa led the forces of the Holy Roman Empire on a long and arduous overland journey. The emperor was drowned while crossing a fast-flowing river in Turkey.

MAMLUK SOLDIERS (C.1190)

The great wealth of Fatimid Egypt meant that Egyptian commanders could field armies with large numbers of regular troops. The core of the regular troops was made up of Turkish slaves, known as Mamluks (from the Turkish word meaning 'owned'). The Mamluk warrior (left) carries the short cavalry bow favoured in Saladin's armies, which was ideal for skirmishing and harassing Crusader forces. He also carries a sword for close combat, although a single-handed axe was also popular. Askari warriors (right) were members of the emir's personal bodyguard. This Askari is armed with a heavy javelin, which was used for a final shock attack before engaging the enemy at close quarters with sword and shield. Both wear mail hauberks.

at times turn violent. Each order had an agreement not to accept men from their rival order.

The Knights of St John began as a charitable order sometime in the 1070s. Their goal was to care for pilgrims to the Holy Land. Booty from the First Crusade, donated to the order, paid for a chain of hospices across the region. Eventually the order took on the duties of protecting the pilgrims and the city of Jerusalem, and became a militant order. Using mercenaries and knights friendly to the order, the Hospitallers garrisoned several fortresses on the route to Jerusalem. After the Crusader army was destroyed at Hattin in 1187, the pope decided to support the various military orders and gave his blessing to the Hospitallers' military role.

THE CAVALRY CHARGE

There is much debate about exactly when the mounted warrior began to charge with the couched lance, i.e. with his weapon held under the arm and braced for a head-on impact. At the time of the Battle of Hastings (1066), some Norman knights were using the lance this way while others thrust downwards with it overarm or rode past and speared enemies out to the side from beyond the reach of their weapons. Some men are known to have hurled their weapons into the mass of their enemies. By 1191 the lance was fairly commonly, though

not exclusively, couched.

The impact of a charge of armoured cavalry was a tremendous thing, and many enemy forces broke before contact. This allowed the men-at-arms to ride down their foes with relative impunity, protected from random blows by their armour. Even if the enemy stood and fought, few could withstand the onslaught of the heavily armoured Western knights.

This was one of the problems the Crusaders faced in the Holy Land. There they met a foe who knew how dangerous the knightly charge could be, and was quite prepared to fall back or even run away from it. The result was that many times Crusader knights hurled themselves at the foe and hit only empty air. As their horses tired and their numbers were whittled down by the fire of horse archers, the men-at-arms would become exhausted and often found themselves dangerously far from their supporting forces.

The Crusader armies of the time included considerable numbers of foot-

soldiers and crossbowmen. Most foot-soldiers were spearmen with armour of leather or quilted cloth and often a light 'helmet' (i.e. a lesser helm) of leather reinforced with metal bands. Their large shields were their main protection. The crossbowmen were provided with quilted jerkins that offered protection against the relatively weak bows of the Saracen horse archers. Their powerful weapons were slow-firing but outranged the Saracen bows.

Saladin's forces at Arsuf were completely different to those of the Crusaders. The backbone of the force was mounted: a mix

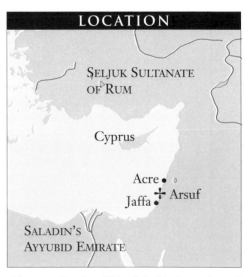

LOCATION

SELJUK SULTANATE OF RUM

Cyprus

Acre ∘
Jaffa ✝ Arsuf

SALADIN'S AYYUBID EMIRATE

After capturing Acre, Richard the Lionheart advanced along the coast of Palestine in order to strike inland to Jerusalem. However, to achieve this objective, he first had to defeat Saladin in battle.

ARSUF

A woodcut of Richard I. Regal and commanding, he is the epitome of the noble mounted warrior of his age. In Richard's case, his deeds were every bit as impressive as his image.

THE OPPOSED FORCES

CRUSADERS (estimated)
Mounted men-at-arms:	1200
Infantry:	10,000
Total:	**12,200**

SARACENS (estimated)
Cavalry:	10,000
Infantry:	10,000
Total:	**20,000**

pike- and javelin-armed Arab or Sudanese footsoldiers and Nubian archers. Ideally the pikemen could protect the archers from an enemy attack while they shot down their opponents, then complete the victory by charging with their pikes. In practice this was hard to coordinate, but the Muslim armies tended to have good discipline and training, and managed combined-arms cooperation better than many European forces of the time.

THE CAMPAIGN

Arsuf was part of the Third Crusade (1189–92), an attempt by a coalition of Christian forces to capture the holy city of Jerusalem from its Muslim rulers. The city had been lost to the Muslims under Saladin (Salah ad-Din Yusuf) after the disastrous battle of Hattin in 1187. Pope Gregory VIII ordered an immediate Crusade to recapture it. The call was answered by Richard I of England (Richard the Lionheart), King Philip II of France (1165–1223) and the Holy Roman Emperor Frederick I Barbarossa (c.1123–90). The 70-year-old Emperor Frederick was drowned during the march across Europe and most of his army turned for home, leaving Richard and Philip to continue.

Capturing Cyprus as an forward base, the Crusaders landed at Acre and besieged the port, capturing it soon after. King Philip returned home at this point but Richard, now in control of a port through which to supply his army, decided to press on to Jerusalem. With him went much of King Philip's force.

Richard's next objective was the port of Jaffa. Marching down the coast, he imposed strict discipline on his force. The army stayed close to the shore to protect its flank and to benefit from the slightly cooler conditions there. The force was arrayed in three columns plus a rearguard. The knights, suffering terribly from the heat, rode in the column closest to the sea. The two outer columns were of infantry. They suffered from the archery of enemy light cavalry who could ride up, shoot, and escape quickly, but the infantry maintained their

of light cavalry equipped with short bows and heavier horsemen able to produce a shock effect with their charge, though not so effectively as the European heavy cavalry. The horse archers of Saladin's force were mainly of Turkish origin. They could attack at close quarters with their light, curved scimitars but these were ineffective against all but the lightest armour. The horse archers were mainly assigned to harass and skirmish with the enemy, though they would swoop down on isolated or broken enemy units to massacre them. The heavy cavalry were mainly of Arab origin. They were equipped with light mail armour and armed with lances, swords and maces. Usually known as *Mamluks*, these heavy Arab cavalry made up Saladin's personal bodyguard and more of the army besides. Their function was to deliver the fatal blow to an enemy force shaken by endless horse archery. To back up the cavalry, Saladin had

discipline and stayed in formation, some men marching with several arrows sticking out of their quilted jerkins. The crossbowmen exacted a steady toll among the horse archers, who could not venture too close to the columns.

Marching under fire in this manner is one of the most difficult of all manoeuvres to carry out. Progress is slow and painstaking, since if the formation breaks up at all the enemy will sweep in and attack. Iron discipline is the key, since the galling fire of the enemy makes individuals want to hurry and opens gaps in the formation for the enemy to exploit. It was particularly impressive that the Crusader army maintained its formation, since discipline in the European armies of the time was very poor. Not only did the knights' warrior instincts tell them to rush out at the enemy but their very way of life had conditioned them to charge at threats regardless rather than plod along hiding behind a screen of common infantry.

For the infantry themselves, the feat is quite remarkable. Often despised by the flower of chivalry they now sheltered, the infantry were forced to bear the brunt of

the enemy's fire for hour after baking hour, and all to protect the precious horses of the knights. They, the infantry, were soaking up arrows to protect animals!

There were plenty of reasons for the formation to fall apart – internal divisions, pressure from the enemy, heat and exhaustion should by all the odds have combined to wear down the Christians' resolve. And yet the Crusaders' discipline held. The formation plodded slowly onward, where possible transferring wounded to

Illustrations of the Third Crusade from a thirteenth-century Venetian manuscript. Note how the noble mounted warrior receives prominence, while the common infantry are relegated to the background.

the ships that followed it down the coast and receiving supplies in return.

On 6 September the Crusader army passed through a wood north of Arsuf, a town north of Jaffa. Had the Saracens fired the wood, it might have become a death-trap, but they did not, perhaps because Saladin had other plans. Thus far the main Saracen force had shadowed Richard's army but made no serious attempt to engage. Now the time was ripe.

DISPOSITIONS

On 7 September the Crusaders had to cover about 10km (6.2 miles) to reach Arsuf, a long day's march in those conditions.

A Crusader footsoldier and sergeant. The spearman's thick gambeson of quilted cloth offered excellent protection against arrows but was uncomfortable to wear in the hot Middle Eastern climate. The sergeant's armour is backed by a similar garment worn underneath the mail.

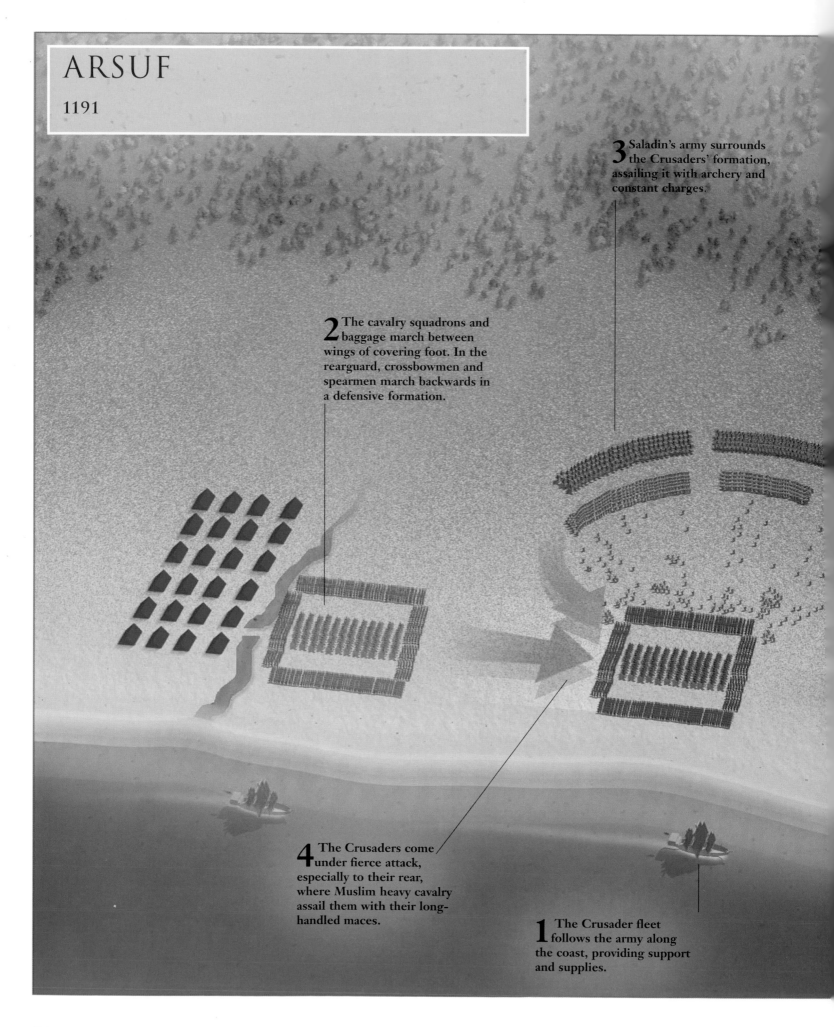

ARSUF

1191

3 Saladin's army surrounds the Crusaders' formation, assailing it with archery and constant charges.

2 The cavalry squadrons and baggage march between wings of covering foot. In the rearguard, crossbowmen and spearmen march backwards in a defensive formation.

4 The Crusaders come under fierce attack, especially to their rear, where Muslim heavy cavalry assail them with their long-handled maces.

1 The Crusader fleet follows the army along the coast, providing support and supplies.

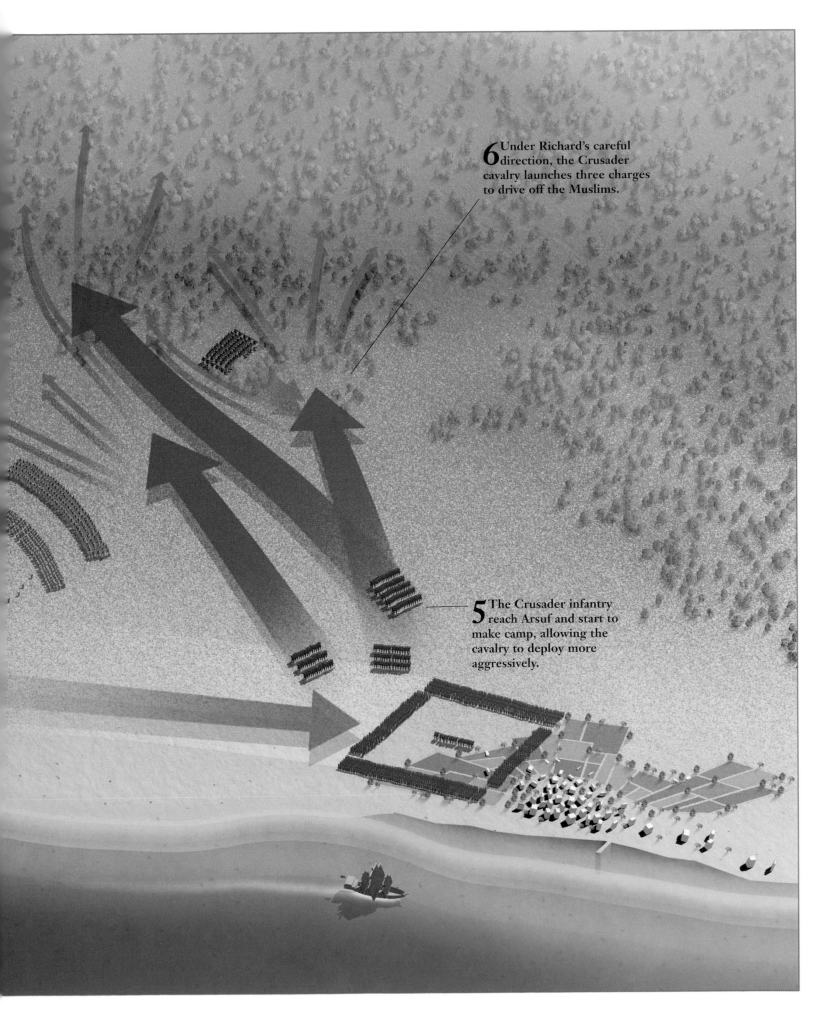

6 Under Richard's careful direction, the Crusader cavalry launches three charges to drive off the Muslims.

5 The Crusader infantry reach Arsuf and start to make camp, allowing the cavalry to deploy more aggressively.

Opposite: Richard the Lionheart leads the great cavalry charge at Arsuf. The impact of heavily armoured men on big horses was awesome and could easily shatter most enemy formations.

Saladin had no intention of letting them reach the town, however. His forces prepared themselves for an attack that would pin the Crusaders against the sea and crush them.

The Saracen formation was typically fluid, with horse archers darting in to shoot in small groups then withdrawing quickly. There was no idea of forming up for battle, just another day of marching and skirmishing. This went on until about 11.00 a.m., at which point the Saracen force attacked in earnest.

The Crusader army was in effect marching in battle formation, organized in a defensive box around its precious supply wagons and the irreplaceable heavy cavalry. In truth the battle had already been going on for days as the defensive formation held off the horse archers and their supporting forces. There had been no serious attack up until that point but now the Saracens were ready to strike.

The forces of Saladin were kept at bay by a fine piece of combined-arms work. Spearmen protected the crossbowmen from direct attack, while the heavy bolts of the crossbowmen exacted a steady toll on the enemy. And in reserve, the threat of the

heavy armoured cavalry prevented the Muslim army from making an all-out assault. For the infantry deployed at the back of the formation, this was in effect a fighting retreat. Most of the time the infantry marched backwards, keeping their shields and weapons facing the enemy. The Crusader army was a 'roving pocket' cut off in enemy territory yet able to continue its march, albeit slowly. The Muslim forces swirled around the human bulwark; ahead, behind and to the left there was nothing but enemies. On the right flank was the sea. The only hope was to march on – and fight on – so the battle became a contest between the pressure exerted by the Muslims and the discipline of the Crusaders.

STEADY PRESSURE

The pressure steadily mounted as the Saracen horse archers came in ever closer and more boldly to shoot. Sometimes the crossbowmen were able to keep the enemy at a distance, but increasingly groups of cavalry were able to race in and attack with lance and sword. Then the spearmen of the Crusader rearguard were forced to engage. Their spears were long enough to be effective against the attacking horsemen and

This Crusader infantry formation of the late twelfth century illustrates how the spearmen braced their spears against the ground while sheltering behind shields to ward off cavalry attacks. The slow-loading crossbowmen then had time to prepare their weapons to drive back any assault. They could even reload in relays, passing the bows forwards to whomever was best placed to shoot.

Bearing a powerful two-headed axe and protected by chain mail, in this illustration Richard I represents the pinnacle of twelfth-century Western military technology. Well-led, Richard's knights were devastatingly effective.

infantry ever lost control of the situation, the knights would have no choice but to engage. They were already itching for a fight; it would not take much more to provoke them into action. Yet somehow, amid the chaos and constant archery, the rearguard held to its task. It is highly unlikely that there was much order to the formation, not with enemy attacks coming in at various points. The scene would be fluid – chaotic even – changing from moment to moment.

Here a band of spearmen is driving a few paces forward, chasing off yet another attack. There a handful of crossbowmen are exchanging fire with horse archers; others load and shoot as fast as they can, covering the retirement of the spearmen back to the column. A gap in the formation is plugged by a handful of infantry just as Muslim cavalry spur at it, hoping to enter the 'box' and cause mayhem. Finally the spearmen regain the main body and struggle to catch their breath. Things are calm for a moment, with only the constant archery taking its toll. But along the line the scene is being repeated as another attack sweeps in …

For the entire morning the rearguard battled on in this manner, holding off attacks at the end of the column while the force as a whole inched forwards. Despite extreme provocation the knights resisted the urge to charge, and the column continued its march towards Arsuf and safety.

As the day wore on, casualties mounted. The whole force was now under fire, and men were falling dead and wounded. Confined within the formation the knights chafed, forced to take casualties and unable to reply in any way. The crossbowmen did their best and the outer column of foot soldiers beat off a series of minor attacks, but the strain was becoming intolerable.

COUNTER-ATTACK

As the army neared Arsuf, the pressure became too much for Richard's knights. The Hospitallers, accompanied by three squadrons of about 100 knights each, burst out of the formation in a reckless charge. Their sudden attack drove back the right wing of the Saracen force, which had been trying to draw such an attack but had ceased to expect it. If Richard did not support the

their shields offered good protection, but they were desperately tired from day after day of marching.

The rearguard could not afford to become embroiled in a mêlée with the attackers. If a group of cavalry broke off and was pursued, even for only a few steps, the spearmen would be quickly surrounded and cut down. So the Crusader infantry was forced to fight a defensive battle. Short rushes to drive off attackers were possible, but it was vital for soldiers to quickly regain the safety of the main force. Dangerous gaps opened up but were sealed by troops who were supposed to be resting inside the defensive formation.

Hoping to draw one of the famously impetuous charges of the Crusader knights, Saladin's forces concentrated mostly on the rear of the column where the Hospitallers and French Royal Guards rode. If the

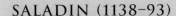

impetuous knights, they would soon be cut off and slaughtered. Yet if he did send more forces after them, he might throw away his whole force. Richard was known for his valour, but he was also a shrewd tactician. His infantry were near to the shelter of the town. Covered by a cavalry charge they could enter and secure the town as a defensive position, protecting the baggage train and giving the army a safe place to retreat to if necessary.

Richard also knew the temperament of his men. They might attack anyway if he did not order it, and without direction their force might be spent for nothing.

Ordering the Templars out, supported by Breton and Angevin knights, Richard launched them at Saladin's left wing. At last given a chance to release their pent-up rage, the knights threw the Saracens back and repulsed a counter-attack by Saladin's personal guard. Now the baggage and its accompanying infantry were entering Arsuf. Richard placed himself at the head of his remaining cavalry, Norman and English knights, and led them at the enemy.

Reeling from heavy blows on both flanks, the Saracen army was shattered by the third charge. Saladin's men scrambled back into the wooded hills above Arsuf leaving behind about 7000 casualties. No less than 32 *amirs* had been killed, almost all of them in the three great charges that broke the army.

SALADIN (1138–93)

Saladin (Salah ad-Din Yusuf Ibn Ayyub) was a courteous and generous individual who was praised even by his Crusader enemies as a man of honour. He was also great warrior and statesman. Representing himself as the champion of Islam, he was able to rally tremendous support which he wielded very effectively. Saladin understood the capabilities and weaknesses of the Crusader armies as well as his own, and shrewdly played to his own forces' strengths. At the Battle of Hattin he was able to draw out the impetuous Crusader knights and isolate them, resulting in a total victory. The same strategy was unsuccessful at Arsuf, but still Saladin was able to keep his force intact and deny the Crusaders their ultimate goal of capturing Jerusalem.

AFTERMATH

The Muslim army returned to the field the following day, resuming its harassing tactics as the Crusaders prepared to push on to their next objective. There was no attempt to launch another full assault, however. Saladin had learned that he could not penetrate the Crusaders' defensive 'box' formation and concluded that he could not draw the impetuous knights out of it either.

Richard the Lionheart did not benefit from his victory at Arsuf. Although he performed a great feat of arms and won a tactical success, his army was not able to take Jerusalem, though a grudging truce was agreed between Saladin and the Crusaders, allowing Christian pilgrims access to the city. Against almost any other Crusader commander, Arsuf would have been another great victory for Saladin. Although defeated in battle he held his army together. Its existence prevented an attack on Jerusalem and brought Saladin an honourable, if less than ideal, outcome to the war.

Tactically, and taken in isolation, Arsuf was a victory for the Crusaders. However, if Arsuf is seen as part of a gradual wearing-down of the European army to make it incapable of capturing Jerusalem, it may be that Saladin came out the strategic victor.

Saladin is depicted here as the wise and kindly father figure who cared for the poor and sick. He was also shrewd and ruthless – an admirable and necessary combination in a leader of his time.

CHÂTEAU GAILLARD
1203–04

THE SIEGE OF CHÂTEAU GAILLARD WAS A LENGTHY AFFAIR IN WHICH A DETERMINED FRENCH FORCE STEADILY DUG AND FOUGHT ITS WAY INTO A HEAVILY FORTIFIED CASTLE HELD BY TROOPS LOYAL TO KING JOHN OF ENGLAND. CHÂTEAU GAILLARD WAS A PARTICULARLY STRONG FORTRESS, AND PROVED VERY DIFFICULT TO CAPTURE.

WHY DID IT HAPPEN?

WHO A French force under King Philip II Augustus of France (1165–1223) besieged an English garrison under Roger de Lacy.

WHAT Determined to take the castle, the French steadily captured the outer and then inner defences.

WHERE Château Gaillard, at the confluence of the Rivers Seine and Gambon in northern France.

WHEN 1203–04.

WHY The castle not only guarded an important river crossing but also represented an insulting challenge to the French king, who wanted to regain lands lost to the English.

OUTCOME The French eventually managed to capture enough of the castle's defences to force a surrender.

Much has been made of the role of the mounted man-at-arms in medieval warfare. This has as much to do with the fact that these men represented the social élite of the time – and therefore determined what was recorded in written and pictorial histories – as with the truth of the matter.

It is also often assumed that warfare in the period was unsophisticated and crude, but this image is not completely accurate. True, many battles were uncontrolled affairs, but this was not the age of the annihilation battle, nor of clever manoeuvres. Instead, war was very much a matter of political interaction. The two main key means of achieving political ends were the raid and the capture of fortresses.

Military jargon of the period had many different words for 'raid', each with a quite specific meaning. Raids were carried out to show up an enemy's weakness, perhaps inciting other nobles to turn on him. They were carried out to destroy crops or other resources, weakening the enemy as a whole. Raids were launched as political bargaining chips – the enemy had to grant concessions or be subjected to more of the same. The raid was an important tool of medieval warmaking, weakening the enemy, and of politics. A raid might lead to a battle, but that was not the object

of the exercise. The political outcome was what mattered.

SIEGE TECHNIQUES
A fortified place, be it a walled town or a great castle, was both a safe haven when under attack and a secure base to operate from. However, a castle or fortress was more than merely a military installation; it was a symbol of power and prestige. A lord who could not defend his castles lost more than the region they controlled; his political reputation might be ruined. Similarly, a

A belfry was a mobile tower popular throughout the ancient and medieval period for assaulting strong walls. It contained several floors to hold attackers. Animal hides were often used to protect the wooden tower from missile fire.

leader who could capture or destroy the strong places of his rivals showed his power to everyone. He was less likely to suffer revolt or challenge in the future.

The main military advantage of a castle or fortification is as a 'force multiplier' against an attacker. A small number of men can hold a fortified area against many times their number. This may deter assault altogether since an attack would involve prohibitive numbers of casualties. If not, the castle's defences impose delay on the attackers and allow the defenders to inflict a great deal of damage.

Techniques and machines were developed to assist in breaching a castle, but at the heart of any attack were men. Not usually the noble cavalry so proudly depicted in song, story and tapestry but common footsoldiers trained to climb, dig and fight their way into a defended place. And opposing them were men similarly determined to keep them out.

With the use of siege engines or siege techniques it was sometimes possible to penetrate a gate or bring down a section of wall. A headlong charge by valorous men into the breaches might be sufficient to force entry, though the cost would be high. More often, a castle assault was a slow and calculated affair, a steady accrual of advantage by the attacker until the defenders' position became untenable. Sometimes treachery played a part in the fall of an otherwise well-defended castle.

Medieval fortress attacks were a complex interplay between besiegers and defenders. Negotiations might be entered into at significant moments, such as when a relief force was beaten off or a critical point fell. Defenders might sally out to bring in food or reinforcements, or even to attack the enemy's camp. Attempts to break the enemy's morale or even to infect the other side with disease were not uncommon. A sufficiently large force could simply sit outside and wait for the defenders to starve, but this could take a long time if the siege lines did not completely isolate the castle, or if it were well provisioned. Any siege was a

dangerous affair, however. Not only did the attacker pin down his army around the castle, robbing himself of mobility, but it was almost certain that disease would break out in his own camp sooner or later.

Despite the inherent difficulties, the reduction of strong places was necessary to campaigning in the medieval period. Not only was an intact fortress a base from which the enemy could raid wherever he pleased, but the possession of a region's fortresses was often seen as a sign that a lord or monarch's dominance over the area was complete. Capturing the fortresses was sometimes the only way to bring a war to a successful conclusion. Whatever the problems, it had to be done.

THE OPPOSING FORCES

Château Gaillard was held by Roger de Lacy, a famous English soldier who held the title of Constable of Cheshire, in the name of King John of England (1167–1216), Richard the Lionheart's brother. It was an extremely powerful castle. Guarded on two flanks by wide rivers, the castle was constructed on a natural rise. The outer approaches were protected by a ditch backed by a wooden palisade, making it difficult to even get near the actual walls.

The castle itself had three main sections. An outer enclosure protected a second

SIEGE WEAPONS

The most frequently used weapons in sieges were various types of throwing and hurling machines. These were roughly of two kinds: those that acted by tension comparable to the action of a bow, and those that worked by torsion, usually through twisted ropes bending back an arm that could be released to hurl an object. These engines varied considerably in size and power. Some were meant primarily to shoot at individuals, others to knock down walls. The catapult (left) was a version of a ballista (see page 67). It also operated like a crossbow with a string to be hauled back. This example has a small sling for throwing missiles such as stones. These could be aimed at specific targets, such as a tower or defended wall, in the hope of having some attritional effect on the defenders.

LOCATION

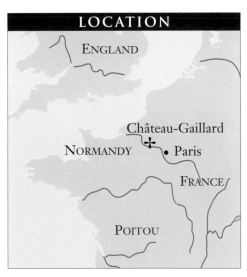

Château Gaillard stood on the frontier between Normandy – then held by the King of England – and the territory of the French king. It lay on a rocky site above the confluence of the Rivers Seine and Gambon.

CENTRES OF POWER

Although the conventional image of medieval warfare is one of thundering lance charges and individual combat between heavily armoured knights, it was by the fall of castles that power truly changed hands. It was in the breach of a wall or atop a belfry that the history of Europe was decided by archery and hand-to-hand combat. Castle assaults were planned and led by the social élite, but they were carried out by ordinary foot soldiers. Similarly the task of defending strong places fell to the common man, often poorly armed and untrained. These ordinary soldiers were the true arbiters of history, for by their actions the fates of kingdoms were decided.

courtyard (or 'ward') which in turn gave access to an inner ward. Each of the wards was surrounded by strong walls with towers. Each must be breached in turn, and each was higher than the last, offering attackers no advantage. The last ward could only be entered by a narrow bridge of natural stone across a steep gully.

De Lacy was charged with denying King Philip II Augustus of France access to the river crossings guarded by the castle, and thereby impeding any campaign he might launch into Normandy. As with any castle, the garrison was not large; the whole point of a castle was to enable small forces to hold off larger ones until assistance could arrive.

DISPOSITIONS

King Philip wished to remove the English from Normandy. The castle at Château Gaillard was the key to the campaign, but he did not move against it directly. Instead he attacked a number of lesser castles in the surrounding area, effectively isolating Château Gaillard and ensuring that his

Opposite: Although King John's unpopularity has been exaggerated by legends and folk tales, there has never been a John II of England. His humiliating defeat in France may well have been a factor in the decision of the barons to force the Magna Carta upon him.

operations were not threatened by nearby forces. Having done as much as possible to prevent the relief of the castle, Philip then set about reducing it by siege. It would be a slow process, for Château Gaillard was a powerful fortress.

The defenders were of course tied to their base, the castle. They could come out to make local counter-attacks, but for the most part they had to simply remain within the defences and try to counter the moves that Philip made. The English took the precaution of destroying the bridge, making a river crossing difficult.

Philip's forces first filled the ditch and broke though the wooden palisade that defended it. This gave access to the castle proper and was necessary before any real

King John of England pays homage to Philip II of France, c.1325–50 (from the Chroniques de France)*. Philip Augustus seized large areas of territory from England after the fall of Château Gaillard, vastly reducing John's power and prestige.*

Lutterell delin.

P. Vanderbanck sculp.

KING IOHN.

2 An English relief force advance up the River Seine but are not able to lift the siege.

4 Philip's men climb up a garderobe (toilet) chute and enter the chapel above. They then let their fellow soldiers into the central bailey, which is captured.

1 Philip II's army approaches from the east in August 1203. He builds trenches to protect his own force and contain the enemy.

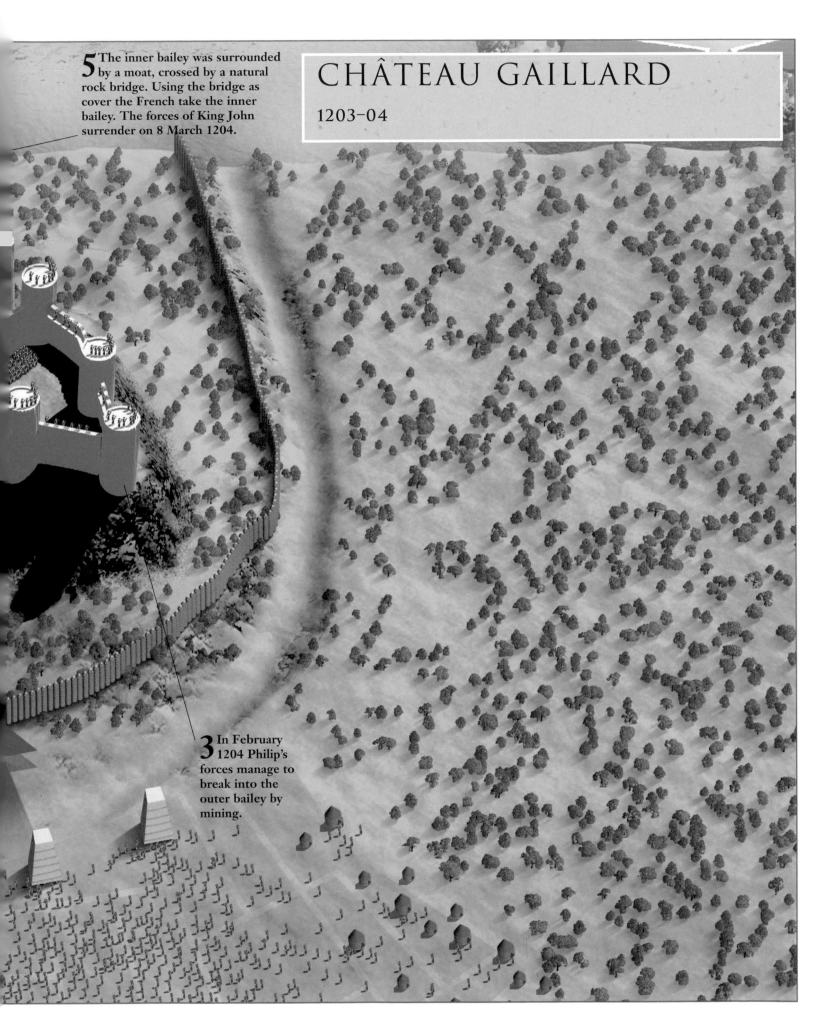

5 The inner bailey was surrounded by a moat, crossed by a natural rock bridge. Using the bridge as cover the French take the inner bailey. The forces of King John surrender on 8 March 1204.

CHÂTEAU GAILLARD
1203–04

3 In February 1204 Philip's forces manage to break into the outer bailey by mining.

The court of Philip II Augustus of France. Both the church and the nobility are prominently depicted, illustrating the undivided support that the king professed to enjoy.

operations could be undertaken. A bridge of boats, defended by ingenious floating towers mounted on boats, was set up to allow the French army to move back and forth. With his communications secure and access to the castle now gained, Philip began the work of reducing its defences.

RELIEF ATTEMPT

The English sent aid to the castle, hoping to drive off the besiegers. The relief attempt was composed of two forces. One was to advance up the river in ships and destroy the bridge of boats. The second would fall on the French land forces and defeat them.

Like so many other plans, the relief went awry. The land attack went in under cover of darkness but was almost wholly unsuccessful. What damage had been done to the bridge was repaired by the time the river force, delayed by the tide, came up. Instead of dividing the attention of the French, the two ill-timed attacks enabled them to concentrate against each in turn and defeat them in detail. By dropping weights onto the English ships

and concentrating archery against them, the French were able to drive off the attack. As the fleet withdrew, cheekily pursued by a handful of Frenchmen sailing in captured vessels, Philip made his opening moves against the castle.

PREPARATIONS

Even in the medieval period, the successful application of technology allowed a small force to achieve results out of all proportion to the size of the unit. The tool in this case was Greek Fire, a nasty mixture of naphtha, pitch and other ingredients that burst into flames when exposed to air. Strapping a number of clay canisters of this flammable material to his body, a Frenchman named Galbert was able to swim to the island behind the castle and place his charges. The resulting inferno enabled the French to storm the island and complete the isolation of the castle.

The siege was going to be a long one, so Philip had housing in the form of crude huts for his troops. He ordered that trenches be

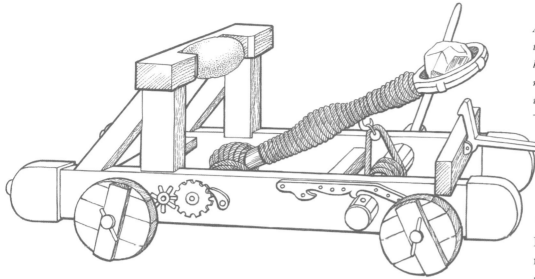

A throwing engine, called a mangonel, worked by the torsion from twisted ropes. The spoonlike arm was hauled back and secured. The spoon was loaded with a rock or other missile. When released, the arm sprang up, struck the bar and hurled the missile.

equipment to attack walls and gates. By February, the first assault was ready.

THE OUTER BAILEY FALLS

In order to get into the bailey, it was necessary to either breach the walls or open a gate. The latter was not likely, though it was possible to eventually batter through one. Philip's assault came from several directions. While siege engines and archers caused casualties among the defenders on the walls, other engines attacked the walls themselves, covered by belfries with a thick sloping roof to protect the men working inside. Miners worked to undermine the walls. This was a fraught business, requiring that a tunnel be dug close under the wall and then collapsed, usually by burning the pit-props. There were many dangers, ranging from early collapse of the tunnel to countermining by the enemy which would result in a desperate close-quarters battle for possession of the tunnels.

dug to defend the camp and that a 'covered way' be set up to allow his men to approach the castle without danger. The covered way was essentially a road dug into a trench and protected by an earth rampart where it faced the castle. This made it difficult for enemy archers in the castle to shoot at troops moving up to their positions or conducting siege works. Philip also set up his siege engines in prepared positions. He ordered that the tops of nearby hills be levelled off to provide good emplacements for them. These threw heavy rocks at the walls in the hope of eventually battering through them and hurled clusters of lighter projectiles to kill or wound the defenders. Meanwhile, Roger de Lacy was concerned that his supplies might not last until a new relief effort could be mounted. He therefore sent all non-combatants out of the castle. In some ways this might be a merciful gesture, but it was also good sense in that it meant several hundred fewer people to feed. At first the French let the refugees through their siege lines, but after a time began to refuse them passage.

The result was that several hundred people ended up trapped between the besiegers and the castle as siege engines and archers exchanged fire over their heads. There they remained for some time,

starving, until Philip relented and gave them food. His men let them through the lines and they dispersed.

King John of England made another attempt to break the siege, this time by raiding Brittany to draw off the French. But Philip declined to give up his hard work to chase the English around the countryside, and remained where he was. Disheartened, King John took ship for England and did not return.

Throughout the winter of 1203–04, the defenders made do with what they had as Philip's men received more supplies. They built belfries, mobile structures designed to protect men while they used rams or other

The ballista was an ancient weapon for shooting bolts. The same word also meant a crossbow, and it worked on the same principle. Here a winch is used to haul back the string, drawing back the bolt in its groove. A trigger then released the missile.

CHÂTEAU GAILLARD

The remains of Château Gaillard today illustrate the powerful concentric defences. The castle dominated the river crossing and represented a formidable obstacle to French aspirations in Normandy.

Mining was hard work but also very skilled. If the tunnel were collapsed in the wrong place or if it ran too deep, it would not damage the wall foundations. If it were too shallow it would fall in. Occasionally a tunnel might be used to gain access to a fortified area, but this was highly unlikely to succeed and rarely tried.

Philip's assault on the first bailey also included the most basic of castle assault techniques: escalade. Foot soldiers ran up to the wall, placed their ladders against it and began to climb. Unfortunately the ladders were not long enough to reach the top. Men became stranded on the top or in the middle of a ladder as others crowded in below, unable to go up or down and under attack by men on the walls. Some of the attackers were able to create footholds in the stonework, and some of them gained the wall. After bitter hand-to-hand fighting enough space was cleared for more men to get onto the wall, and the defenders were forced back. As more Frenchmen gained the first bailey it became obvious that it could not be held. Those of the defenders who

could fled back to the second bailey and prepared themselves for a new assault.

THE SECOND BAILEY FALLS

The cost in time and lives to gain the outer bailey had been high, but Philip was prepared for this. Sieges, especially of such a strong castle, were always expensive. He was quite prepared to pay a high price for the other baileys too. However, if another way presented itself then Philip would happily take it.

Sometimes it was possible to get into a castle by trickery, bribery or by taking advantage of the treachery of someone inside. Occasionally, a clever soldier among the attackers might be able to take advantage of a mistake by the garrison or a flaw in the defences. Château Gaillard had such a flaw. Enterprising soldiers found that they could crawl through the chute of a garderobe (a toilet) and from there clamber up into the second bailey's chapel. Setting fire to the chapel door, the Frenchmen were able to break out into the bailey and incidentally caused a great deal of confusion. They reached the bailey gate and opened it, admitting a powerful assault force. By the time the fighting was over the second bailey was a burned-out ruin and the defenders had retreated to the final sanctuary of the third bailey and the keep.

MINING THE THIRD BAILEY

The third bailey was extremely well defended, even though the garrison was down to approximately 150 men by now. The only access was over a rock formation, which bridged the steep gully in front of the walls. Assault across the bridge was suicidal, escalade was impossible and the gully made it unlikely that siege engines could be brought up to the walls. The only way in was mining. Perversely, the rock bridge worked in favour of the attackers, who were able to use it as shelter from the defenders' increasingly desperate rain of missiles.

At last, on 6 March 1204, the French were able to break into the inner bailey. One custom of fortress assaults that survived for many centuries was that once there was a 'practicable breach' in the wall, i.e. one that could be used for an assault with a realistic chance of success, the garrison commander could surrender with honour. Indeed, he was expected to. A force that surrendered when the wall came down could usually expect mercy and possibly the honours of war. If they refused and made it necessary for the attackers to endure the hell of an assault, there was little chance of quarter. At Château Gaillard,

The castle walls, rising from a steep ditch, were impossible to approach with siege engines or ladders. Archers on the circular tower could sweep the base of the wall from behind the protection of the ramparts.

the remaining defenders decided to surrender the castle. There was nothing more they could do. A last stand would simply have cost more lives – including their own – and achieved absolutely nothing.

The siege had lasted about eight months, starting in August 1203. However, the active phase of the operation, in which Philip's carefully planned assaults gradually reduced the castle's defences and forced its surrender, took only a month.

AFTERMATH

Having captured Château Gaillard, Philip launched a campaign into English-held territory. English prestige and morale had suffered badly. Not only had they lost their fine castles but the relief attempt had resulted in total defeat. Normandy did not put up much of a fight, and afterwards Philip took Rouen and pushed on all the way to the coast. His campaign gained him several provinces including Anjou and Touraine. English holdings in France were greatly diminished. Château Gaillard's commander, Roger de Lacy, returned to England to begin work reinforcing his own castle at Pontefract.

In England, where King John was already unpopular, the fall of Château Gaillard

meant the loss of even more prestige. A king who could not even keep control of his own castles, and who failed to come to the assistance of loyal lords holding out under siege in his name, was a weak king. It is likely that the humiliation of Château Gaillard played a part in the decision of the English barons to challenge King John. This in turn led to one of the most important events in English history: the signing of Magna Carta.

Mining a wall was an ancient and common way of passing it. The idea was to tunnel under the wall, supporting the roof of the tunnel with props. When the tunnel was complete the props were fired and it collapsed, bringing down the wall with it. The attackers at ground level could then get in.

CONSTANTINOPLE
1203-04

THE VENETIAN AND FRENCH FORCES THAT SET OUT ON THE FOURTH CRUSADE WERE 'DETOURED' AND ASSAULTED THE CITY OF CONSTANTINOPLE IN BOTH 1203 AND 1204, MARKING THE LARGEST AMPHIBIOUS ATTACK IN THE MIDDLE AGES TO THAT DATE. THIS BATTLE SHOWED WESTERN MILITARY INGENUITY AND COORDINATION AT ITS BEST.

WHY DID IT HAPPEN?

WHO A French Crusader army numbering about 12,000 accompanied by 8000 Venetians led by the Doge Enrico Dandolo (c.1122–1205), opposed by the larger garrison of Constantinople, commanded by the usurper Emperor Alexius III (d. 1211).

WHAT The Crusader army launched a two-pronged assault against a heavily fortified city.

WHERE Constantinople, modern Istanbul, Turkey.

WHEN July 1203, April 1204.

WHY The Crusader army, in debt to Venice, sought to solve its financial woes by restoring the exiled Prince Alexius (d. 1204) to the throne of the Byzantine Empire.

OUTCOME Venetian seaborne forces and French Crusaders attacked the city. Much of it was burned, the usurper fled and the Crusaders installed Prince Alexius as Emperor Alexius IV.

By the early thirteenth century, it was generally accepted that the Byzantine Empire was past its prime. The empire's main military recruiting grounds had been lost to the Turks in the course of the eleventh century, and the emperors increasingly relied on diplomacy and mercenaries. There is little evidence of a training programme for men-at-arms comparable to the education of Western knights. The Byzantine navy was also decrepit, since most Byzantine trade was carried by the fleets of the Italian city-states. Worse, emperors could rarely count on the complete loyalty of their commanders and troops. Internal rivalries and factions were especially a problem in 1203: Emperor

Alexius III had deposed and blinded his brother, Isaac II Angelos. Many believed that the true ruler was Isaac's son Alexius, who had escaped to Western Europe to beg for help in regaining his throne.

The Crusader force was composed of two elements: French knights and footsoldiers, and Venetian sailors, oarsmen and marines. Each group was arguably the most professional of its time, the one by land and the other by sea. French knights had won an enviable reputation for their skill and discipline, including an ability to coordinate the battlefield tactics of heavily armed knights and footsoldiers, especially crossbowmen. The Venetians, for their part, aimed to dominate the Mediterranean, and

This fourteenth-century manuscript illumination depicts the Venetian Council of Ten. The doge and nine others sit in discussion, while four scribes sitting in the front take notes.

their galley fleet had proved its value and effectiveness in a large number of encounters throughout the twelfth century, including the assault of several cities. Key to Venetian success was the flexibility of their tactics. The Venetians fought in the typical style of medieval galleys, relying on the oarsmen to bring the vessel into action and marines to disorganize the enemy with a barrage of arrows, rocks and other projectiles before boarding enemy ships for hand-to-hand combat. Venetian fleets had also experimented with amphibious warfare in the twelfth century, though, achieving high proficiency at landing fighting men who were ready to engage with land enemies immediately.

THE CAMPAIGN

Pope Innocent III proclaimed the Fourth Crusade in 1201. The expedition was intended to liberate Jerusalem from Muslim control, perhaps by way of an attack on Alexandria. But the French nobles who organized the expedition made a serious error of judgement. Intending to facilitate travel to the Holy Land, they made a treaty with Venice, by which the Venetians, in return for a per capita payment, were to provide transport for 33,500 men and 4500 horses, besides providing 50 armed galleys to protect the transports. Many Crusaders decided to journey to the East by other routes, however. Only about 12,000 Crusaders turned up at Venice in the summer of 1202, leaving an enormous bill to be paid for the ships the Venetians had constructed in good faith and at great expense.

The Venetians offered the Crusader leadership, a consortium of French nobles, a way to fulfil their obligations. Their leader, Doge Enrico Dandolo, declared that the city would wait for its payment if the Crusaders helped the Venetians with a military problem of their own, the reconquest of Zara, until recently a Venetian possession on the eastern shore of the Adriatic. Despite protests that Crusaders should not attack a Christian city (whose ruler was himself a Crusader), they had no choice but satisfy the Venetians, taking Zara after a brief siege.

The conquest of Zara did not solve the Crusaders' monetary problems, though. It

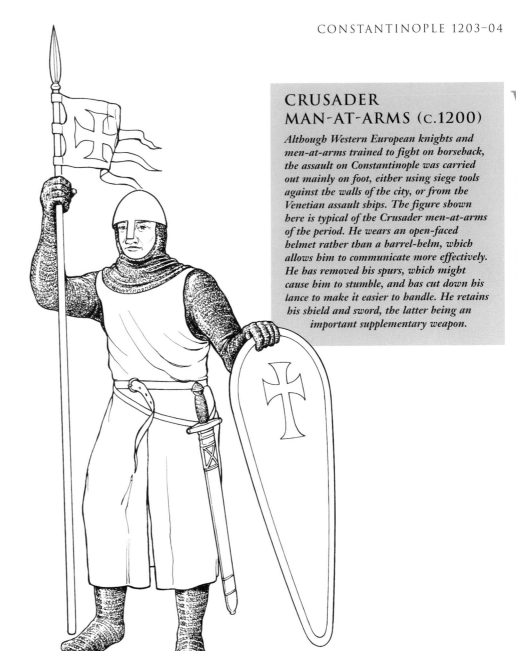

therefore seemed to be a heaven-sent opportunity when a Byzantine prince, Alexius Angelos, came and asked the Crusaders to help him gain his rights – his father, Isaac II Angelos, had been deposed and blinded in a palace coup. In return, Alexius promised to pay the Crusaders' debt to Venice and aid them on their Crusade. So the Crusaders set out for the Christian city of Constantinople, where, to their surprise, they found the people unwilling to accept Prince Alexius' claims. So they prepared to attack, to win his rights by force.

DISPOSITIONS

Medieval Constantinople was a hard nut to crack. The city was famous for its defences. It was built on a promontory that projected into the sea and was thus surrounded by water on three sides. The whole was also encircled by massive walls. The Land Walls

CRUSADER MAN-AT-ARMS (C.1200)

Although Western European knights and men-at-arms trained to fight on horseback, the assault on Constantinople was carried out mainly on foot, either using siege tools against the walls of the city, or from the Venetian assault ships. The figure shown here is typical of the Crusader men-at-arms of the period. He wears an open-faced helmet rather than a barrel-helm, which allows him to communicate more effectively. He has removed his spurs, which might cause him to stumble, and has cut down his lance to make it easier to handle. He retains his shield and sword, the latter being an important supplementary weapon.

LOCATION

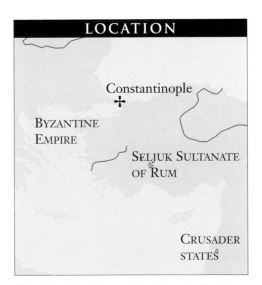

Constantinople

BYZANTINE EMPIRE

SELJUK SULTANATE OF RUM

CRUSADER STATES

The old capital of the crumbling Byzantine Empire, Constantinople guarded the entrance to the Black Sea, the rich lands of which had attracted raiders and would-be conquerors as far back as the ancient Greeks.

were particularly strongly fortified, and on two of the sea sides assault was impossible – on the Bosporus and Sea of Marmara fronts of the city the walls rose almost directly from the water, and attackers would also have to cope with the rough open sea.

The only conceivable weak spot was the Golden Horn, the harbour of Constantinople. On that side of the city, ships were sheltered from the open sea; there were also small beaches between water and walls, where attackers could gain a precarious foothold for an assault with scaling ladders. The authorities of Constantinople had long dealt with the threat from within the Golden Horn, though, by running a great iron chain across the mouth of the harbour, anchored at either side by strong towers. Ships could only enter if they paid a fee to have the chain raised.

For their attack, the Crusaders planned a strategy that would employ both land and sea contingents as efficiently as possible. The first step was to gain control of the Tower of Galata at the harbour mouth. To do so, they planned an amphibious assault, the largest such operation in medieval history up to that time.

THE FIRST ATTACK

The assault on Constantinople began on 5 July 1203 with the effort to take the Tower of Galata at the mouth of the Golden Horn. French Crusaders and their horses were loaded into their transport ships, which were then towed towards the land by galleys (the transports were roundships, propelled by sails, and could not trust to the wind to get them to their agreed position). The transports were run aground on the beach

This fifteenth-century Western European woodcut of Constantinople conveys a good impression of the city's powerful system of defences.

The conquest of Constantinople, 1203. Shallow-draught Venetian-style galleys like this were well suited for attacks on beaches, and proceeded to outwit the defending Byzantines, who were not expecting a seaborne invasion.

before the small suburb of Galata.

Although Greek soldiers were massed on the beach to contest their landing, the Venetian ships were well suited to this sort of amphibious assault. The holds of the transports had doors that could open into ramps, which facilitated loading and unloading. The ramps also made it possible for the French knights to saddle and mount their horses while still aboard the ships, riding out ready to attack the enemy. The Crusaders drove off the Greeks on the beach in short order, a success that can be credited to Venetian ingenuity and French horse-handling skills, but also to Greek military disorganization and unwillingness to fight. The Crusaders then camped for the night.

The next day opened with a Greek surprise attack on the Crusader camp, which was beaten off. The Crusaders then stormed the Tower of Galata by means of the siege ladders they had brought along.

THE SECOND STAGE

Their ships now safe from interference by troops in the Tower of Galata, the Venetians proceeded to deal with the chain across the harbour mouth, breaking it by ramming it with their largest ship, which had been specially reinforced for the purpose. Some Byzantine warships were present in the Golden Horn and tried to prevent the

Venetian vessels from entering. But the Byzantine Empire no longer had an effective war fleet.

The ships were decrepit and the forces aboard them inadequate; they were soon beaten and the Crusaders proceeded into the harbour, where they began to fortify a camp as if for a long siege. Such a strategy was impossible, however. The Crusaders had almost no supplies left, and everything to fear from the forces in the city, which seem to have outnumbered them by a considerable margin. The Westerners suffered a series of sallies from the city, responding with counter-attacks, for several days. The Venetian and French leaders soon settled on a bold plan to assault the city, implementing it as soon as their preparations were complete.

THE ASSAULT

On 11 July the French Crusaders set off from their camp to march around Constantinople towards the Land Wall, where in an assault it would be possible to use their horses effectively and fight with familiar tactics. They had to rebuild a bridge that the Greeks had destroyed, but Emperor Alexius made few other attempts to harass them while on the march, showing a lethargy that has mystified historians. A large Greek force gathered outside the walls to combat the French when the main assault came on 17 July.

The troops of Count Baldwin of Flanders (1172–1205), who led the land

CONSTANTINOPLE

1203–04

5 A large Byzantine force exits the city to engage the French Crusaders, pressing them so hard they have to summon the Venetians for support.

4 Venetians break into the city near the Blachernae Palace. They are soon forced to withdraw, to support their French allies.

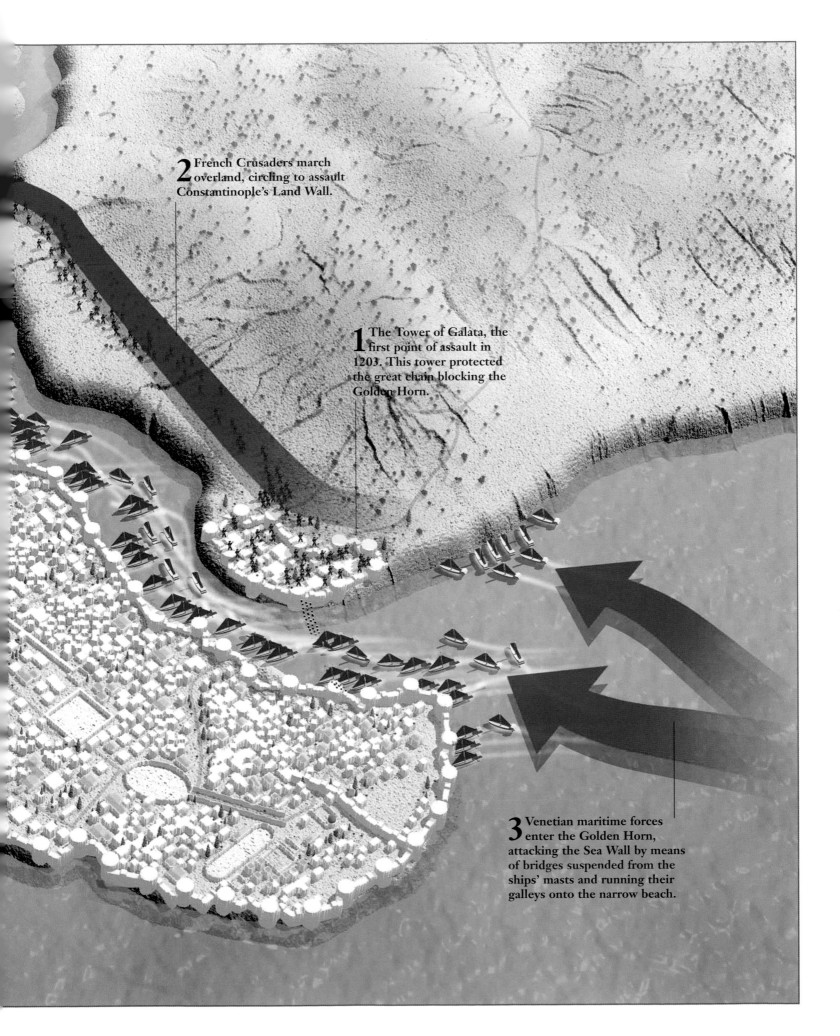

2 French Crusaders march overland, circling to assault Constantinople's Land Wall.

1 The Tower of Galata, the first point of assault in 1203. This tower protected the great chain blocking the Golden Horn.

3 Venetian maritime forces enter the Golden Horn, attacking the Sea Wall by means of bridges suspended from the ships' masts and running their galleys onto the narrow beach.

assault, succeeded in raising a few siege ladders against the wall, but the attack was soon beaten off in heavy fighting, both on and before the wall. Meanwhile, the Venetians had prepared their own naval assault. The Sea Wall of Constantinople that faced the Golden Horn was less imposing than the Land Wall, but still stood 9m (30ft) high with heavy towers at regular intervals. There was no shortage of defenders, both archers and engineers working catapults, some so large that they launched stones heavier than a man.

The Venetians' preparations were meticulous. They covered their ships with hides, to protect them from Greek Fire, a highly combustible chemical compound.

They also padded their ships with timber and vines, providing some protection from the catapults on the walls. They then proceeded to launch a two-pronged attack. Galleys were to beach before the walls, so their men could disembark and erect siege ladders to scale the walls. Much more unusually, the larger roundships were converted into floating siege towers. The seamen built plank bridges, broad enough for three men abreast, then attached them to the masts so they could be swivelled and latched onto the wall – if the ship could get close enough.

Venetian forces succeeded in capturing large segments of the Sea Wall, thanks in part to a variety of mobile siege towers mounted in the larger Venetian ships. Screens to protect their troops from missile fire helped the attackers get close to the wall.

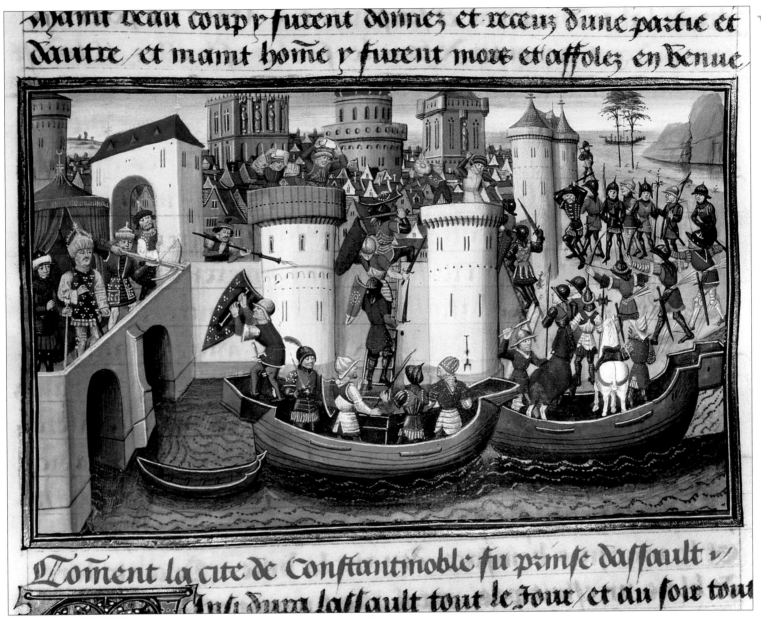

A favourable wind did indeed allow the roundships with their portable bridges to approach the wall. Their chance of success in face of a strong defence seemed slim, though, so the Venetian commander, the Doge Enrico Dandolo, decided to employ the galleys to draw at least some of the fire from the roundships. Dandolo, although old and blind, had the loyalty of the Venetians. He ordered the beaching of the galleys and, when the crews hesitated, ordered his own flagship to set an example, running it up onto the beach and sending his men against the walls with ladders.

The other Venetians would not allow their elected ruler and their city's banner to remain in such danger, and raced to follow. The roundships and galleys worked extremely well together. Several roundships managed to hook their bridges onto towers and send their men pouring onto the walls of Constantinople. They then opened the gates for the galley crews that had landed on the beaches. In this way the Venetians gained a large section of the Sea Wall.

Despite their gains, the Venetians did not enter Constantinople. Instead, they were forced to withdraw to lend support to the French Crusaders, who found themselves in serious difficulties at the Land Wall. While withdrawing, though, the Venetians set fires that spread and consumed a large part of the city.

The battle was won, however. Emperor Alexius III, despairing of his ability to hold his throne in face of such determined assault and the growing hatred of his own people, fled that very night. The city gates were

This fifteenth-century manuscript illustration depicts the capture of Constantinople in 1203. The dress, armour and city walls in the illustration bear little resemblance to the actual siege, being more representative of the period in which it was drawn.

This nineteenth-century engraving of the Crusaders' entry into Constantinople, by Gustave Doré (1832–83), captures the horror that many people have expressed over the centuries at this Christian conquest of a Christian city.

soon peaceably opened, and Prince Alexius was admitted to be crowned as co-emperor with his father Isaac.

AFTERMATH

The new emperor, Alexius IV, failed to keep his promises to the Crusaders, probably lacking the resources to do so. Betrayed and disillusioned, the Crusader force attacked Constantinople again in April 1204, this time taking the city by storm, subjecting it to a vicious sack, and establishing a Westerner, Baldwin of Flanders, as the new Byzantine emperor (although he was captured in battle the following year and died a prisoner). The

Crusade leaders were excommunicated for attacking a Christian city, and the Crusade never reached the Holy Land.

The consequences of the two assaults on Constantinople were catastrophic for the Byzantine Empire. The city was stripped of its wealth, and 60 years of Latin rule so sharpened antagonism between Catholics and Orthodox Christians that the Greeks were ultimately more willing to accept conquest by the Ottoman Turks than to ally themselves with the hated Westerners. The empire never regained its territory or its financial strength, weakening it fatally just as the Ottomans began their rise.

The French Crusaders carried a great deal of booty home with them. Nevertheless the ultimate winners in this conflict were the Venetians. The Italian city-state established itself as the pre-eminent naval power in the Mediterranean, claiming sweeping trading privileges in Byzantine territories and taking full advantage of the fleet that had been constructed for the Fourth Crusade. Venice created a highly militaristic trading empire in the eastern Mediterranean, seizing a series of bases by

applying the tactics they had developed so effectively at Constantinople.

The Battle of Constantinople in 1203 is perhaps most important as a demonstration of skills current in Western Europe by this time, rather than for its innovations. The meticulous planning and tight discipline of the assault show beyond a shadow of doubt that Western soldiers and sailors, when well led and coordinated, could execute complex tactics with absolute professionalism, whether by land or by sea.

This seventeenth-century painting by Domenico Tintoretto (1560–1635) shows the conquest of Constantinople. While it vividly expresses Venetian pride in the event, the artist's depiction is historically inaccurate in several respects.

BOUVINES
1214

ON 27 JULY 1214, AT THE BRIDGE OF BOUVINES, WEST OF TOURNAI, IN THE COUNTY OF FLANDERS, A BATTLE WAS FOUGHT THAT INVOLVED MOST OF THE MAJOR PRINCIPALITIES OF WESTERN EUROPE. PHILIP II AUGUSTUS (1165–1223), KING OF FRANCE, DEFEATED AN ALLIED ARMY LED BY THE HOLY ROMAN EMPEROR OTTO IV OF BRUNSWICK (C.1180–1218).

WHY DID IT HAPPEN?

WHO The French led by King Philip II met the allies under Holy Roman Emperor Otto IV.

WHAT The battle was fought in three phases: cavalry vs. cavalry; cavalry/infantry vs. cavalry/infantry; infantry vs. infantry.

WHERE At Bouvines near Tournai in northern France.

WHEN 27 July 1214.

WHY Several French princes rebelling against Philip II were joined by King John of England (1167–1216), who had lost lands to Philip, and Otto IV, because Philip was supported by Pope Innocent III (1160–1216).

OUTCOME: Philip II Augustus's patient tactics easily defeated the allied princes, who rushed into battle without waiting for the arrival of their entire army and without any united leadership.

To the participants, the Battle of Bouvines was a worldwide conflict, for nearly every ruling magnate in northwestern Europe took part there, with Pope Innocent III, Prince-bishop Hugh de Pierrepoint of Liège, and King John of England anxiously awaiting the results. Except for the battles of the Crusades, no medieval battle can compare with Bouvines for its European scope and participation.

On one side fought Otto IV of Brunswick, the Holy Roman Emperor, with his barons – the Counts of Tecklemburg, Katzenellenbogen, and Dortmund – and their armies. Joining Otto was William, Earl of Salisbury, half-brother of King John of England. William Long Sword, as he was known, was there to command the troops sent from England, and to be in charge of the large amount of money donated by King John to the allies. Ferrand of Portugal,

Count of Flanders and Hainault, also fought with his large force of knights and footsoldiers, and he was joined by several other rebellious nobles of France, including Reginald of Dammartin, Count of Boulogne, and Hugo, Baron of Boves. Also present at Bouvines was Willem, Count of Holland, Hendrik I, Duke of Brabant, and the Counts of Limburg and Lorraine, with many lesser counts, dukes and nobles, 'bellicose men, expert in military matters', in the eyes of the contemporary English chronicler Roger of Wendover.

King Philip II of France, known to history as Philip Augustus, a cognomen given him by his biographer, Guillaume le Breton, opposed them. The historian Clarius would later eulogize Philip as 'the most victorious king, who as a son of the Holy Mother Church stands as a defender and protector of Catholicism'. Philip and

The Battle of Bouvines was a favourite subject of French painter Horace Vernet (1789–1863) who specialized in portrayals of the victories of great French generals. Now hanging in the Musée du Château at Versailles, this painting shows the victorious King Philip II Augustus of France at the end of the battle.

his army were supported by the pope and the Prince-bishop of Liège, who also sent troops to fight with the French.

The Battle of Bouvines was a large battle, fought with sizeable armies on an extensive battlefield. Modern historians do not agree with the numbers recorded in early narrative sources – some of which place each side at 80,000 – but they do agree that it was fought by armies of between 10,000 and 20,000.

Both armies also fielded large cavalry forces, with perhaps as many as 1200 dubbed knights fighting with the French force and 1500 with the allies. However, the numbers of infantry greatly exceeded those of the cavalry; in the Flemish army, they may have totalled more than four times those of the cavalry. The allies' forces also seem to have outnumbered the French, although not by a large amount. Nor did the allied generals use these larger numbers to any advantage.

CAUSE OF THE CONFLICT

Each of the allies seems to have had his own reason for opposing Philip Augustus in the war that ended with the Battle of Bouvines. King John's reason was probably the most simple: Philip had been capturing English lands in France since he returned home from the Third Crusade in 1191. Trying to regain these lands had cost John's elder brother, Richard the Lionheart, his life in 1199 at the siege of Chalus. A defeat of Philip would return these lands to the English crown.

Otto IV's conflict was more with the pope than it was with Philip. Crowned by Innocent III as Holy Roman Emperor in 1209, confirming his election as King of Germany the year previously, Otto quickly earned Innocent's anger by claiming and then attacking the Kingdom of Sicily. The pope promptly excommunicated the emperor, freeing the Germans from allegiance to him and inciting his enemies to rebellion. Innocent's suggested replacement was his ward, Frederick of Hohenstaufen. The rebellion had gone increasingly against Otto for four years. Opposing Philip, who was supported fully by the pope, was a means for Otto to regain his credibility as ruler of Germany.

As for those French princes who opposed their king, it is difficult to locate a principal cause for their rebellion. Certainly Philip Augustus' strength as a ruler limited the sovereignty of all his barons. Some of the more powerful ones felt independent enough to oppose their king. Ferrand of Portugal, despite being Count of Flanders and Hainault only since his marriage to the Countess, Joan of Constantinople, in 1212, was the strongest of these, and thus served as the rebels' leader. His special disrespect for the king was shown in his refusal to accompany him on an invasion of England in 1213, since such a course would have been economically damaging to his counties' cloth industries. Thus an alliance with King John of England, Otto IV of Brunswick, and other rebellious French lords was logical.

THE CAMPAIGN

The day before the battle, Philip Augustus' army was in Tournai, 20km (12.4 miles) east of Bouvines. Although Tournai was in the County of Flanders, the townspeople had chosen not to rebel against the king with their count, Ferrand of Portugal. (Throughout the Middle Ages, even during the Hundred Years War when enemies surrounded the town for several decades, Tournai would always remain faithful to the French king.) At Tournai, Philip Augustus and his military leadership held a council of war. They determined to march towards the allied army and to try to bring them to battle as soon as possible. But they also determined to find favourable terrain on which to fight.

The allies started the day of battle only about 12km (7.4 miles) to the southeast of the French, at Mortagne. According to the French chronicler known as the Minstrel of Reims, it was only at Mortagne that the allied leaders were informed of the

THE ORIFLAMME

This French knight bears the Oriflamme, the sacred silk standard of France. The Oriflamme was traditionally dated to Charlemagne and only taken from St Denis Cathedral when facing heretics or rebels, the latter being the case in 1214. It was thought that when it was taken out in battle, God was with the French. The Oriflamme's divine inspiration prompted more ferocious and heroic actions from the French soldiery, especially at Bouvines.

LOCATION

Philip Augustus and his French army, being pursued by an equally large coalition of forces from the Holy Roman Empire, decided to do battle outside Bouvines, a small town in northern France.

BOUVINES

This late medieval illumination, found in a manuscript of the Grandes Chroniques de France and currently housed at the Bibliothèque Nationale in Paris, shows the charge of French King Philip Augustus against Holy Roman Emperor Otto IV of Brunswick. However, although both rulers were on the battlefield, they never directly faced each other.

Le .x. Coment othon assembla son ost a valencennes . Et coment il vindrent or tennez a bataille pour ce qui cuidierent le roy seurprendre despourueuement .

THE OPPOSED FORCES

FRENCH (estimated)
Mounted men-at-arms:	1300
Infantry:	4–5000
Total:	**5300–6300**

ALLIES (estimated)
Mounted men-at-arms:	1500
Infantry:	6000
Total:	**7500**

Opposite: The Battle of Bouvines, in 1214, was decided in favour of King Philip Augustus in one of the most important encounters of the Middle Ages. There the French king's armies fought against and defeated a coalition of forces from the Holy Roman Empire, England and rebellious French principalities. This highly romanticized engraving of Moreau de Tours, created in the nineteenth century, shows the obeisance to Philip of the defeated soldiers.

proximity of the French army, and in hearing this news they rejoiced, as 'they believed they had them in their net'. Confident that they could easily defeat the French, the allies were concerned only with fighting them and not with where the battle was to take place or if the terrain would favour them. They marched in pursuit of the French army.

At Bouvines Philip found the favourable terrain he had been searching for. He stopped on the other side of the bridge over the Marcq River at Bouvines, next to the Roman road on which his army had been marching. At the small church in Bouvines, the king celebrated mass with his barons, 'fully armed' and prepared for war. He then addressed them, in words recorded by the Minstrel of Reims:

'Lords, you are all my men and I am your Sire … I have much loved you and

brought you great honour and given you largely of what was mine. I have never wronged or failed you but I have always led you rightfully. For God's sake, I beg you all today to protect my body and my honour, and yours as well. And if you think that the crown would be better served by one of you, I agree to it and want it with good heart and good will.'

The French barons answered: 'Sire, for God's sake, we do not want any King but you. Ride bravely against your enemies, we are ready to die with you.' They then left the church, unfurled their banners, including the Oriflamme, only to be unfurled against enemies whom the king regarded as heretics or rebels. To the French, the Counts of Flanders and Boulogne and the Baron of Boves were rebels. They were also heretics, as Otto IV of Brunswick had been excommunicated by

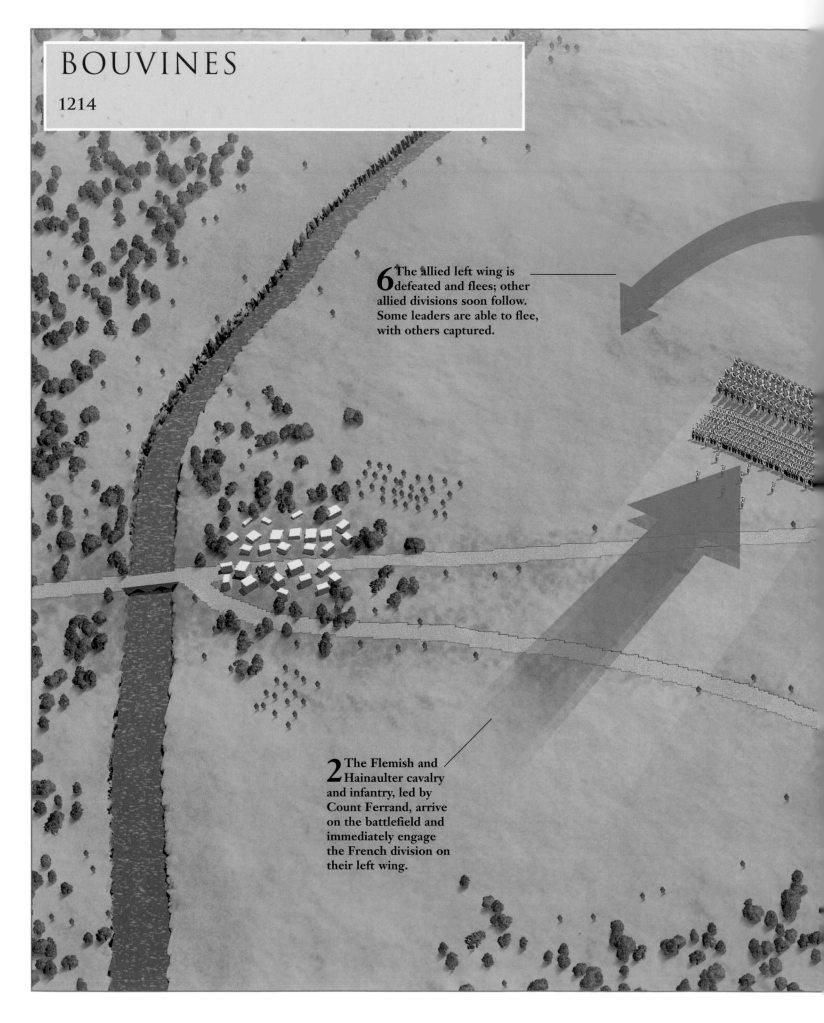

BOUVINES

1214

6 The allied left wing is defeated and flees; other allied divisions soon follow. Some leaders are able to flee, with others captured.

2 The Flemish and Hainaulter cavalry and infantry, led by Count Ferrand, arrive on the battlefield and immediately engage the French division on their left wing.

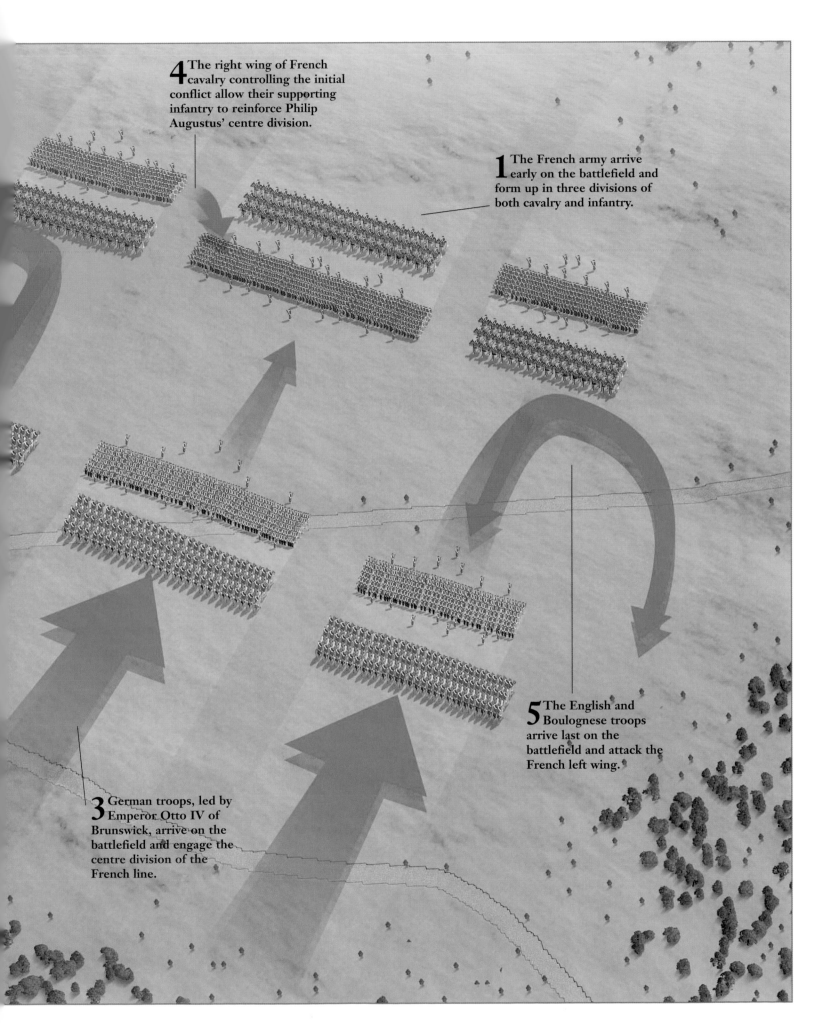

4 The right wing of French cavalry controlling the initial conflict allow their supporting infantry to reinforce Philip Augustus' centre division.

1 The French army arrive early on the battlefield and form up in three divisions of both cavalry and infantry.

3 German troops, led by Emperor Otto IV of Brunswick, arrive on the battlefield and engage the centre division of the French line.

5 The English and Boulognese troops arrive last on the battlefield and attack the French left wing.

Of the several French nobles rebelling against Philip Augustus, none was more powerful than Ferrand of Portugal (1186–1233). Having gained the County of Flanders by marrying Countess Joan of Constantinople, Ferrand was captured at Bouvines and imprisoned in Paris for 12 years. This fourteenth-century illumination depicts the count in a fictional fight against the king.

Pope Innocent III, and it was forbidden to side with an excommunicant.

DISPOSITIONS

The *Relatio Marchianensis de pugna Bouvinis*, likely the earliest account of the battle and written by either an eyewitness or from eyewitness accounts, reports that Philip demonstrated an important characteristic of good generalship, humility, a trait that was not duplicated in the leaders of the enemy forces: 'Seeing that his adversaries were pursuing him terribly, like enraged dogs, and also bearing in mind that he could not retreat without too much dishonour, [Philip] put his hope in the Lord and arranged his army into military echelons as is customary for those who are about to fight.'

His was a calculated strategy. The king realized that the terrain at Bouvines – a large,

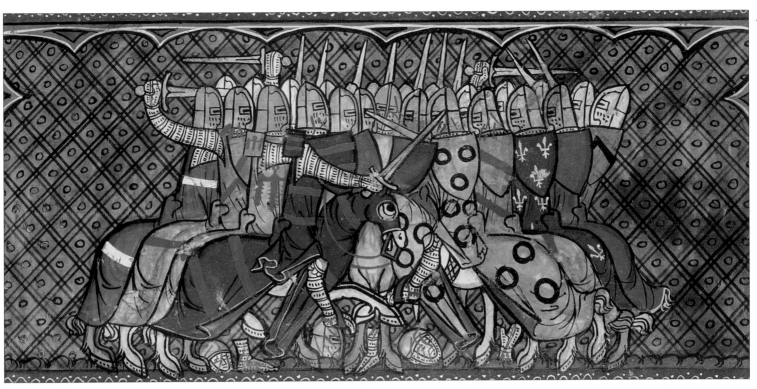

Because of its scope and participants, the Battle of Bouvines was depicted in numerous contemporary illustrations. Here the French and allies' armies are shown embroiled in cavalry combat in an illumination painted c.1335 in a manuscript of the Grandes Chroniques de France.

flat area surrounded by river and marshes – offered him several advantages, and he ordered his army in three large divisions, cavalry and infantry in each division. They were impressive warriors. Again, the author of the *Relatio Machianensis* writes:

'The knights and the auxiliaries, armed and arranged into ordered echelons, prepared in all haste for the battle. The horses' bridles were tightened by the auxiliaries. The armour shone in the splendour of the sun and it seemed that the light of day was doubled. The banners unfolded in the winds and offered themselves to the currents; they presented a delightful spectacle to the eyes.'

The allied army was pursuing the French at a very fast pace. Of course, the cavalry rode in front. When their leaders heard that the French had stopped at Bouvines, their pace picked up even more. This stretched the allied army out for quite a distance. One modern historian, J.F. Verbruggen, estimates that the length of the

allied column might have reached as much as 10km (6.2 miles).

Military wisdom would have suggested that the Flemish vanguard halt their march and wait for the rest of the allied forces to catch up. This would have united the whole allied army, thereby allowing them to exploit their numerical superiority. But those in the van did not follow this more cautious path. Instead, they formed their own units and marched onto the field. A second part of the army joined them at Bouvines before the battle began, but throughout its course further allied soldiers continued to arrive, some not reaching the field until the fight was over.

The left wing of the allies, filled mostly with Flemish and Hainaulter cavalry, under the leadership of Ferrand of Portugal, faced a French right wing composed of heavy cavalry supported by lighter horsemen, led by the Duke of Burgundy and the Count of

This French knight wears arms and armour typical of the early thirteenth century. A full helm obscures his face, adding to the menace of his appearance. Intimidating the enemy by one's appearance has always been a useful weapon in the armoury of a soldier.

Champagne. In the centre of the allied forces was Emperor Otto, his German barons, and their cavalry and infantry – in almost equal numbers. They faced Philip Augustus' main body, also both cavalry and

BOUVINES

On the battlefield, the nobility were identified by their coat-of-arms. In this way, knights could tell friend from foe and were also able to spot a high-standing prince who would bring a rich ransom if captured. The fleur-de-lys (top left) was first adopted by Philip II; later the English kings incorporated the symbol into their royal heraldry as an indication of their claim to the French throne.

infantry, commanded by the king himself. Finally, on the allies' right wing, Reginald of Dammartin and William Long Sword commanded a division of their own soldiers and also several bands of mercenaries whose services had been purchased with English money. Although it is known that there was cavalry in this division, it seems to have been primarily composed of infantry, the numbers of which increased throughout the battle as allied infantry soldiers arrived, this wing being closest to the road. These soldiers faced a French left wing composed of both cavalry and infantry and led by the Counts of Ponthieu and Dreux and the Bishop of Beauvais, among others.

THE BATTLE

The Battle of Bouvines began with a clash between the allied left and French right wings. This was in the form of a simultaneous cavalry charge – horse against horse, lances couched – as if a tournament mêlée was being fought. Again, the *Relatio Marchianensis* provides the best account: 'The first French echelon attacked the Flemings with virility, breaking their echelons by nobly cutting across them, and penetrated their army through all impetuous and tenacious movement.'

As was the case often with such horse-on-horse combats, the fighting was over quite quickly; the *Relatio Marchianensis* continues: 'The Flemings, seeing this and defeated in the space of an hour, turned their backs and quickly took to flight.' In this phase of battle, the experienced French cavalry appears to have faced little competition from their counterparts. No infantry are recorded as having been involved in this combat.

While the cavalry battle was being fought on his right, Philip Augustus delayed

his own attack. Once more one can see in this only his military experience and leadership expertise. He had ordered his infantry in front of his cavalry and, as such, he knew that a defensive posture was preferable to an offensive charge. However, the emperor who faced him was not willing to await the outcome of the fighting next to him. He charged recklessly into the centre of the French line. Initially, the Germans pushed the French troops back, the energy of the charge even knocking the king from his saddle. But, the French lines held; they did not break or flee. Guillaume le Breton, who was probably also an eyewitness to the battle, recounts what happened:

'While the French were fighting Otto and the Germans, German footsoldiers that had gone on ahead suddenly reached the King and, with lances and iron hooks, brought him to the ground. If the outstanding virtue of the special armour with which his body was enclosed had not protected him, they would have killed him on the spot. But a few of the knights who had remained with him, along with Galon of Montigny who repeatedly waved the standard to call for help and Peter Tristan who of his own accord got off his steed and put himself in front of the blows so as to protect the King, destroyed and killed all those sergeants on foot. The King jumped up and mounted his horse more nimbly than anyone would have thought possible. After the King had remounted and the rabble that had brought him down had all been destroyed and killed, the King's battalion engaged Otto's echelon. Then began the marvellous fray, the slaying and slaughtering by both sides of men and horses as they all were fighting with wondrous virtue.' Eventually, the German attack petered out, with the French infantry, supported by the cavalry who were lined up as their reserve, regaining their lost ground and then pushing their opponents back. In the midst of the engagement, Otto's own horse was wounded and, turning away from the fighting, it fled, taking the emperor with it. The second phase of the battle had also gone to the French.

About the time the first phase of the battle was ending, and shortly after the second phase had begun, the third phase began. Once more, the allies took the initiative, charging their right wing into the French left. And, reinforced by their constantly arriving infantry, they continued to fight long after the other two allied divisions had broken and run. The fighting here was much more evenly balanced, causing Guillaume le Breton to admire the allied leaders there:

'Count Reginald of Boulogne who had been in the fray continually was still fighting so strongly that no one could vanquish or overcome him. He was using a new art of battle: he had set up a double row of well-armed foot soldiers pressed closely together in a circle in the manner of a wheel. There was only one entrance to the inside of this circle through which he went in when he wanted to catch his breath or was pushed too hard by his enemies. He did this several times.' However, eventually, as these French soldiers began to gain reinforcements from the other two victorious divisions, the remaining allies left on the field – some cavalry with a lot more infantry – began to tire and weaken. Yet, only after the Count of Boulogne's horse was killed under him, trapping him in the fall, did they finally cease fighting. According to Guillaume le Breton, at this time only six knights remained by his side. The other allies had fled or surrendered.

AFTERMATH

Surprisingly, despite the length of the encounter and the numbers who fought at the Battle of Bouvines, only 169 allied and two French knights are reported to have been killed, suggesting the strength of the armour of their time. Contemporary sources record no figures for infantry deaths, but it is suggested that they, equally well armoured, also lost only a few. Many more were captured and would see the inside of Philip's dungeons, including five barons – Ferrand of Flanders, William, Earl of Salisbury, Reginald of Boulogne, Willem of Holland, and the unnamed Count of Tecklemburg – 25 other nobles, and 139 knights. Ferrand was not freed until 1227. Emperor Otto IV of Brunswick, Hendrik of Brabant, and Hugo of Boves managed to escape, but for Otto IV and Hugo of Boves

it was but a short respite. With his defeat at Bouvines, Otto IV had lost all credibility as emperor. Innocent III and the German princes who opposed the Otto had been proven right in an 'ordeal by battle'.

Although he attempted to regain his former position, Otto quickly found that his erstwhile German allies had turned against him. Frederick II now found no opposition in ascending the German throne. Knowing that he would be summarily executed if caught, Otto IV lived on the run for four years, harboured by friends, until he died of natural causes in 1218. Hugo of Boves did not live even that long. Trying to reach the safety of London after the battle, he is reported to have fallen overboard during a storm in the Channel and drowned. English losses were more geographical. Of the once-large Angevin Empire in France, John was only able to hold onto Gascony, and then just barely, thus setting the stage for the Hundred Years War, which began more than a century later.

Two illuminations on the Battle of Bouvines painted c.1335 and found in a manuscript of the Grandes Chroniques de France. *The first shows a fictional combat between Ferrand, Count of Flanders, and King Philip Augustus. The second depicts the captive Ferrand being led by the victorious king into Paris.*

LEIGNITZ
1241

THEY RULED THE GREATEST LAND EMPIRE THERE HAS EVER BEEN. FROM KOREA IN THE FAR EAST TO THE SHORES OF THE BALTIC, FROM THE ARCTIC CIRCLE TO THE TIP OF INDIA THE MONGOLS WERE SUPREME. POPES, KINGS AND EMPERORS HAD NO ANSWER TO THE SCALE OF THEIR STRATEGY OR THEIR DISCIPLINE ON THE BATTLEFIELD.

WHY DID IT HAPPEN?

WHO A Mongol army comprising two *touman* (20,000 warriors) under Baidar on an 'diversionary raid' was confronted by an army of Silesians, Germans and the Holy Orders of 20–30,000 men under Henry II of Silesia (d. 1241).

WHAT Mongol skirmishers repulsed the initial allied assault but the Silesian army renewed the attack and the Mongols feigned retreat drawing the allied cavalry into the heart of the army. Here they were attacked from both front and flank. Beaten and routed they then carried away the infantry waiting in reserve.

WHERE Leignitz, now in modern Poland, between Prague and Breslau.

WHEN 9 April 1241.

WHY The Mongols attacked all who did not submit to them.

OUTCOME The allied army was utterly destroyed and the Mongols slaughtered everyone in the Oder valley as a lesson to the rest.

The first Mongol attack on Europe came in 1221 when they passed northwards through the mountains between the Black and Caspian Seas. After ravaging modern Russia for three years they retired to the central steppes after the longest march in history and laden with plunder. Twelve years later, in 1236, they returned and again ravaged Russia. The news was spread by one Friar Julian but few listened unless they were on the front-line like King Bela IV of Hungary (1206–70). He took in Cuman refugees from the Mongol hordes and allied them to his cause. Meanwhile the Mongols rested in a great tented city in the Don valley while their leaders squabbled over drinking precedence, a dispute which was resolved only through reference to the vizier at the Mongol capital of Karakorum.

In 1240 they were ready to move again and raided deep into the Russian heartland destroying even mighty Kiev. Overwintering near Przemysl on the modern border between Poland and the Ukraine they were on the move again, following a plan that would have been awesome in any age, but in early medieval Europe must have seemed supernatural. In fact it was masterminded by the Mongol general Subedei. Three *touman* would hold down the already beaten Russians, while the remaining 10 *touman* would advance on a 1000km (621-mile) wide front heading west between the Black Sea and the Baltic. The target was Hungary. Two *touman* under Baidar and Kadan would sweep northwest into Poland and Lithuania on a diversionary raid and then move south to support the main effort. One, under Siban would skirt the northern edge of the Carpathian mountains and enter Hungary from the north. Batu with perhaps four *touman* would force the passes through the

The Mongol Empire in 1300 was the greatest land empire the world has ever seen. At its height, it stretched from Southeast Asia in the east to Poland in the west. Under the leadership of Genghis Khan's grandson, Batu, the Mongols first entered Europe in 1237, capturing the plains of western Russia in just a single winter.

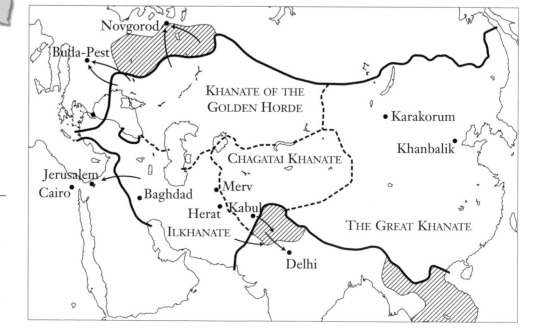

mountains in Transylvania to arrive from the east. Meanwhile the architect of the plan, Subedei, would advance along the banks of the Danube and appear from the south. If the response to the southern attacks appeared too strong for the combined eight *touman* they were to withdraw until the northern force arrived in the enemy's rear. Not even the German attack on the Soviet Union in World War II matched this level of strategic planning.

THE CAMPAIGN

In keeping with Mongol tradition Batu wrote to both King Bela of Hungary and Frederick II, the Holy Roman Emperor, demanding the surrender of their kingdoms and payment of a tenth of everything for the upkeep of the Mongol army – or face the destruction of everything. This was so audacious a demand it could hardly be believed and the Christian princes continued their relatively petty squabbles. The Holy Roman Emperor, of whom Bela was a vassal, was arming his men in a dispute with the pope, who was doing the same, over the emperor's disobedience and his atheist and libertine views.

The north, preoccupied with tensions between the Teutonic Order, the princes of Poland and attacking either pagan tribes or Orthodox Russians, was taken completely by surprise when Baidar and Kadan's army arrived. King Bela, however, had started fortifying the Carpathian passes and putting out scouts in the direction of the Mongol hordes. It was to no avail; he assembled his army in February but there were deep divisions between factions and disputes raged even as the Mongols were in the passes. By mid-March the Mongols were through and Hungarian towns and fortresses were falling to the invaders and being burnt. By the end of March the Mongols were at the gates of Pest. However, they did not attack, but withdrew.

King Bela should have sat tight but he did not. He and his huge divided army followed. On the banks of the river Sajo at Mohi the 100,000-strong Hungarian army camped for the last time. The chained wagons encircling their encampment became their own trap. Batu's four *touman* and Subedei's two *touman* had combined and

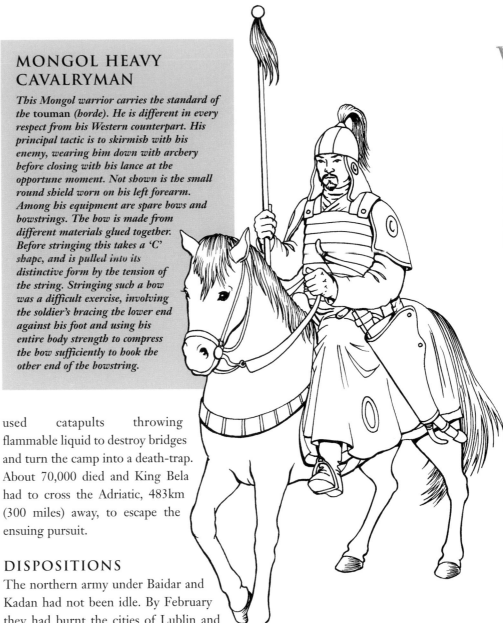

MONGOL HEAVY CAVALRYMAN

This Mongol warrior carries the standard of the touman *(horde). He is different in every respect from his Western counterpart. His principal tactic is to skirmish with his enemy, wearing him down with archery before closing with his lance at the opportune moment. Not shown is the small round shield worn on his left forearm. Among his equipment are spare bows and bowstrings. The bow is made from different materials glued together. Before stringing this takes a 'C' shape, and is pulled into its distinctive form by the tension of the string. Stringing such a bow was a difficult exercise, involving the soldier's bracing the lower end against his foot and using his entire body strength to compress the bow sufficiently to hook the other end of the bowstring.*

used catapults throwing flammable liquid to destroy bridges and turn the camp into a death-trap. About 70,000 died and King Bela had to cross the Adriatic, 483km (300 miles) away, to escape the ensuing pursuit.

DISPOSITIONS

The northern army under Baidar and Kadan had not been idle. By February they had burnt the cities of Lublin and Zawichost (Volodymyr) on the road to Warsaw. Next was Sandomir, taken with barely a fight. This was not going to plan. They were supposed to be drawing forces towards themselves and away from the main action in Hungary. But no one wanted to come out and fight. They had to try harder. Promising to rendezvous at Breslau 322km (200 miles) to the west, Baidar and Kadan split the army making each part a more tempting target. Kadan's *touman* rode west and attacked Mazowiecki. Baidar headed into the setting sun and towards Cracow. Baidar got the result he wanted. Leading elements came within a few kilometres of the city, captured some slaves and booty and retired slowly back to camp. The Polish commander of the garrison couldn't resist the temptation and led a large portion of his force in pursuit. The Mongols feigned panic and routed leading the garrison even further

LOCATION

The Mongols succeeded in battle by degrading first the cohesion then the morale of their enemy. This was made easier by their reputation, which intimidated many foes before battle was joined.

LEIGNITZ

away from the city. Then 18km (11 miles) from the gates the Mongols turned the panicked rout into a trap and the Poles were caught. Most were killed but enough were allowed to escape back to Cracow and

The artist of this fourteenth-century miniature has depicted both the garrison and Mongols in European dress and equipment. The 'handle' on the end of the crossbows is actually a foot stirrup used to hold the weapon down while the string is attached to a hook on the shooter's belt, thus cocking the bow ready to fire.

spread total and unfeigned terror. When the rest of the *touman* arrived the city was deserted. Cracow was burnt to the ground.

Baidar now had to cross the River Oder. The bridges had already been destroyed so there was a delay while his men collected boats. By the time they arrived at Breslau the inhabitants had already burnt the city and sought refuge in the castle. News now reached him that all the hard work was beginning to pay off.

Henry of Silesia had formed an extensive alliance and was at Leignitz, a

mere day's ride for a Mongol. Also King Wenceslas of Bohemia (1205–53) was on his way with another army 50,000 strong. Baidar sent messages to Kadan and Batu as his *touman* raced to get to Leignitz before the two armies could unite.

THE OPPOSING FORCES

Henry's army included his own Silesians plus contingents from the Holy Orders: Teutonic Knights, Templars and Hospitalars, few in number but strong in determination. There were also some

Germans from the settlements in Lithuania and the survivors from Cracow. They comprised knights, sergeants and footsoldiers, about 25,000 in all. Apart from the Holy Orders most were poorly trained feudal levies. Henry's army was organized into four 'battles': Bavarian goldminers from Goldburg led by Boleslaw Syepiolka; Polish levies and the Cracow survivors commanded by Sudislaw, whose brother had died outside Cracow; the Teutonic Knights spearheaded the contingent from Oppeln with Duke Miccislaw at their head;

and finally the Templars and Hospitalars fronted the Silesian army led by King Henry. Apart from the Goldburg contingent which was all infantry, each battle seems to have been made up of both infantry levies and mounted knights.

The Mongols also included men from many different tribes and cultures. But all had been subsumed into the higher Mongol organization. Surrounded by veterans with thousands of miles on horseback and numerous raids and battles behind them, they could not fail to fight well. The army was raised from one man in ten, first from the Mongol heartlands then the conquered territories as the empire grew. Each warrior had to provide his own weapons and horses. He might lead two or three spares on campaign and feed himself from what he could hunt, carry or find. He was expected to serve for as long as required – there was no time limit. Mongol organization was decimal in form. The smallest unit was ten men, then 100, 1000 and the 10,000-strong *touman*. The horses of a unit were all of the same basic colour.

A typical Mongol horse archer. He is mounted on a pony of 13 to 14 hands, which had immense stamina. He was equally able to fire to his left side, right front and to the rear. His only blind spot was his rear right.

THE BATTLE

The Mongols sent forward their *Mangudai* light cavalry, proficient in feigned flight. They were met by Henry's Silesian cavalry who were of such bad quality they ran from the *Mangudai* who had planned to run away themselves. Henry sent forward the Polish cavalry and Teutonic Knights. These succeeded in slowly 'forcing' back the *Mangudai* but too slowly so he joined in himself with the rest of his cavalry. The *Mangudai* now ran away.

Mistaking this for a rout the knights followed and pursued deep into the deadly embrace of the Mongol army. The cavalry on their flanks closed in, showering the knights with arrows. They even set fire to a smokescreen they had prepared in the path of the knights after they had ridden over it. Thus, for the remaining infantry the

<table>
<tr><td colspan="2">**THE OPPOSED FORCES**</td></tr>
<tr><td colspan="2">MONGOLS (estimated)</td></tr>
<tr><td>*Mangudai* cavalry:</td><td>1000</td></tr>
<tr><td>Horse archers:</td><td>11,000</td></tr>
<tr><td>Heavy cavalry:</td><td>8000</td></tr>
<tr><td>**Total:**</td><td>**20,000**</td></tr>
<tr><td colspan="2">ALLIES (estimated)</td></tr>
<tr><td>Knights/men-at-arms:</td><td>8000</td></tr>
<tr><td>Light cavalry:</td><td>3000</td></tr>
<tr><td>Infantry:</td><td>14,000</td></tr>
<tr><td>**Total:**</td><td>**25,000**</td></tr>
</table>

LEIGNITZ

1241

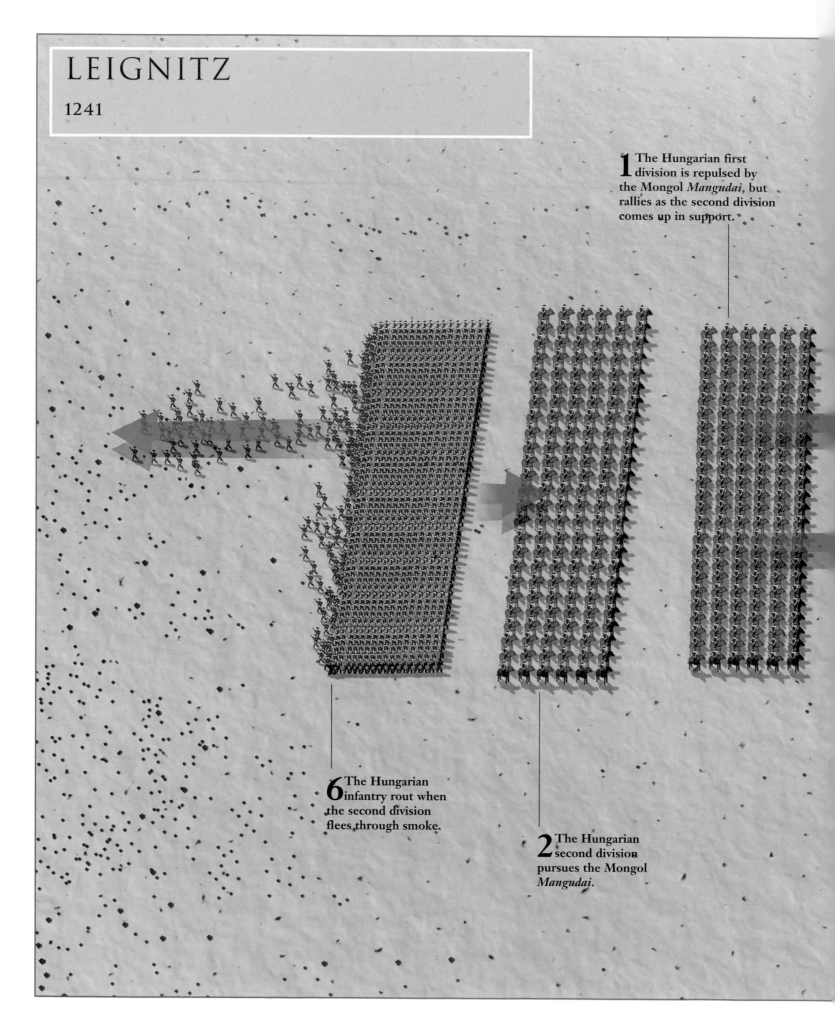

1 The Hungarian first division is repulsed by the Mongol *Mangudai*, but rallies as the second division comes up in support.

6 The Hungarian infantry rout when the second division flees through smoke.

2 The Hungarian second division pursues the Mongol *Mangudai*.

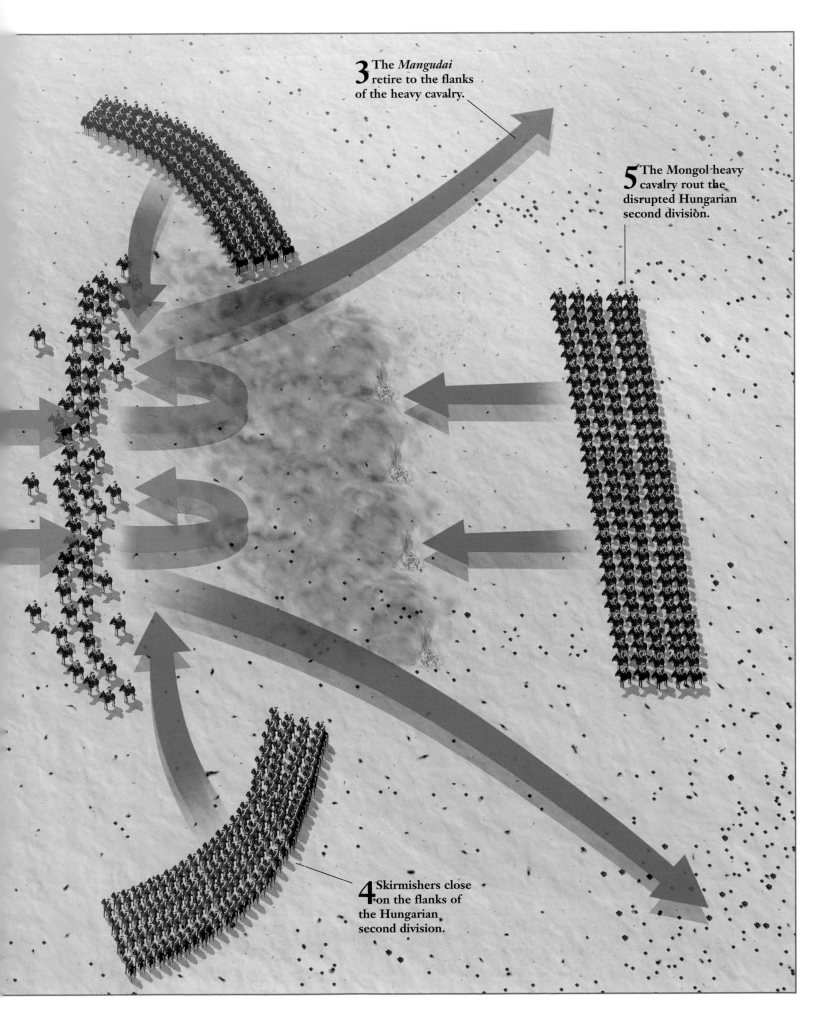

3 The *Mangudai* retire to the flanks of the heavy cavalry.

5 The Mongol heavy cavalry rout the disrupted Hungarian second division.

4 Skirmishers close on the flanks of the Hungarian second division.

LEIGNITZ

This sixteenth-century miniature shows a Mongol chieftain wearing loose, comfortable clothing, probably silk. His quiver and bowcase are suspended from his belt. The Mongols shaved the crown and back of the head but kept long plaits at the sides.

in to regenerate the area. If Leignitz was taken with their victories at Mohi and Hermannstad the same week, the Mongols were now in a position to sweep into Western Europe. They consolidated their hold on Hungary but did not cross the Danube all that summer. They burned Pest, the twin town of Buda. News embellished by the fancies of the medieval mind spread as far west as France. There was an attempt to raise a Crusade against the invaders but the fighting between pope and emperor continued. Even Austria, now taking its turn in the front line, had to contend with an invasion from the emperor.

In reality there was no coordinated resistance plan, no army assembling to stop the deadly tide. The pope died, and so did his 80-year-old successor before he could be crowned. The Danube froze that winter and Batu crossed on Christmas Day and captured and destroyed modern Esztergom, while Kadan did the same to Buda and Zagreb. Their scouts reached the outskirts of Vienna and Venice. Austria was next and perhaps Italy after that. But the Mongols didn't have it all their own way. A Croatian army beat them at Grobnok a mere 80km (50 miles) southeast of Trieste.

Only fate could offer Europe a respite and it did. The great Khan Ogedai (reigned 1229–41), the son of Genghis Khan (1167–1227) died in Karakorum, 5683km (3500 miles) to the east on 11 December 1241. The news arrived in mid-March 1242 and the princely commanders of the armies were obliged to return to elect his successor, just like the cardinals electing a new pope. The Mongol tide ebbed, leaving everything drowned in blood on the way. The Christians did manage to send a delegation – three friars, Stephen, John and Benedict – from the pope's new capital at Lyon in France (where he had been forced to skulk by the Holy Roman Emperor) to speak with the Mongol lords. Stephen was too ill to complete the journey. But John and

knights would have appeared to be swallowed up. And then there was the awful wait before worst fears were realized. The knights reappeared, a few to begin with, but soon followed by the rest – routed.

The best the area had, lords and masters over all they surveyed, had been beaten by heathens by some unknown means. The infantry couldn't stand it, they too routed and the Mongols pursued. Relentless pursuit by an enemy mounted on faster horses, as the Mongols were, was an awful thing. There was no escape, no time to hide, no let-up in the killing. This is when armies

are utterly destroyed. In half a week the Mongols had slaughtered three armies totalling 150,000 men. The year 1241 was a good one for the harvester of souls.

AFTERMATH

In Poland, along the Oder River, the population was all but exterminated. The Grand Master of the Teutonic Order escaped, but Henry did not. To keep a tally of the dead during the pursuit the Mongols cut an ear off each of their victims and collected them in sacks. There were nine of them, large ones. Settlers had to be brought

Benedict arrived at Batu's camp at Sarai on the banks of the Volga while at Karakorum Kuyuk was about to be crowned khan. From Batu's camp they moved on to Karakorum taking 15 weeks to travel the 4023km (2500 miles).

The new khan, disinclined towards Christianity, did not accept the pope's message kindly. If he was not accepted as overlord by the European princes he would 'know them as his enemies'. More than two and a half years after leaving, the friars returned to Lyon full of the ominous threats of the khan.

Meanwhile the Mongol hordes turned their attention to the Muslim world of the Middle East, and it was here that they met their match. The *Mamluk* troops of Egypt routed the Mongols at Ain Jalut in 1260, at Albistan in 1277 and at Homs in 1281. Further invasions were attempted over the following decades. But, effectively, Europeans had the Muslims of Egypt to thank for saving their lands.

This fifteenth-century Persian painting shows the figure on the left controlling his horse with his knees while using his lance two-handed in a fighting style that goes back more than 1000 years. Although the lance loses some of its transferred momentum through the flexibility of the soldier's arm muscles, the technique allows the cavalryman to use the lance as a stabbing weapon in the post-charge scrum.

PEIPUS
1242

ALEXANDER NEVSKII, REVERED IN SOVIET PROPAGANDA, WAS CAUGHT BETWEEN CATHOLIC INTOLERANCE AND PAGAN INDULGENCE. HOWEVER, HE KNEW WHO TO KNEEL BEFORE AND WHO HE COULD FIGHT. HE ACCEPTED THE MONGOL YOKE AND AT LAKE PEIPUS DEFEATED THE TEUTONIC KNIGHTS AND THEIR ALLIES.

WHY DID IT HAPPEN?

WHO A Russian force of 5000 under Alexandre Nevskii (1220–63), opposed a Crusader army of perhaps 1000 under Bishop Hermann von Buxhoved of Tartu (d. 1248).

WHAT The power of the knightly charge was dissipated by mounted archery and the remaining knights overwhelmed by the more numerous enemy.

WHERE Lake Peipus, on the border between modern Estonia and Russia.

WHEN April 1242.

WHY The Russians had launched a raid into enemy territory in revenge for one by the Crusaders and were in the process of withdrawing when they were caught by the pursuing Crusaders.

OUTCOME Almost half of the Crusaders were killed, a few were captured and even fewer escaped.

Christianity spread from Palestine along two distinct northerly routes. To the northwest it travelled through the communication routes of the Roman Empire and became the Catholic Church. Due north it progressed through Armenia and Greece to Russia and became the Greek and Russian Orthodox Churches. When these two great arms of Christianity reached the Baltic, progress stalled as they encircled the pagan peoples of Poland, Lithuania, Livonia and Estonia.

Denmark, then on the rise and ruling Norway as well as the country we recognize today, expanded into the area and annexed modern Estonia around 1100 AD. But this was not so much a religious move, as simply an extension of Danish power to secure trading outlets. The first notion of a Baltic Crusade was preached in 1198, but the response was poor and progress patchy. So in 1204 the Bishop of Riga, Albert von Buxhoved, formed a military order, the Sword Brethren, in order to boost enthusiasm for the Crusader movement.

In 1224 they wanted to attack the pagans in Estonia, especially their fortress of Tartu, which was subject to the rule of the Orthodox Russian city of Pskov, in turn subject to Novgorod. The assault was joined by one of Albert's brothers Hermann. Although bitterly contested, the attack was

successful and Hermann became the Christian Bishop of Tartu. This put the bishop and the Sword Brethren in conflict with the Danes who had designs of their own on the area. Ten years later the pope dispensed a Solomon-like judgement and gave Estonia to the Danes and Latvia to the

Alexandre Nevskii (1219–63), Russian boyar (prince), lionized in a Soviet propaganda image. He had many disagreements with Novgorod's city council and nearly did not help them in their struggle with the Teutonic Knights. He later accepted Mongol suzerainty and ruled in their name until his death.

Teutonic Knights. Unfortunately the Sword Brethren plus some visiting Crusaders and 200 Russians from Pskov were all but wiped out in 1237 at the battle of Siauliai in Lithuania against the pagan Kurs. The remnants of the order had little option but to merge with the new military order in the area, the Order of the Hospital of St Mary of the Germans of Jerusalem, better known as the Teutonic Knights. They had been founded when the Crusaders attempted to recapture Acre from the Muslims in 1190 following the Battle of the Horns of Hattin and only arrived in the area with 20 knights and 200 sergeants in 1230. After a shaky start they had became the primary Catholic military force around the Baltic. But they were still principally concerned with affairs in the Holy Land from where the Grand Master frequently called for his subordinates to attend upon him. Thus it was that in 1242 the knights were commanded not by their local commander or his second-in-command but by the third-ranking leader Andreas von Felben.

Encouraged by the Crusaders' capture of the Byzantine capital and seat of the Greek Orthodox Church in 1204, the pope demanded that Orthodox Novgorod accept the Latin creed. But Novgorod had other problems – the Mongols, to name several thousand, who had first raided in 1223. Also, following the battle of Siauliai the Lithuanian tribes had united under the leadership of one Mindaugas and the Crusaders were seen as being a counter to them, allowing the Russians to focus on the far greater threat of the Mongols. In 1237 they penetrated further north than ever before, and Novgorod, now governed by Alexandre Nevskii, submitted rather than risk annihilation. Although the army retired up to its horses' knees in Russian mud the Mongols retained a loose suzerainty over the city-state.

THE CAMPAIGN

The Crusaders planned a three-pronged invasion in line with each individual contingent's ambitions. The Swedes would sail the length of the modern Gulf of Finland and land near the site of modern-day St Petersburg. They hoped this would

NOVGOROD POLK INFANTRYMAN (c.1240)

Russia was first settled by the Vikings travelling along its rivers. They met the nomadic tribes who roamed the steppes. So Russian arms and armour reflect both Western (Norse) and Eastern influences: long-handled axes, spears and round shields from Scandinavia, lamellar armour, Norman-style teardrop shields, and conical helmets from the East. This infantryman wears chain mail armour with a sleeveless, waist-length quilted tunic and a round, Turkic-style breastplate. He has a simple Norse-style conical helmet with a nose guard, and is armed with a long-handled axe.

limit the encroaching Orthodoxy amongst the Finnish tribes and secure their own trading routes to the Russian heartland. The Danes, supported by visiting Crusaders, would attack along the coast from their northern Estonian border through Narva and towards Koporye. The Teutonic Knights and their allies would capture the city of Pskov at the southern tip of Lake Peipus. The three forces were separated by 241km (150 miles) of the most inhospitable terrain, utterly incapable of supporting each other. Nineteen kilometres (12 miles) a day were as much as a force could hope to achieve in that environment. Here we can see the hand of an unmilitary man, William of Modena, the Pope's envoy sent to patch up the dispute between the Danes, the Sword Brethren and the Buxhoved brothers.

He also organized the Crusade, perhaps to unite the different parties. In 1240 the Swedes set sail, a year before the other invasions. Their force included Norwegians, some Finnish tribesmen and a few Teutonic Knights. They made camp on the southern

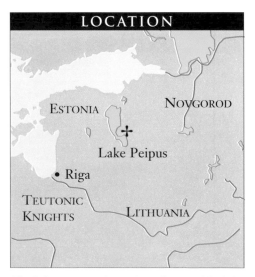

LOCATION

The Baltic coast was the northeast frontier of Catholic Europe. Germanic settlers spread along the coast then pushed inland, overpowering the pagan tribes. Here they met the Orthodox Christians of Russia.

People have always needed heroes and role models. Although never canonized, Alexandre Nevskii is depicted here as the central figure on a Russian Orthodox icon – an object of worship. The style of this image can be traced back to the Byzantine Empire and thence to Imperial Rome.

bank of the River Neva – and here hesitated. Alexandre Nevskii, however, did not. He mobilized the local men from the pagan tribes and, together with his own *druzhina* (roughly equivalent to a Western lord's retinue), launched a dawn attack on the Swedish camp. It was totally successful and the Swedes were swept back to their boats.

Over winter the Danish thrust got under way. By this time the forces of Novgorod had dispersed amid internal bickering and the Danes had considerable success. There were sporadic raids which penetrated to within 30km (19 miles) of Novgorod but the main effort along the southern shore of

the Gulf of Finland captured the Novgorod outpost at Koporye. Here the Crusaders started building a castle, which was completed by April 1241 (it cannot have been much more than a tower). About the same time the awful tales of the Mongol defeat of the Hungarian host at Leignitz, huge by comparison with the forces operating in this area, must have reached them, but Novgorod's earlier submission to the Mongols paid off and they were left alone. Now the third prong of the attack was launched towards the southern tip of Lake Peipus and the fortress of Izborsk. The small army included Teutonic Knights

Opposite: The Holy Orders were led by a Grand Master who owed his allegiance to the pope and could treat on equal terms with kings. The Grand Master of the Teutonic Order is pictured here with one of the Sword Brethren in thirteenth-century mail armour.

PEIPUS

1242

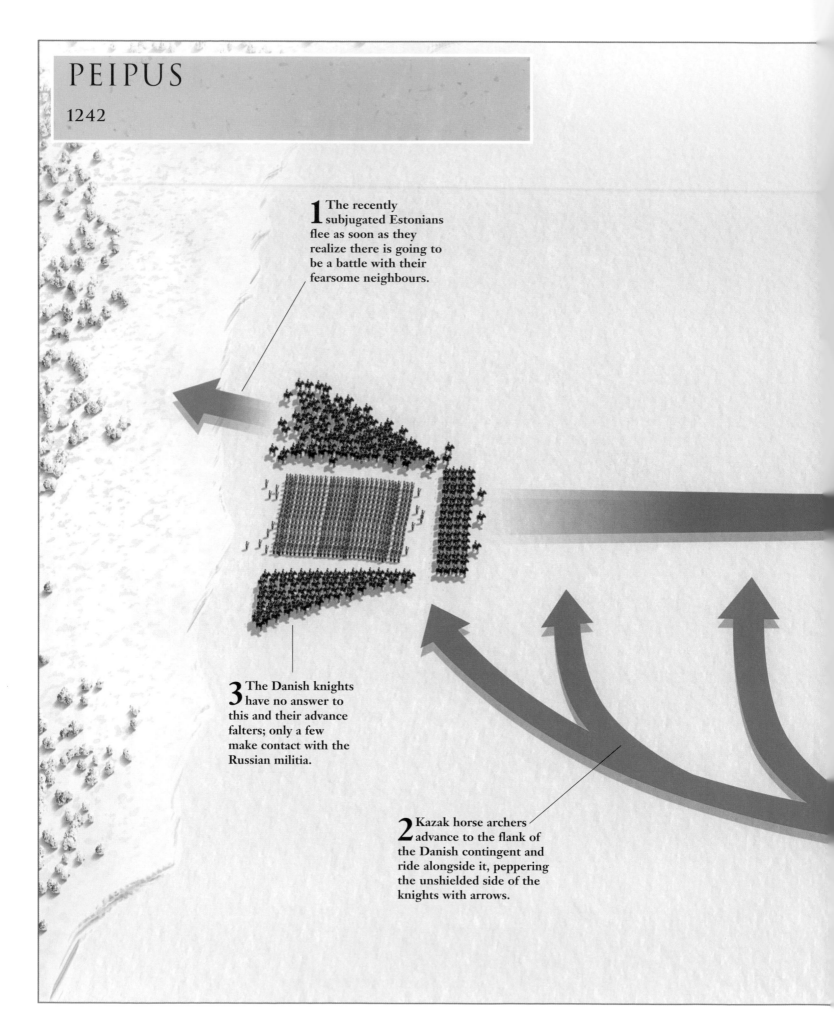

1 The recently subjugated Estonians flee as soon as they realize there is going to be a battle with their fearsome neighbours.

3 The Danish knights have no answer to this and their advance falters; only a few make contact with the Russian militia.

2 Kazak horse archers advance to the flank of the Danish contingent and ride alongside it, peppering the unshielded side of the knights with arrows.

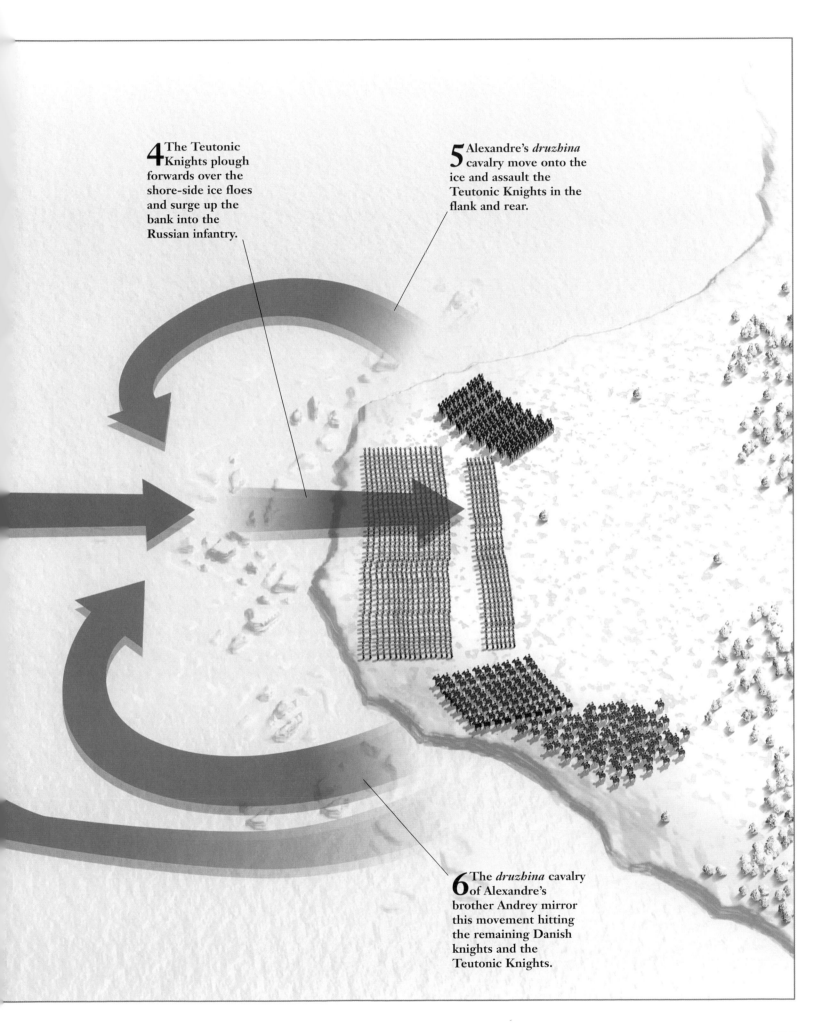

4 The Teutonic Knights plough forwards over the shore-side ice floes and surge up the bank into the Russian infantry.

5 Alexandre's *druzhina* cavalry move onto the ice and assault the Teutonic Knights in the flank and rear.

6 The *druzhina* cavalry of Alexandre's brother Andrey mirror this movement hitting the remaining Danish knights and the Teutonic Knights.

PEIPUS

THE OPPOSED FORCES

RUSSIANS (estimated)

Druzhina cavalry:	800
Novgorod polk cavalry:	200
Novgorod polk infantry:	800
Tribal infantry:	2000
Kazak/Cuman horse archers:	1200
Total:	**5000**

CRUSADERS (estimated)

Teutonic Knights:	20
Men-at-arms:	200
Danish knights:	300
Estonian infantry:	500
Total:	**1020**

under their local commander, Andreas von Felben, Danish troops under two princes, the subjugated tribesmen from Tartu and Estonia and some renegade Russians – about 1000 in all. The fortress was taken by storm. However, the Danish King Waldemar had died in April and when the news reached the army the Danish princes and their contingent of perhaps 300 returned home.

Possibly encouraged by this weakening of the Crusaders' force the town militia, or *polk*, of neighbouring Pskov mounted a counter-attack and met the invaders in the field on 16 September 1241. The 600-strong militia was defeated and chased back to their town, which soon surrendered, some of the citizens fleeing to Novgorod. A tiny force was left to garrison the town, two knights of the order and probably 20 sergeants, in line with other Teutonic

Russian infantry and Danish knights engage in hand-to-hand fighting in Sergei Eisenstein's 1938 epic movie Alexandre Nevskii. *The movie is a wonderful spectacle but should not be treated as an authoritative source for the events, weapons or tactics.*

garrisons, and the *druzhina* of the local mayor. While the knights were busy around Pskov, Alexandre re-established his position in Novgorod and speedily moved his *druzhina*, local troops and tribal levies to recapture the now-fortified town of Koporye from the Germans and Danes. Then moving south he joined with his brother Andrey's *druzhina* from Suzdal and Novgorod's own *druzhina* militia; about 3000 *druzhina* plus perhaps 2000 local and tribal troops, vastly outnumbering the Crusaders around Pskov. By now winter had set in and temperatures were regularly below −5°C (23°F). He recaptured Pskov without a fight on 5 March 1242. But he did not stop there. Bypassing the fortress at Izborsk he raided deep into the territory south of Tartu. This was a true raid for revenge, not an attempt to provoke the Crusaders into battle. The Russians fanned out, causing as much damage and chaos as they could. Campaigning at this time of the year in Russia is risky. This is the eve of the thaw when roads will turn to mush and everything slithers to a halt, as Hitler's troops discovered in the last century.

Nevertheless the Crusaders turned out to counter the raid. The available forces included 20 Teutonic Knights, perhaps 200 men-at-arms, Danish royal knights, the militia from Tartu and Estonian tribal levies. Bishop Hermann commanded the army. As they approached, the dispersed Russian forces moved to join up but one small flanking force was caught and all but wiped out at a bridge by the village of Mooste. The survivors warned Alexandre and he turned his army eastwards across the still-frozen Lake Peipus. The Crusader victors of this skirmish also took their news to Bishop Hermann with their army. They too turned east across the ice somewhat to the north of the Russians and following them on a parallel course.

THE BATTLE

The Russians reached the further shore first and turned north to await the Crusaders from firm ground on the beach at a place called Raven Rock. The prevailing wind in this area is from the west, and this plus the tendency of ice to thaw and refreeze forced the ice to build up into wave-like ridges on the eastern shore, thus forming an area of broken ground in front of the deployed Russians. Alexandre positioned his infantry, armed with a mixture of spears, bows and axes, in the centre. On his flanks he placed his cavalry with horse archers, probably Kazak or Cuman mercenaries from the Russian steppes.

The Estonian levies, forced to fight by their masters, fled from the field at the sight of the Russian army without making any contribution. The outnumbered Crusaders then did what they knew best. They formed a 'Boar's snout', a blunt wedge formation

with the best troops, Teutonic Knights, at the front, and charged. This cannot have been easy with horses slipping on the ice, so it is doubtful they managed the full momentum of the classic knightly charge. All the same despite the slippery and uneven ice and the arrows of the enemy they struck the militia in the centre of the Russian line with great force, driving into their lines and killing many. But in such a mêlée neither the militia nor the Crusader knights could see what was happening on the flanks.

As the knights were cutting down the militia in the centre, the Russian cavalry was falling on their flanks. The horse archers were concentrated on the left, where their arrows would have more effect on the

shieldless right sides of the Danish knights led by their princes who had the place of honour on the right of the Crusader army. Suffering serious casualties, many of the Danes began to turn and fall back across the lake. The remaining knights continued to drive into the Russian foot but were in turn struck at great disadvantage by the *druzhina* cavalry. With the limited peripheral vision provided by their helmets and their own

The helmet of Alexandre Nevskii, Russian hero and boyar (prince) of Novgorod. It is important to remember that the tools available to the craftsman who made this superb piece of armour were simply hammers, chisels and files.

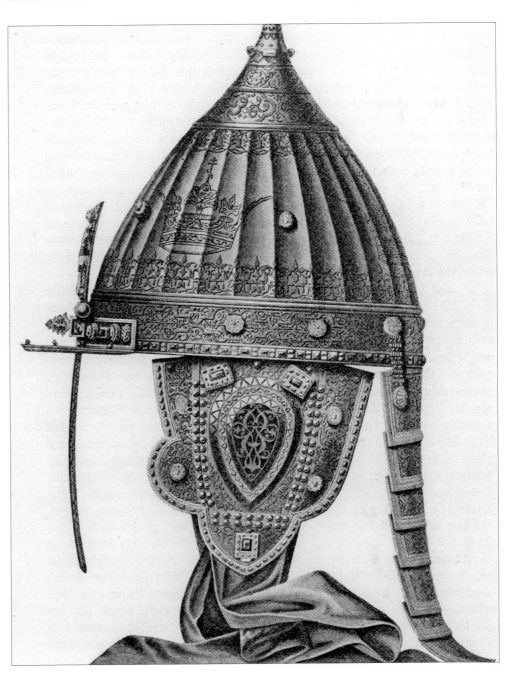

concentration on the enemy in front, many of them would have been cut down, unaware of this new foe. It was too much. Those Crusaders who either could not or would not escape fought on until they were beaten. Six Teutonic Knights were captured plus 44 other Danish and German men-at-arms. The small Crusader force left 400 bodies on the ice. Those that fled were pursued only to the far shore of the lake.

And what of the legendary breaking of the ice and drowning of knights? Lake Peipus is remarkably shallow, and gently shelving beaches interspersed with dense reed-beds form the edge of the lake. The depth in places is as little as 30cm (12in).

In this scene from Eisenstein's black-and-white movie, the Teutonic Knights and supporting footsoldiers are sporting black crosses on their white shields. Within the Teutonic Order, personal coats-of-arms were forbidden and beards were compulsory. The footsoldiers in this still from the movie are rather too well equipped for their lowly station.

The ice at that time of year is between 20 and 50cm (8 and 20in) thick, enough to support the weight of a small car, although there can be pockets of thin ice in the lee of rocks and reeds. Therefore any knights who did drown in the rout probably did so as the result of falling off their horses for some other reason rather than the spectacular version in the famous film *Alexandre Nevskii* (1938), directed by Sergei Eisenstein.

AFTERMATH

The casualties on both sides were high. The Crusaders lost 45 per cent of their force and the following year the Estonian tribes threw off the yoke of their Danish overlords. The Russian militia bore the brunt of their casualties but the numbers are not recorded. Poor planning and understanding led to the failure of the 1241 campaign that culminated in the Crusaders' defeat at Lake Peipus. The three-pronged attack was atrociously timed and the difficulties of campaigning in the broad, underpopulated terrain with newly conquered and converted

allies were not appreciated, the conclusion being that faith is no substitute for common sense. Of course the woes of the Teutonic Order did not end there. They offered to withdraw from the conquered lands and exchange prisoners, for they were desperately short of manpower now. This was accepted by Novgorod and a 20-year peace ensued. Almost immediately the order was faced with a revolt 644km (400 miles) in their rear when Duke Swantopelk and the Prussians rose in rebellion. The revolt lasted for 11 years before a peace treaty was concluded. This period included two year-long truces and a further two serious defeats for the order at Rensen in 1244 and Krucken in 1249. At both of these battles the Grand Master was killed. It was not until 1254 that the knights felt strong enough, with an army of 60,000, to cautiously return to the offensive and advance on Balga in modern Poland which they had last held in 1242.

The year after the Battle of Lake Peipus the Estonians also rose in open revolt

against their Danish overlords. They were subdued again and revolted again, the last occasion being in 1343. In 1346 the Danes sold the troublesome province to the Teutonic Order.

Fortunately for Alexandre Nevskii and the people of Novgorod, the Mongols, who had caused such havoc in nearby Poland, returned to the steppes to approve the accession of Ogedai as their new khan. However, they continued to maintain a governor near Kanev and a military presence of around 60,000 men. Under and after their overlordship Novgorod grew to

become the largest single, albeit underpopulated, Christian state in the region. Rivalled only by Lithuania, it also remained the last western bastion of Orthodox Christianity. However, it didn't stop the two Nevskii brothers falling out. Andrey rose in revolt against the Mongols and Alexandre ruthlessly crushed him on their behalf. For this service he was created Grand Prince of Russia, founding the Tsarist line. Novgorod and other cities that had not been destroyed continued under the relatively benign rule of the Mongols – they at least tolerated different religions.

The Battle on Ice *(1942; oil on canvas) by Vladimir Aleksandrovich Serov (1910–68). In Soviet Russia, Alexandre Nevskii was a popular hero, and his victories were exploited to the full in World War II propaganda. This is in part because he came from a pre-Tsarist era, but also because he repelled German invaders from the West.*

MALTA
1283

THE BATTLE OF MALTA WAS ONE OF THE GREAT SEA FIGHTS OF THE THIRTEENTH CENTURY. IT WAS THE FIRST TRIUMPH OF A NEW NAVAL POWER – ARAGON – IN BATTLE AGAINST A COMMITTED ENEMY. MALTA ALSO PROVIDES AN IDEAL EXAMPLE OF MEDITERRANEAN GALLEY WARFARE IN THE LATER MIDDLE AGES.

WHY DID IT HAPPEN?

WHO An Aragonese-Catalan fleet under Admiral Roger of Lauria (c.1245–1304), opposed by an Angevin fleet under the command of Admirals William Cornut (d. 1283) and Bartholomew Bonvin.

WHAT The battle took place between the fleet of King Charles I of Sicily (1227–85), a French prince who was also Duke of Anjou, and that of King Pedro III of Aragon (1239–85).

WHERE The Grand Harbour of Malta, near modern-day Valletta.

WHEN 8 June 1283.

WHY The Angevin fleet had been ordered to Malta to relieve the garrison there. An Aragonese fleet pursued the Angevins and confronted them in the harbour.

OUTCOME After a day-long battle, the Angevins were badly defeated. Contemporary reports tell that 3500 Angevins were killed, including one of their admirals, while nearly 1000 were captured. Aragonese casualties were less than 10 per cent.

During the later Middle Ages, galleys dominated naval warfare in the Mediterranean. They were long, slim warships of shallow draft, propelled by about 100 oars; the ships were also equipped with sails, which were not used in battle. Unlike ancient fighting ships, medieval galleys did not have rams. Instead, the typical style of fighting was to lessen the enemy's resistance by means of an intensive shower of arrows, javelins and other projectiles, followed by an attempt to board the enemy vessel. Such fighting depended on several factors to be successful. The sailors had to be able to bring the ship to the most advantageous position, by preference presenting their own bow or sterncastle to the enemy's side, allowing them to hurl missiles from the greater height at the fore and aft of the ship. The skill of marines was also very important, both in the initial missile exchanges and in boarding. Most important of all, though, a number of independently operated ships without easy means of communication had to be brought to coordinated action during the literal ebb and flow of battle, so a talented admiral with a sound grasp of tactics was even more vital for victory than was a gifted general in a medieval land battle.

Now protected by impressive sixteenth-century fortifications, the Grand Harbour of Malta is one of the finest harbours in the Mediterranean and the subject of contention as late as World War II.

The Angevin ruler of Sicily, Charles I, had badly mismanaged his fleet. Although he invested large sums in shipbuilding, the recruitment of crews was poor. Mercenary crossbowmen were hired from Genoa and Pisa, and seamen for the most part came from Provence and the Regno. These poorly paid and often unwilling men showed little enthusiasm for fighting, and the diversity of languages spoken led to poor communication in action. The infantry usually consisted of heavily armoured Frenchmen, even knights, whose equipment was more suited to land warfare than to fighting on a heaving deck. Worse, King Charles made the office of admiral hereditary rather than an appointment for experienced sea captains. At Malta in 1283 the two Angevin admirals were nevertheless experienced men from important merchant families of Marseilles, but it is unclear why there was a divided command. By 1283, the Angevin fleet's lack of coordination was clear, as at the Battle of Nicotera (14 October 1282), during which the various Angevin units failed to support each other and scattered without resisting the enemy.

By contrast, the Aragonese navy called into being by King Pedro III was a surprisingly innovative and integrated fighting force. Much of the credit for its success must go to Pedro's admiral, the Italian Roger of Lauria, who although he was often outnumbered never lost a naval engagement and who was moreover a great administrator. Shortly before the War of the Sicilian Vespers (the name given to the conflict between Aragon and the house of Anjou for control of the Kingdom of Sicily) began in 1282, the Aragonese started building galleys with significant modifications. For over a century, the standard Mediterranean galley had been rowed by 104–108 oars; the new Aragonese galleys were increased in size to 112–124 oars. This made the ships heavier and slower, usually a disadvantage in galley warfare, but the new vessels also had high bulwarks for the men to shelter behind, as well as forecastles and sterncastles raised higher and protected more strongly than was normal in the Mediterranean. All these innovations were intended to take advantage of the high-quality Catalan

crossbowmen that were available to the fleet.

Catalan crossbowmen, about 30 for each of the largest galleys and fewer for the smaller ships, were regarded as the best in the Mediterranean. Many of them had experience of land war. They were also well equipped: at the Battle of Malta each had two 60cm (2ft) crossbows and one 30cm (1ft) crossbow, as well as 300 bolts for each type of bow. In addition, they had leather armour, iron caps and short swords for boarding. They were supplemented by Aragonese light infantry, the *almogavars*, trained in Spanish border fighting and experienced in the use of javelins and spears. These troops were ideally suited to naval warfare, being lightly armoured and more nimble than their Angevin counterparts. What is more, the Aragonese fleet had a considerable esprit de corps. Roger of Lauria personally recruited both sailors and marines all the time he was admiral, besides meticulously assuring their pay and adequate supplies of food and water.

THE CAMPAIGN

The Battle of Malta was part of the War of the Sicilian Vespers, a conflict between the princes of Anjou, a junior line of the French royal family, and the royal house of Aragon for control of Sicily and southern Italy, fought between 1282 and 1302. The war is especially noteworthy since every major battle was fought at sea.

Duke Charles of Anjou had claimed the throne of Sicily in 1266. His administrators and high taxes soon alienated the populace. A rebellion began on 29 March 1282 in the city of Palermo, at about the time of evening prayer (vespers), thus giving the war its name. King Pedro of Aragon, who had a claim to Sicily, made common cause with the rebels.

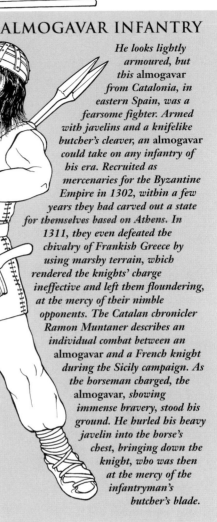

ALMOGAVAR INFANTRY

He looks lightly armoured, but this almogavar from Catalonia, in eastern Spain, was a fearsome fighter. Armed with javelins and a knifelike butcher's cleaver, an almogavar could take on any infantry of his era. Recruited as mercenaries for the Byzantine Empire in 1302, within a few years they had carved out a state for themselves based on Athens. In 1311, they even defeated the chivalry of Frankish Greece by using marshy terrain, which rendered the knights' charge ineffective and left them floundering, at the mercy of their nimble opponents. The Catalan chronicler Ramon Muntaner describes an individual combat between an almogavar and a French knight during the Sicily campaign. As the horseman charged, the almogavar, showing immense bravery, stood his ground. He hurled his heavy javelin into the horse's chest, bringing down the knight, who was then at the mercy of the infantryman's butcher's blade.

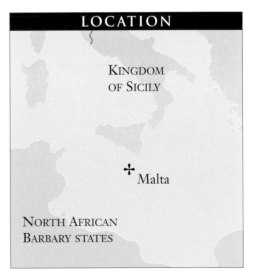

LOCATION

KINGDOM
OF SICILY

✝ Malta

NORTH AFRICAN
BARBARY STATES

Malta's position south of Sicily in the middle of the Mediterranean made it highly desirable as a naval base. It was a key to control of the Kingdom of Sicily, which included southern Italy.

The military situation was still very fluid in 1283, despite the Aragonese capture of 22 Angevin galleys at the Battle of Nicotera the preceding autumn. Control of Malta was of central importance, since the island, with its excellent harbour, was ideally located to stage a naval invasion of Sicily. An Angevin garrison had retained precarious hold of the harbour fortifications since the beginning of the war, pinned down by a local insurrection and an Aragonese contingent that had arrived to attack them.

Thus the Angevin fleet's order to sail to the relief of the garrison on Malta in late April/early May of 1283 was a military necessity. Eighteen galleys and nine smaller vessels were dispatched. They arrived at the Grand Harbour of Malta on 4 June, drawing their ships up onto the shore at Dockyard Creek.

The Aragonese fleet, commanded by Roger of Lauria, pursued this relieving force with 21 galleys. He reached the Grand Harbour late in the day on 7 June and sent a *barca* (a small, oared vessel) into the harbour to reconnoitre; this ship successfully passed unnoticed between the two Angevin ships that had been set to guard the harbour mouth, but had tied up on either side.

THE FIRST ATTACK

Upon learning his enemy's dispositions, Roger of Lauria's first challenge was to bring the Angevin fleet to battle. The Angevins were beached stern-first on the

In this illustration from a fifteenth-century Italian manuscript, successful Aragonese soldiers disembark from Naples with their Angevin prisoners.

shore. It was impractical to attack them while they remained in that position, since the beached ships could easily be reinforced by land and even if a ship were captured it could not be carried off. So Roger did the 'chivalrous' – and sensible – thing: instead of launching a surprise attack he entered the Grand Harbour with his ships at dawn, and ordered that trumpets be blown to rouse the sleeping enemy. The Angevins then rowed their vessels out to accept the challenge, and the battle was fought within the harbour.

The Aragonese admiral ordered his ships to advance in line abreast, the vessels linked with cables long enough to allow the galleys to be rowed but still able to keep the

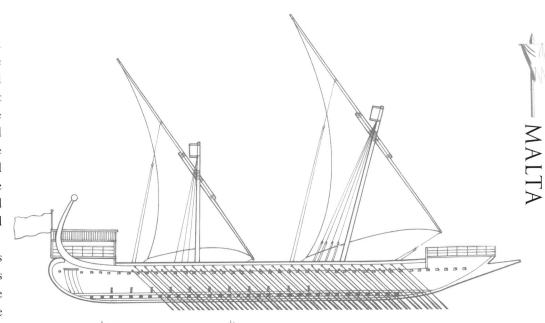

Above: *Reconstruction of a* taride *built for King Charles of Sicily in 1278. Roomier than a war galley, a* taride *could transport horses for amphibious assaults.*

Left: *This illustration shows a hypothetical distribution of rowers in a Mediterranean galley of the High Middle Ages.*

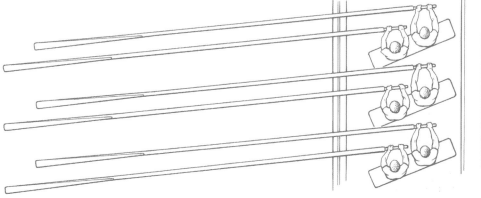

ships from scattering in the current. This was a common Mediterranean fighting tactic of the time.

As the fleets closed range, the Angevin fighters launched a barrage of javelins, arrows, stones and even powdered lime to blind their enemies – the traditional opening move of a medieval galley fight. But, unusually, Admiral Roger ordered his men to limit their response. Instead of returning fire with everything at their command, only the crossbowmen were allowed to reply to the enemy. The rest of the Aragonese fighting men were ordered to shelter from enemy missiles. It is clear from an account of the Battle of Rosas in 1285 that the new Aragonese ship design did indeed provide an unusual degree of protection from missiles: the ships in 1285 were so much higher than those of their opponents that the Angevins were unable to board them. Thus the Aragonese marines were able to remain relatively unscathed in the initial assault.

By about noon the Angevins had run out of ammunition. A chronicler reports that

they even threw the mortars and pestles that they used for grinding lime, a suggestion of their increasing desperation at their inability to create so much disorder that they could board the Aragonese ships. At that point the Aragonese marines were unleashed. They still apparently had a large supply of crossbow bolts, which were used to good effect by the expert Catalan archers. As the range closed, javelins and stones were added to the barrage.

Unlike the Aragonese, the Angevins did not have effective bulwarks to protect them from missile attack, and the greater height of the Aragonese ships also made their shooting much more effective.

CRISIS POINT

The Angevin ships were driven into disarray by the missile attack, rapidly losing their cohesion as an integrated fighting unit. Thus, ship by ship, the Aragonese drew near enough that their marines were able to board and continue the fight hand-to-hand.

The fighting was fierce; despite the disorder of the Angevins, they still

THE OPPOSED FORCES

ARAGONESE (estimated)
Galleys:	21
Sailors and rowers:	c.4000
Catalan crossbowmen:	c.500
Aragonese infantry:	c.1000
Total:	**21 galleys, 5500 men**

ANGEVIN (estimated)
Galleys:	18
Smaller vessels:	9
Sailors and rowers:	c.6000
Genoese and Pisan crossbowmen:	c.600
Provençal infantry:	c.1200
Total:	**27 ships, c.7800 men**

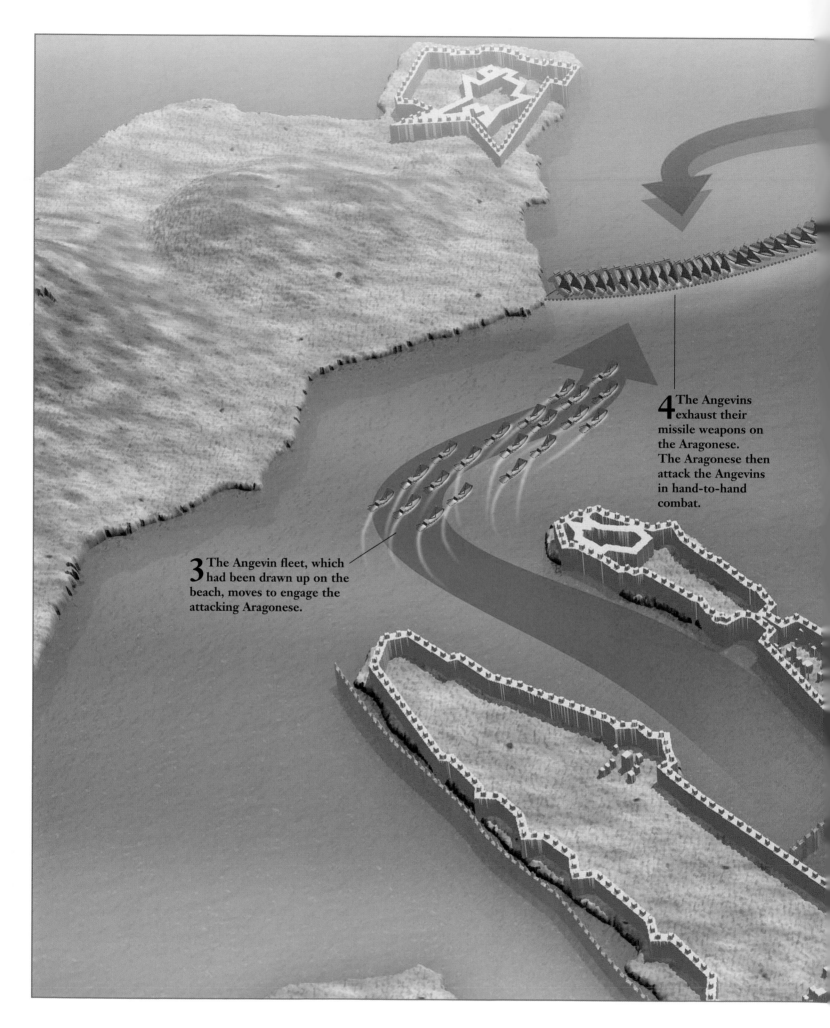

4 The Angevins exhaust their missile weapons on the Aragonese. The Aragonese then attack the Angevins in hand-to-hand combat.

3 The Angevin fleet, which had been drawn up on the beach, moves to engage the attacking Aragonese.

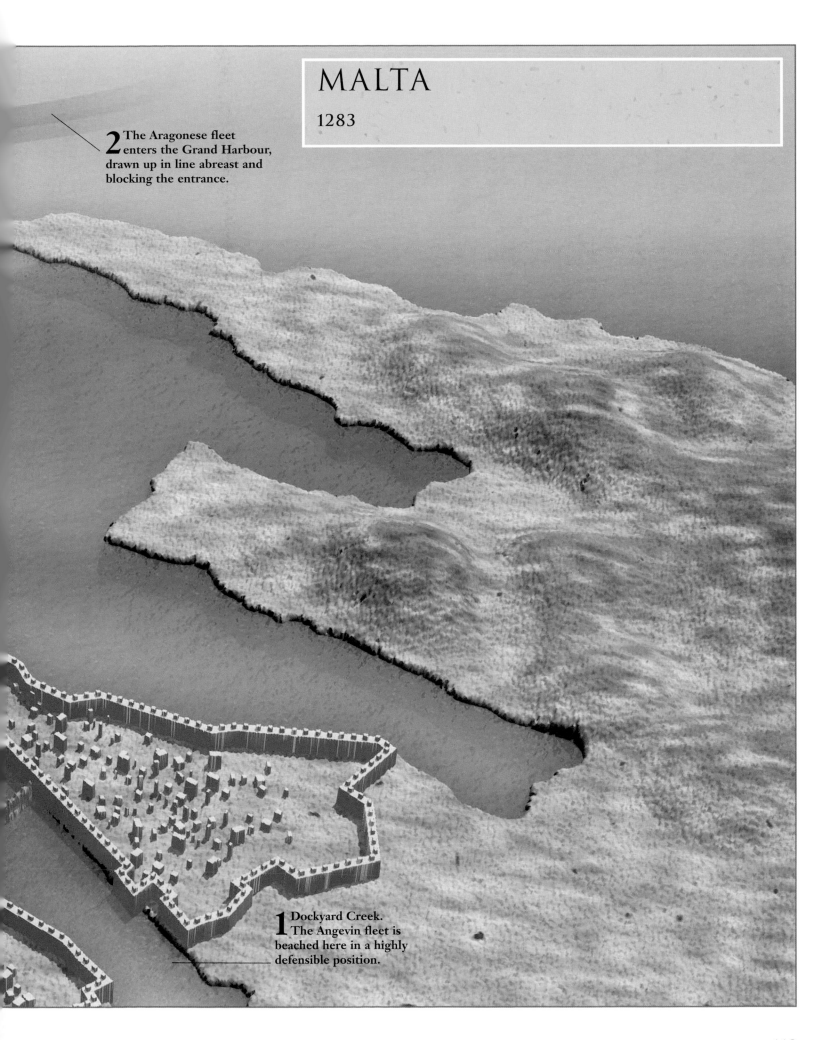

MALTA
1283

2 The Aragonese fleet enters the Grand Harbour, drawn up in line abreast and blocking the entrance.

1 Dockyard Creek. The Angevin fleet is beached here in a highly defensible position.

A Romantic-era depiction of Charles I of Anjou, first of the Angevin kings of Sicily. Charles had grand plans to reassemble the Latin empire established in the eastern Mediterranean by the descendants of the Fourth Crusade.

outnumbered the Aragonese in both ships and men. The battle continued until dusk, but gradually the more suitable equipment of the Aragonese fighters began to tell. It is likely that the better training of the ships' crews also played an important role, making it possible for two ships at a time to attack an enemy galley or prevent disengagement, which would have given the Angevins a breathing space in which to regroup. The battle was assuredly brutal. Medieval naval warfare was in many respects comparable to land armies taking a fortress by storm.

Quarter was not usually given to the losers, whose best hope of survival was to swim for it – in an age in which few people were taught to swim. The casualties of the hand-to-hand fighting included the Angevin admiral Cornut.

Finally, at dusk Bonvin, the surviving Angevin admiral, broke free of the Aragonese fleet and fled. He took with him a few, maybe seven, damaged galleys, of which two later had to be abandoned because they were no longer seaworthy. The Catalan chronicler Ramon Muntaner reports that 3500 Angevin mariners and marines were killed and nearly 1000 more were captured. By contrast, after the battle Roger of Lauria recruited some 288 replacements, so his casualties must have been fewer than 10 per cent.

AFTERMATH

The Battle of Malta was not decisive. Roger of Lauria was able to lead a series of raids against Angevin positions in late 1283 and the first half of 1284, with between 36 and 40 galleys under his command. A new Angevin fleet of about the same size was soon built, however. The fleets met at the Battle of Naples on 5 June 1284 – and Aragon won again, capturing King Charles' son in the battle.

However, even that encounter did not break Angevin sea power. A still larger battle was waged on 23 June 1287, called the 'Battle of the Counts' because of the number of important French nobles with the Angevin fleet. In that encounter, the Angevin fleet dissolved when attacked, the Genoese admiral in particular fleeing with his entire squadron. The Aragonese seized 44 galleys that day, and about 5000 prisoners. Finally the war was ended by treaty in 1302, the Angevins retaining control of the southern Italian mainland and recognizing the ruler of Aragon as king of the island of Sicily.

The Battle of Malta did not change the face of European warfare. The higher and more solid Aragonese galley style did not pass into general use: the ships' slowness and clumsiness was too often a disadvantage. There was no general change in tactics, and after the battle as before, war at sea was conducted using a combination of preliminary barrage followed by boarding. Instead, the Battle of Malta is perhaps most instructive as a well-documented example of the many factors that went into galley warfare in the later Middle Ages. Several lessons can be learned from it. Perhaps most importantly, naval warfare could only be waged effectively by strong governments that were able to build and provision fleets and hire the professionals to operate them. In that regard, the Aragonese and Angevins were relatively equal. Beyond that, however, good leadership was essential, and equipment suitable for fighting at sea.

The Angevins might be criticized for their failure to adopt the Aragonese innovations – higher galleys and better defences – that served them so well at the Battle of Malta and elsewhere. But in fairness, it is very unlikely that the Angevins could have used such new construction plans effectively. The Aragonese leaders had suited their ships to the resources they had available, in particular highly trained and highly motivated Catalan crossbowmen, the best in Europe. The French could not produce a comparable force. Pisan and Genoese crossbowmen were skilled, but less likely to carry a fight to the bitter end. Thus the Angevins had to rely on the greater mobility of their lighter-weight, quicker ships. The Aragonese leaders had taken a gamble that, thanks especially to good leadership, paid off in the unique circumstances of the late thirteenth century.

A statue was erected to honour Roger of Lauria in the city of Tarragona, Aragon. Roger was an extremely successful admiral for the Aragonese cause.

BANNOCKBURN
1314

THE BATTLE OF BANNOCKBURN PITTED AN OUTNUMBERED FORCE OF SCOTS PIKEMEN AGAINST THE DEADLY COMBINATION OF ENGLISH ARCHERS AND MEN-AT-ARMS. THE STAKES WERE HIGH: THE OWNERSHIP OF THE CRITICAL CASTLE AT STIRLING WOULD BE DECIDED BY A DAY OF BATTLE.

WHY DID IT HAPPEN?

WHO An English army numbering 18,000 under King Edward II (1284–1327), opposed by 9500 Scots under King Robert the Bruce (1274–1329).

WHAT The main action took place between blocks of Scottish pikemen and heavily armoured English cavalry.

WHERE 1.6km (1 mile) southeast of Stirling Castle, Scotland.

WHEN June 1314.

WHY Marching to relieve Stirling Castle, the English army was intercepted by the Scots.

OUTCOME The English were caught in marshy ground while trying to outflank the Scots, who attacked aggressively and broke the English army.

Scotland had long fought for her independence from English rule. The result was a series of raids, battles and skirmishes as the conflict flared up and died down. Both sides knew the capabilities of their foes and had tried to develop a fighting system to effectively deal with them.

On both sides, the social élite rode to war encased in armour and bearing a sword plus other weapons including the lance, mace and axe. These men-at-arms included noblemen and knights as well as professional soldiers of high status in the service of the great lords. These heavily

In this romanticized nineteenth-century illustration Edward II is depicted at his coronation as a wise and noble figure. His martial prowess is suggested by the crowned helm by his side. In reality Edward lacked the vision and determination of his father and his son.

armoured cavalry represented the main striking power of the armies of the time. They tended to be courageous and skilful but ill-disciplined and prone to bickering among themselves over questions of honour and precedence. This situation is all but inevitable when social status is tied to prowess in war.

KNIGHTS VERSUS PIKEMEN

There were far more men-at-arms on the English side than among the Scots, for the simple reason that England was richer and had a larger population. Supporting an élite warrior in vastly expensive armour required the effort of a large number of more lowly individuals. England simply had a bigger budget and thus could put more men-at-arms in the field.

To offset the English advantage in heavy cavalry, the Scots had developed a fighting system that made excellent use of unarmoured footsoldiers. Instead of simply rounding up peasants and herding them into action in the hope they might do some good, the Scots deployed formations of uniformly equipped soldiers with a specific aim in mind. These formations were essentially blocks of unarmoured men equipped with long pikes.

A pike is a clumsy weapon which is of little use to an individual warrior. But although too long and unwieldy for individual combat, the pike comes into its own when deployed in a massed formation. For every man in the front rank, there are several sharp points projecting forwards, creating a vicious hedge of blades which has sufficient reach to hold cavalry at bay and will plunge into an enemy infantry formation before their shorter hand weapons can come into play.

The heyday of the pike had come and gone a thousand and more years before, when the Greeks clashed with their foes in vast phalanx formations that might contain as many as 20–30,000 men. The pike had been discredited when the Greek fighting system fell out of favour, but it remained an effective weapon when used properly.

At 4m (13ft), the Scots pike was far shorter than the ancient Greek *sarissa* (which could often be up to 7m/24ft in length), making it easier to manoeuvre and permitting formations to quickly change facing at need. The great downfall of the Greek phalanx was its inflexibility. It could crush whatever was ahead of it but if attacked from the flanks it was impossible to manoeuvre to deal with the problem. The Scots used much smaller formations called *schiltrons*, which were able to manoeuvre freely in attack. When necessary they could create an all-round hedge of pike points.

The pike is more effective than might be supposed against an armoured man. If he can be induced to rush forward and impale himself upon it, all well and good, but if the pikeman can charge home, the impact is almost as great. When the pike head strikes a solid target and does not immediately slide off a shield or armour plate, the shaft will flex somewhat, storing energy to add to that of the pikeman's forward rush or pushing arms. The shaft will only bow so far, however, before it springs forward. This releases the stored energy in the form of forward movement of the point, giving the pike added penetration against armour or flesh.

VOLUNTEERS

The Scots pikemen differed from the rabble militia normally fielded by the English in another fundamental way. They were an organized volunteer force, bound by loyalty – to each other, to their leaders and to the cause of Scottish independence. These troops had confidence in themselves and in their companions and also had something to gain from

LOCATION

Bannockburn lies just to the southwest of Stirling Castle, a position which is strategically crucial in Scotland. The Battle of Bannockburn was fought over possession of the castle.

SCOTTISH PIKEMAN (c.1300)

Scottish pikemen around the year 1300 were equipped very simply, with minimal armour often consisting of little more than a leather helmet and shield. Many would not even have had helmets. But when tightly packed together in schiltron formation, they proved capable defeating the English heavy cavalry charges. The Scottish formation at Bannockburn would have been recognizable to the Picts of half a millennium earlier: massed pikes with swords and shields plus others carrying axes and bills.

King Robert the Bruce's relationship with his peasant spearmen is captured in this Victorian engraving. Much less well armoured than their English opponents, they nevertheless possessed the morale and the weaponry to overwhelm their enemy.

winning. They also knew what happened to a *schiltron* that broke up, having seen or heard of their countrymen being ridden down by enemy cavalry. Survival, and victory, depended on standing firm together.

On the English side, the heavy cavalry was backed up by a force of infantry and, much more importantly, by archers. The combination of these troops had been the downfall of Scots armies in the past, when the *schiltrons* were broken up by a steady rain of arrows to which they could not reply, then mown down by the cavalry to complete the disaster.

The English king, Edward II, knew well how to use the formidable force of archers he had inherited from his father, Edward I (1239–1307). However, the Scots knew what to expect and their leaders had deliberated on what they might do to avoid defeat by a combination of archery fire and cavalry shock.

THE CAMPAIGN

Stirling Castle occupied a critical location in southern Scotland, dominating the only bridge across the River Forth. Controlled

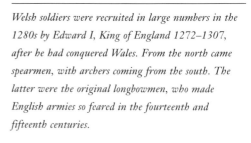

Welsh soldiers were recruited in large numbers in the 1280s by Edward I, King of England 1272–1307, after he had conquered Wales. From the north came spearmen, with archers coming from the south. The latter were the original longbowmen, who made English armies so feared in the fourteenth and fifteenth centuries.

by the English, it barred the passage of Scots forces into England and provided a base for operations against what the English kings considered to be rebels against the crown. If Scotland was to be free and independent, Stirling Castle would have to be taken from the English. Indeed, its fall would be a powerful symbol to the Scottish people, perhaps winning greater support for the cause of independence. Thus Stirling Castle was more than materially important to both sides. Its ownership would influence morale and might even be the deciding factor in the campaign.

Scots forces advanced on Stirling and laid siege to the castle. By the convention of the time the castle commander, Sir Robert Mowbray, made an agreement with the besiegers that if relief were not forthcoming by Midsummer's Day then the castle would be surrendered. There was nothing dishonourable or even unusual about such

an arrangement, which would mitigate the horrors of siege warfare somewhat. Essentially, the English king was honour-bound to send support to his vassals in such situations, and if he was unable or unwilling to do so then they were not required to fight to the death for his possessions (in this case, the castle at Stirling).

Since Stirling was so important, it was obvious to Robert the Bruce that King Edward would march to its relief. If his force made contact with the castle, the convention to surrender would be void, and the chances of a successful siege or assault were not great. It was clear that the Scots would have to defeat the English in the field and prevent them breaking through.

Allowing King Edward to advance through the empty and unproductive region to the south, thus extending his supply chain, Robert the Bruce elected to offer battle just short of the castle. This ensured

THE OPPOSED FORCES

SCOTS (estimated)
Mounted men-at-arms:	500
Pikemen:	9000
Total:	**9500**

ENGLISH (estimated)
Mounted men-at-arms:	1000
Infantry:	17,000
Total:	**18,000**

King Robert the Bruce slays Sir Henry de Bohun and breaks his best battle-axe in the process. Such romantic clashes between champions are the stuff of legend – but it was common clansmen armed with cheap pikes that won the day.

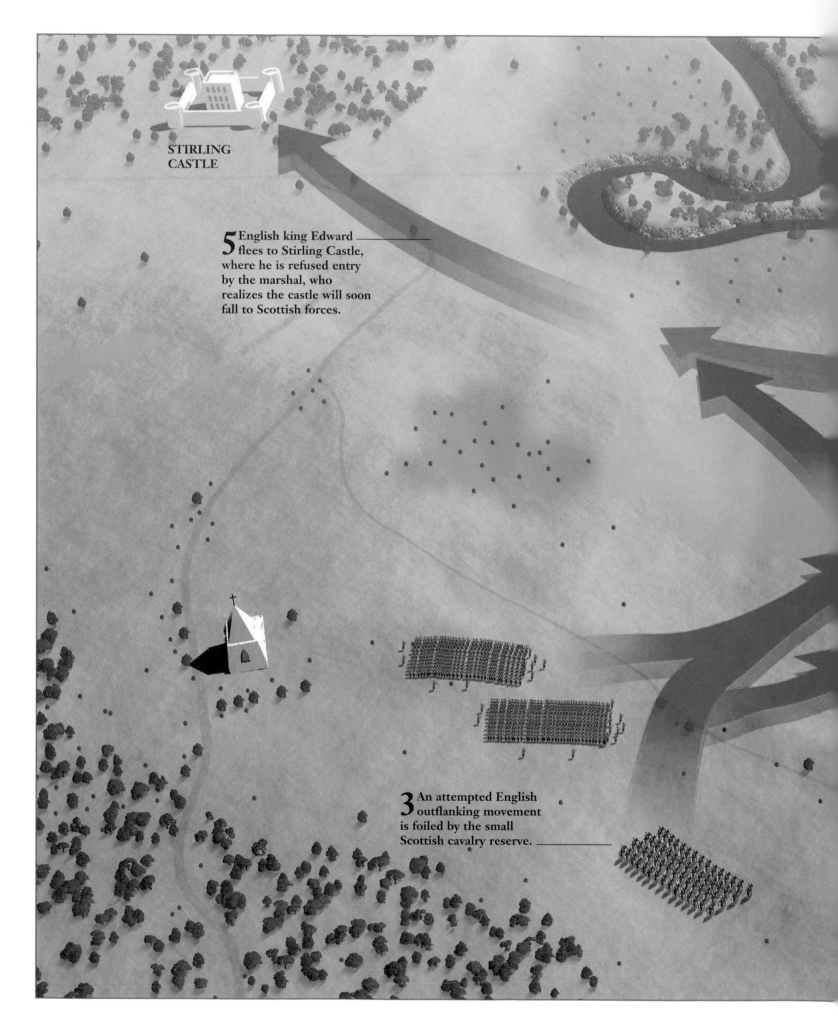

STIRLING
CASTLE

5 English king Edward flees to Stirling Castle, where he is refused entry by the marshal, who realizes the castle will soon fall to Scottish forces.

3 An attempted English outflanking movement is foiled by the small Scottish cavalry reserve.

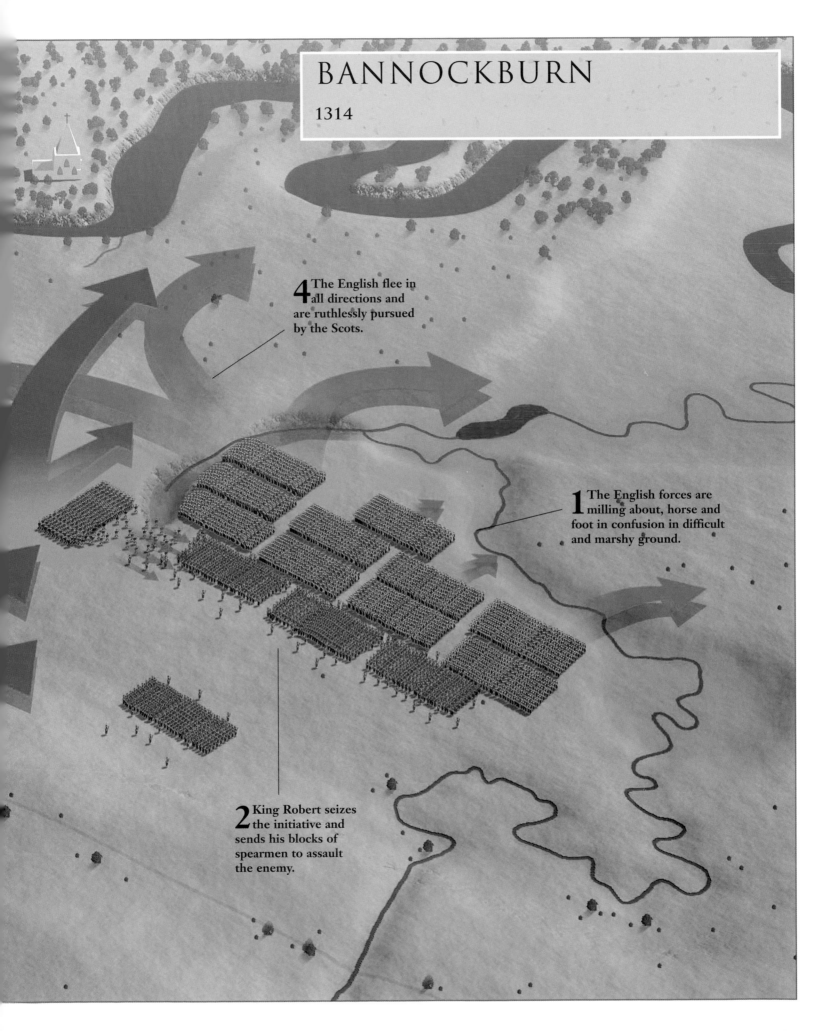

BANNOCKBURN
1314

4 The English flee in all directions and are ruthlessly pursued by the Scots.

1 The English forces are milling about, horse and foot in confusion in difficult and marshy ground.

2 King Robert seizes the initiative and sends his blocks of spearmen to assault the enemy.

This illustration shows a Scottish schiltron – *led by Robert the Bruce – standing firm in the face of cavalry attack. In reality there would be fewer armoured men in the pike formations than depicted here, and Robert would most likely have been leading his cavalry.*

that the English would be intercepted and that the battle would take place on terrain of the Scots' choosing, but it allowed no second chance if the day went badly.

DISPOSITIONS

The Scots army deployed for battle 1.6km (1 mile) from the castle and awaited the approach of the enemy. Rather than the more usual formation of three divisions (or 'battles'), the Scots were drawn up in four large blocks of pikemen, each numbering 2000–2500 men. Three of these made up the front line, under King Robert's brother Edward, Earl Douglas and the Steward of Scotland respectively. The fourth unit was in reserve under the personal command of King Robert. In addition, there was a small reserve of about 500 cavalry under the Marshal of Scotland, Sir Robert Keith, which waited to the rear. The Scots line was anchored at its flanks on the village of St Ninian and the Bannock Burn (stream). The pikemen dug pits, known as 'wolf traps', and strewed caltrops, triangular iron spikes designed to injure horses, to their front. Both measures were meant to break up a charge and had been well tried

throughout history. After that they rested as best they could.

The English priority was to relieve Stirling Castle, not to defeat Robert the Bruce in open battle. To this end, a force of about 300 men-at-arms under Sir Robert Clifford attempted to break through to the castle in an immediate assault. They were intercepted by about 500 pikemen, who positioned themselves across the road to the castle. If they reached it the surrender agreement would be void and the garrison free to launch an attack on the Scots army. Rushing out in advance of his comrades, a

lone English knight, Sir Henry de Bohun, decided to open the battle all alone. Charging at King Robert, who had not yet switched from his light riding horse to his battle charger, Sir Henry was met by the Scots king's furious counter-attack. Avoiding the lance thrust, King Robert slew Sir Henry with a single blow to the head, smashing the impetuous knight's helm and his own battle-axe in the process.

Clifford's force assaulted the *schiltron* but no doubt inspired by their leader's example the Scots stood firm. Several knights were killed trying to break into the *schiltron*, and at length the English force retired to where the remainder of King Edward's army was deploying for battle. The troops had been marching all morning and were weary even before the deployment began. By the time his forces were in some kind of order, Edward decided it was too late to attack that day.

Apparently disheartened by events thus far King Edward decided to attempt to outflank the Scots during the night. The English army spent the night slogging through the marshy ground along the banks of the Bannock. As dawn broke the English were across the river but in terrible disorder. Mired in the marsh, the heavy cavalry were unable to move quickly and – worse – they were between the archers and the Scots pikemen.

THE SCOTS ATTACK

Not one to pass up such an opportunity, Robert the Bruce unleashed his pike columns down the slight slope at the English vanguard before they could form up. The archers did what they could, shooting over the cavalry, but probably caused as many casualties among their own men as the enemy.

The first clash was a terrible thing. Men were pierced through, or bowled over to lie helpless in the marsh where they drowned

EUROPEAN CROSSBOWMAN

This crossbowman wears the typical helmet and mail armour of the professional European soldier around 1300. Although the longbow was a much more effective weapon, crossbowmen, who required much less training to be effective, were popular since they could be raised for a single season or campaign and then disbanded. For this reason, the crossbow remained the primary missile weapon in most parts of Europe throughout the fourteenth century. Like the longbow, most crossbows were made of yew. The 'claw' on this man's belt assists in making it quicker and easier to cock the weapon.

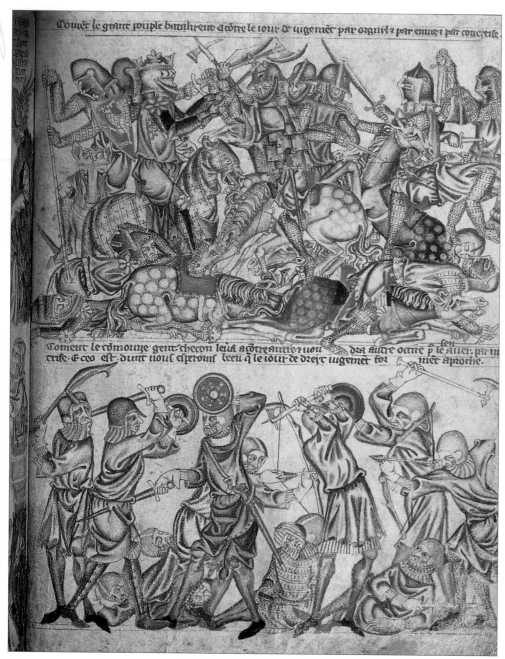

This half-page from the Holkham Picture Bible *(mid-fourteenth century) is entitled, 'How the lower classes fight'. As well as showing a range of swords and pole-arms, it accurately represents the archers' bows as thick and knotty staves.*

arrows into the massed Scots formations. For a short time, the archers were able to fulfil their purpose – that of breaking up the *schiltrons* – and it looked as though the tide might just turn.

However, Robert the Bruce had provided for such an eventuality. His cavalry reserve had been briefed to deal with the threat presented to the pikemen by English archers. Rather than seek out combat with their social equals, as armoured cavalry were expected to do at the time, the Scots cavalry were used in the most effective manner possible – as a mobile striking force hitting whatever target would do the most good. Sir Robert Keith, Marshal of Scotland, led his 500 cavalry in a charge against the flanking archers. Normally such a thing would have been prevented by the English cavalry, but they were being massacred in the marsh nearby and were thus powerless to intervene. Assailed at close quarters with lance and spear, sword and axe, the archers were quickly scattered or cut down and the pendulum swung once again in the direction of the Scots.

Bodies of English cavalry were able to break away from the mêlée and to make a number of small, local charges. However, these were delivered in a confused and ineffective manner against troops trained and equipped to repel a headlong, massed cavalry attack over open ground. Handfuls of men-at-arms, however valiant, struggling up through a marsh were unable to make any impression.

THE FINAL MOMENTS

The end came suddenly. The English cavalry, pushed back against their infantry, had caused great disorder even among those bodies that had managed to form up. The Scots pushed grimly on into the mix of foot and horse, until suddenly the English broke and fled. Once the rout had started it spread swiftly, with men scattering in all directions.

As the English army disintegrated, the Scots pursued vigorously. King Edward and some of his escort were able to reach Stirling Castle, where they asked for sanctuary. Ironically, the king had achieved in utter defeat what his army was not able to do in battle. Knowing that he was bound to

or were dispatched by the rear ranks of the Scots force. Horses stampeded, causing further chaos in the rear of the English.

Although the English fought back valiantly, they were in desperate straits and under attack by a foe who showed no signs of letting up. Men in the rear could not assist their comrades at the front. They could only await their turn and resist as best they could.

COUNTERSTROKES

Realizing what was happening, and perhaps out of self-preservation, some of the English archers ran clear of the mêlée and established themselves on the right flank, where they loosed a murderous hail of

surrender the castle very soon and that this would mean handing over his king to the Scots, the garrison commander refused to allow the royal party to enter.

AFTERMATH

The Battle of Bannockburn was not so much won by the Scots as lost by the English. Other battles had shown that the combination of archers and heavy cavalry could defeat the Scots pike formations in most circumstances.

Robert the Bruce can be credited with creating a situation where he had a real chance of victory despite the odds, and with recognizing that his English foe had handed him a splendid opportunity. The tactic of maintaining a cavalry reserve and using it to disperse the enemy archers marks him as a commander well above average for his era.

In the end, however, Bannockburn was won by the courage and aggression of common Scotsmen who were not afraid to launch a headlong attack when the opportunity presented itself, and who kept on pushing until victory was theirs.

The English lost 22 barons, 68 knights and around 1000 infantry in the battle itself. Many more were killed or captured in the pursuit that followed. King Edward was eventually able to reach safety at Dunbar Castle. The Scots lost about 500 infantry and two men-at-arms. Stirling Castle surrendered as agreed shortly after the battle. The English defeat at Bannockburn ensured that Scotland remained independent from England, at least for the time being. However, the pattern of Scots defeat at the hands of English archers supported by men-at-arms was soon resumed.

In this eighteenth-century magazine illustration, Edward II, King of England, is denied entry to Stirling Castle by the garrison commander, following the defeat at Bannockburn. Bound by an agreement to surrender the castle that very day, Sir Robert Mowbray was placed in the unenviable position of refusing his king sanctuary within the walls. King Edward eventually gained the sanctuary of Dunbar Castle. Many of his nobles were not so fortunate.

SLUYS
1340

THE BATTLE OF SLUYS WAS ENGLAND'S FIRST MAJOR VICTORY IN THE HUNDRED YEARS WAR. THE GREATEST NAVAL BATTLE OF THE EUROPEAN MIDDLE AGES, SLUYS DEMONSTRATED DECISIVELY THE ADVANTAGE OF ENGLISH LONGBOWMEN OVER THE CROSSBOWMEN EMPLOYED BY FRANCE, WHILE FREEING ENGLAND FROM THE THREAT OF INVASION.

WHY DID IT HAPPEN?

WHO An English fleet of 120–160 vessels, under the command of King Edward III (1312–77) and carrying an invasion force, opposed by 213 French ships led by the admirals Hugh Quiérat and Nicholas Béhuchet.

WHAT The battle took place between the French and English fleets, the fighting taking the form of sustained projectile exchanges followed by boarding.

WHERE The estuary of the Zwyn River near Sluys, 16km (10 miles) from Bruges, now in Belgium.

WHEN 24 June 1340.

WHY The French fleet blocked the mouth of the Zwyn, intending to prevent the disembarkation of English troops. The English fleet attacked, hoping to break through and sail upriver to Bruges.

OUTCOME Crippled by a poor defensive strategy and inadequate numbers of soldiers aboard their ships, the French were massacred by English archery and hand-to-hand fighting.

Kings Philip VI of France (1293–1350) and Edward III of England both believed that naval warfare was best pursued with galleys, oared vessels that were not dependent on wind to manoeuvre. In 1340, however, both sides had to rely on cogs – merchant roundships propelled by sails rather than oars. The French king had hired a large Genoese galley fleet at the onset of the Hundred Years War, but suffered a mutiny that left him with only 22 French royal galleys – 18 of which were burned in

An undated woodcut of Philip VI of France, the first French king of the house of Valois, in profile. After 1337, Philip's reign was dominated by the opening phases of the Hundred Years War with England.

an English raid early in 1340. Philip was thus reduced to a defensive fleet strategy that could be carried out using impressed merchant ships, rather than the grand invasion of England he had planned. King Edward of England tried desperately to hire Venetian galleys to protect his projected invasion of France via Flanders, but his offers received only evasive responses from Venice. He, too, had to rely on merchant vessels, with forecastles and sterncastles added to act as fighting platforms from which soldiers could shoot arrows or hurl javelins and stones at the enemy.

Thus, in terms of ships, both the English and French fleets felt themselves to be at a disadvantage. The French government soon proved to have superior organizational resources, though. Upon adopting a defensive policy aimed to block English invaders from the Flemish coast, King Philip built up a 213-ship 'Great Army of the Sea' composed mostly of cogs; merchants were paid for the use of their ships, and sailors received their wages promptly. This orderly collection of ships forms a strong contrast to the English fleet: King Edward demanded merchant shipping to

carry his army to the Continent in an increasingly hysterical tone as his 1340 invasion was repeatedly delayed when the transport failed to appear. He finally collected somewhere between 120 and 160 ships, mostly privately owned merchantmen.

Despite its smaller size, the English fleet had two great advantages over the French force: it was intelligently commanded (although the battle displays little tactical sophistication), and the English ships had a

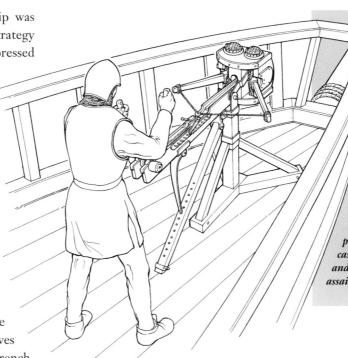

Left: Fitted for war, this fourteenth-century merchant cog is typical of the ships that fought at Sluys. It has castles at the fore, the stern and the masthead. Later, this style of ship would be fitted with the world's first naval cannons.

LOCATION

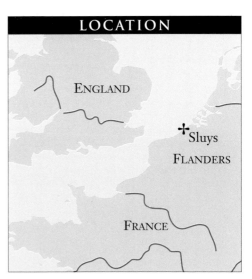

Flanders was Edward III's ally in his war against France. By landing his army there, Edward could join forces with Flemish troops for a joint invasion of northern France.

127

Edward III was head of the church, head of state and England's commander-in-chief, as this nineteenth-century illustration indicates in his dress and posture.

EDWARD III AND THE HUNDRED YEARS WAR

The Hundred Years War, which was to dominate Edward's reign, began in 1337. Disputes over English holdings in France, trouble between the great Flemish weaving cities (allies of the English) and their French overlords, and French aid to the rebellious Scots were the chief causes of the war. Edward's assumption of the title of King of France in 1340, based on a claim through his mother, was an immediate provocation to the French monarchy. Edward fought in many battles in the war, including Sluys (1340) and the famous Battle of Crécy (1346), as well as in the successful siege of Calais (1346–47). A peace was concluded by the Treaty of Brétigny (1360), under which Edward was awarded a large ransom for the French King John II, who had been captured by Edward the Black Prince at the Battle of Poitiers (1356). The treaty also conceded large amounts of French territory, including Aquitaine and Calais. In 1369, in response to heavy taxation of his nobles by the Black Prince, Charles V of France renewed the war, and the French, under Bertrand du Guesclin, Constable of France, won back much territory. A truce followed in 1375. Within two years both King Edward and the Black Prince were dead, and hostilities were not resumed until 1415, when King Henry V (1388–1422) reasserted the English claim.

great many professional soldiers on board – men-at-arms and longbowmen – intended for the summer's land campaign. By contrast, the French were able to muster only about 150 experienced men-at-arms and fewer than 500 crossbowmen; the fleet also included more than 19,000 men from maritime towns, who may have been good sailors but especially lacked skill in archery. The presence of soldiers was decisive in medieval naval war, which was conducted by means of missile barrages (arrows, javelins, rocks, etc) against the opposing ship and then an attempt at boarding.

THE CAMPAIGN

The Battle of Sluys was the first major battle of the Hundred Years War, waged between England and France in an intermittent fashion between 1337 and 1453. By 1340 the rulers of both countries had suffered severe setbacks – of a fiscal rather than a military nature, as each discovered that the resources of a medieval state were simply inadequate to their ambitions. Philip VI of France had planned a major invasion of England in 1339, only to have his fleet dispersed by a storm and then the mutiny of his Genoese galley crews.

This led him to adopt a defensive strategy suitable to the merchant ships on which he had to rely, with the intention of preventing an English landing along the Flanders coast. For his part, Edward III had bankrupted himself in the first years of campaigning and scraped together a new expeditionary force for the 1340 fighting season. Some of this force was dissipated when adequate shipping failed to appear at a number of rendezvous; Edward's largest royal ships were also unavailable during the planning stages of the campaign since they were stationed along the southern English coast to repel a threatened French invasion. Neither state was able to afford anything like a professional navy.

King Edward had not fully anticipated the implications of Philip's naval setbacks, apparently remaining ignorant of the fact that Philip's 'Great Army of the Sea' had taken up a position on the Flanders coast until 10 June 1340, just days before he intended to sail with his army. Despite the advice of his senior administrators, Edward was unwilling to forego his plans for the year. Instead, a flurry of orders forced nearby ports to produce additional merchant ships for use as transports, horses

were disembarked to make room for more fighting men, and the royal ships were ordered to join the expedition. Edward managed to pull together a fleet of 120–160 vessels. They were mostly merchantmen forced into royal service, and because of their rapid impressment were probably less prepared for naval warfare than their French counterparts. Compensating for this weakness, the ships carried a large number of soldiers (besides baggage, the queen and her attendants, and war materiel). The fleet sailed for Flanders on 20 June.

DISPOSITIONS

The English found the French fleet arrayed in a defensive position, completely blocking the mouth of the Zwyn estuary, which in the fourteenth century was about 4.8km (3 miles) wide (thanks to silt deposits, the site of the battle is now farmland). The French admirals, apparently anxious that the English might sneak by them and effect a landing,

Archers firing at a butt, 1300–40, from The Luttrell Psalter. *Although the longbow was the most effective weapon of the Hundred Years War, proficiency with it could only be achieved after many hours of practice.*

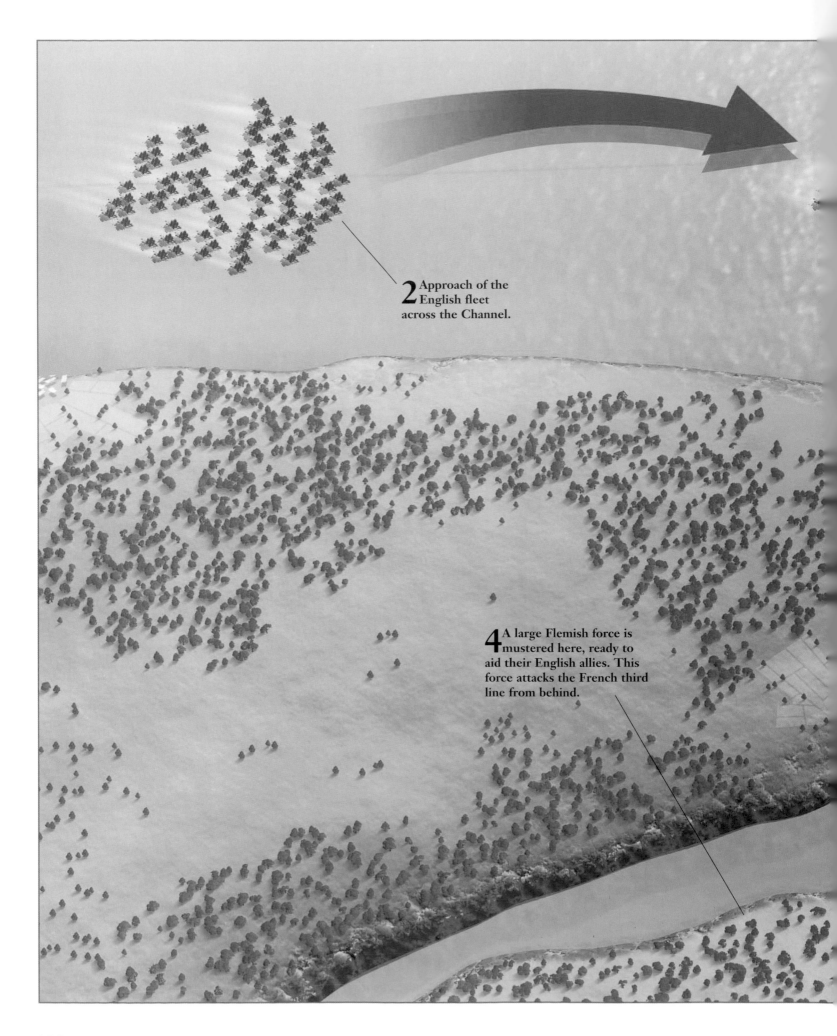

2 Approach of the
English fleet
across the Channel.

4 A large Flemish force is
mustered here, ready to
aid their English allies. This
force attacks the French third
line from behind.

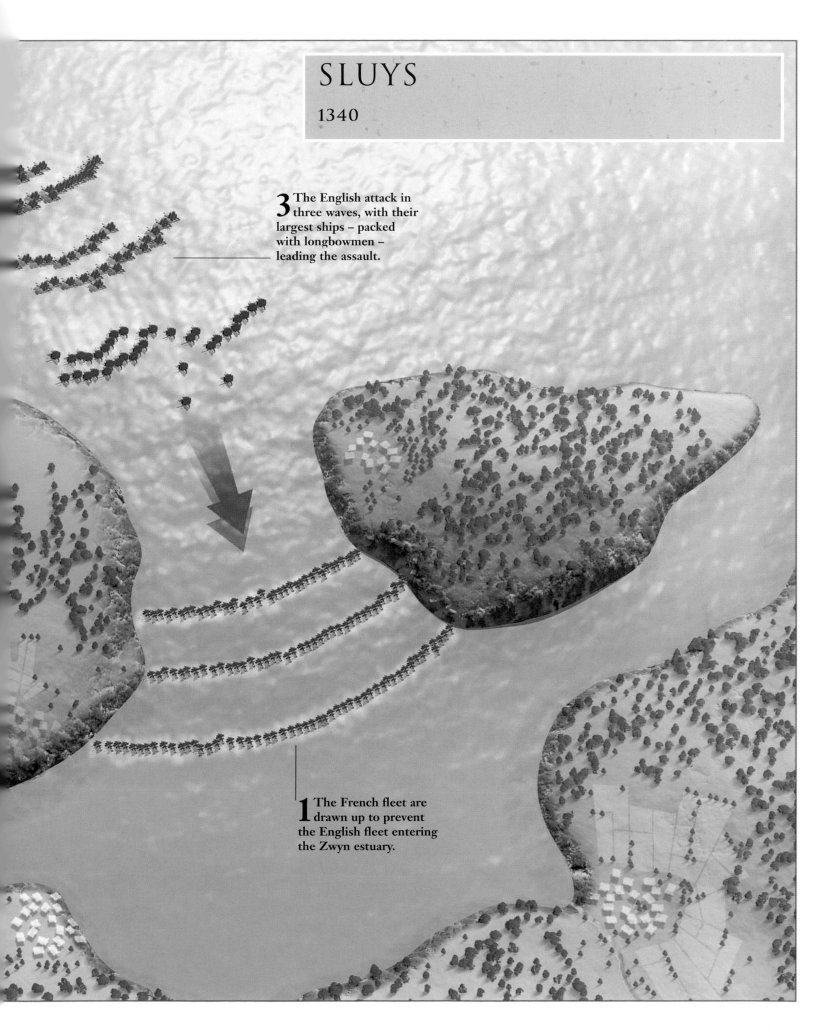

SLUYS

1340

3 The English attack in three waves, with their largest ships – packed with longbowmen – leading the assault.

1 The French fleet are drawn up to prevent the English fleet entering the Zwyn estuary.

SLUYS

THE OPPOSED FORCES

ENGLISH

Ships (mostly cogs):   c.120–160
Archers (estimated):   3–4000
Men-at-arms (estimated):   1500
Sailors and other fighters: unknown
**Total: c.120–160 ships,
c.5500 soldiers plus an unknown
number of other men.**

FRENCH

Galleys: 6
Oared barges: 22
Royal sailing ships: 7
Merchantmen: 167
Spanish and Flemish ships: 11
Crossbowmen: c.500
Men-at-arms: c.150
Sailors and other fighters: c.18,500
Total: 213 ships, c.19,150 men

chained their ships to each other to form three long lines. They ignored the protests of experienced French captains who urged that the French fleet sail out to meet the English on the open sea where there was room to manoeuvre and warned that the wind blowing into the mouth of the river would wreak havoc among the chained ships.

The prophets of doom were correct. When the English fleet approached the French on 24 June, Edward was in no hurry to attack, delaying until the sun would no longer be in his men's eyes during the onslaught, at about 3.00 p.m. In the meantime, the French ships, the vast majority of them sailing vessels, began to be blown off-station and to drift eastwards in the current. Soon the French ships were fouling each other and the French line had fallen into disarray. The French admirals finally saw their error and ordered the ships unchained from each other. The ships then began to edge westwards again to reblock the river mouth. Thus, even though the French fleet appeared to be imposing – the chronicler Froissart said the ships looked like a row of castles – in reality, the French ships were badly prepared for the English attack when it came.

THE ATTACK

The English fleet was marshalled into three lines for its approach, King Edward placing the largest ships in the front line, including his own flagship, the cog *Thomas*. The style of naval fighting of the time called for shipboard soldiers to pummel the enemy with projectiles as the range closed, then if possible to grapple with an enemy ship that had been thrown into disorder by the wounding or killing of its personnel and board it. The English force at Sluys had an enormous advantage in this sort of warfare. The ships were loaded with men-at-arms

The final stage of a sea battle between two northern European fourteenth-century cogs approaches. The cogs did not normally use oars, so sails had to be employed even during battle. Archers and crossbowmen were widely employed in a battle of attrition that often ended when one ship boarded the other and killed or captured its crew.

and especially longbowmen intended for the invasion, so English firepower vastly outclassed anything the French could produce. While the French had plenty of men to throw stones or javelins from the mastheads and castles – neither effective at a range of more than about 9m (10 yards) – they had mustered fewer than 500 professional crossbowmen. And the crossbowmen they had available proved to be far inferior to the English longbowmen in a rapid attack.

Not only were the English archers' arrows more accurate and could wound or even kill at more than 90m (100 yards), in a situation where speed counted, trained longbowmen could loose up to 12 arrows a

minute, much faster than a crossbowman. Also important in a sea fight, English bow strings affected by the damp could be replaced in a moment, unlike the more complicated mechanism of a crossbow.

The French put up as strong a defence as possible – Edward III himself received a crossbow bolt through his thigh – but the combination of low firepower and initial disarray was too much for the French sailors and soldiers. In addition, as the afternoon progressed the French crews were forced to fight with the sun in their eyes. The first of the three French lines was destroyed in quick order; the tall ships from the English first line were then able to move on against the smaller, tightly clustered ships of the

This fifteenth-century manuscript illustration from Froissart's Chronicle *shows the close, ship-to-ship combat of the Battle of Sluys, 1340. Naval warfare in the Medieval period was a much more carefully planned affair than this illustrstion suggests, with tactics playing a crucial role in deciding the outcome of a battle.*

Taken from the late fourteenth-century manuscript Chroniques d'Angleterre *by Jean de Wavrin, this illustration shows French ships moored at Sluys in the days before the battle.*

French middle line. This difference in height gave the English barrage an even greater advantage.

ENCIRCLEMENT OF THE FRENCH

During the initial English assault, King Edward's rather reluctant Flemish allies had merely watched the action from the banks of the Zwyn rather than participating. When the English advantage became apparent, though, the Flemings came out in ships from Sluys and other harbours on the Zwyn and proceeded to attack the French third line from the rear. The battle broke down into a series of skirmishes between individual ships. Most of the fighting was over by about 10.00 p.m., although two ships continued to fight until dawn. Froissart tells that when the final French ship was taken, 400 corpses were counted on its deck.

Since their escape route was blocked, the French losses were devastating. The English captured 190 of the 213 French ships engaged in the battle; almost the only vessels to escape were the oared galleys and barges, which could manoeuvre much more effectively than the English ships, reliant as the latter were on the wind. Between 16,000 and 18,000 Frenchmen lost their lives at Sluys, making it the bloodiest naval battle of the Middle Ages. Losses were so great because, unlike in land fighting, it was unusual to give quarter to enemies when boarding a ship: there was no secure place to stow prisoners. Besides, the psychological impact of the desperate hand-to-hand struggle must be considered. A fleet action was less like a field battle, more like the storming of a castle on land, an event also normally marked by wholesale slaughter. Thus the only hope left for crewmembers of a losing ship was either to present such a rich appearance that overexcited men would find them worth taking for ransom, or to take to the water. But in this battle even the faint hope of reaching land by swimming was vain: the Flemings lined the west bank of the Zwyn and clubbed to death the French survivors who crawled onto land. Even the two French admirals perished. Quiérat was killed in the course of the battle, while Béhuchet was taken prisoner. He was at first intended for ransom, but when Edward discovered that the admiral had led a series of devastating raids against the English coast the previous year he ordered that Béhuchet be hanged from the yardarm of his own ship.

AFTERMATH

The immediate effect of the Battle of Sluys was to allow Edward III to disembark his army unopposed and proceed to wage a summer campaign against the French. The total victory of the English also certainly reinforced the loyalty of Edward's Flemish allies, who had received an impressive confirmation of English military power. Neither of these results had a long-term impact on the course of the war, though. Instead, the most important consequence of Sluys was that it effectively ended any threat of a French invasion of England, essuring that the Hundred Years War would be fought on French rather than English soil.

The Battle of Sluys was also the first large-scale demonstration of the devastating effectiveness of the English longbow, in this case against the more cumbersome and slower crossbow. Thus the engagement at Sluys provided an important prelude to the Battle of Crécy in 1346, when similar tactics were successfully employed against heavily armed cavalry.

Although it was arguably the greatest battle of the Hundred Years War, the celebration of the Battle of Sluys fell victim to the military values of its own time. For while the chronicler Froissart provided a description of the battle and it received brief

mentions in other sources, Sluys failed to catch the popular imagination in the way the smaller and less significant land battles of Crécy, Poitiers and Agincourt did. Sluys, despite the personal leadership of Edward III, was essentially a lower-class battle without the romanticism involved in defeating the leaders of European chivalry on a battlefield. Modern authors have in general followed the medieval prejudice, neglecting the largest-scale military event of the Hundred Years War and England's greatest medieval victory.

This early twentieth-century illustration shows the coronation of King Edward III in 1327 at Westminster, London, by Archbishop of Canterbury Walter Reynolds (d. 1327).

CRÉCY
1346

THE BATTLE OF CRÉCY WAS THE BEGINNING OF THE END FOR THE ARMOURED CAVALRYMAN WHO HAD DOMINATED WARFARE FOR CENTURIES. PITTING A TIRED AND OUTNUMBERED ENGLISH FORCE COMPOSED MAINLY OF ARCHERS AGAINST THE FLOWER OF FRENCH CHIVALRY, CRÉCY WAS THE SHAPE OF THINGS TO COME.

WHY DID IT HAPPEN?

WHO An English army numbering 9000 under King Edward III (1312–77), opposed by some 30,000 French troops under King Philip VI (1293–1350).

WHAT The main action took place between defensively positioned archers and dismounted men-at-arms, attacked by mounted men-at-arms.

WHERE The village of Crécy-en-Ponthieu, near Abbeville, France.

WHEN 26 August 1346.

WHY The English army, marching to link up with Flemish allies, was caught and brought to battle by a vastly superior French force.

OUTCOME Repeated French charges were slaughtered by intense archery. Over 10,000 casualties were inflicted by the English, for the loss of about 100 men. The French army attacked until after nightfall, then collapsed and scattered.

In the 1300s, the mounted man-at-arms was king of the battlefield. Either a titled nobleman holding the rank of knight or above, or a professional soldier in the service of such a noble, the man-at-arms represented the maximum possible fighting power that could be concentrated in a single soldier. He prepared for war all his life, honing his skills in training and testing them in tournaments against his peers. Even his leisure pursuits – hunting, falconry and so forth – were martial and warlike. Secure in his armour of partial plate (heavy metal plates and helm with lighter mail over the joints), the man-at-arms could cut down his foes with axe, mace, lance and, of course,

A bust of Edward III from Westminster Abbey shows the king as a wise patriarch. Edward III was a strong ruler and a considerable military tactician. His victory at Crécy demonstrated the superiority of combined arms over the headlong cavalry charge.

the sword. Little or nothing could stand in the way of the knightly charge, and battle had become a disorganized affair where individual acts of courage and skill were prized far more highly than tactics.

However, the English had discovered that a combination of men-at-arms and longbow-equipped archers was extremely potent. Archers were expected to be able to loose six shafts a minute at the very least, and these would be well-aimed out to an effective range of about 250m (273 yards). The longbow had an extreme range of about 350m (383 yards). Good archers were appreciated by the English kings. Poachers, normally sentenced to death if caught, were offered a pardon if they would serve as archers in the king's armies. On campaign, the archer was paid for his services. At the time of Crécy the going rate was two to four pence per day, while an esquire (a man-at-arms who was not a knight or higher noble) received one shilling a day.

ARMS AND STATUS

A very different situation prevailed in France. There, the man-at arms was everything. Militia would be raised for any campaign but they were ill-armed, untrained and little more than a rabble. If by some miracle the infantry actually achieved something on the battlefield instead of scattering straightaway, they were liable to be ridden down by their own side as hot-blooded knights, eager to attack, saw any delay in charging as an affront to their honour. There was thus little incentive for the French infantryman to fight well, and even the foreign mercenaries fielded by many commanders were viewed with suspicion and contempt. This in turn led to further lacklustre performances which reinforced the view that the only troops worth anything on the field were noblemen in armour, raised in a warrior culture and determined to prove their worth by deeds of valour and reckless aggression.

The reasons for this apparently strange conduct are enshrined within the culture of France at the time. Military activity was linked to social status, and status was to a great extent influenced by personal performance in war. By restricting military training and equipment to a small social

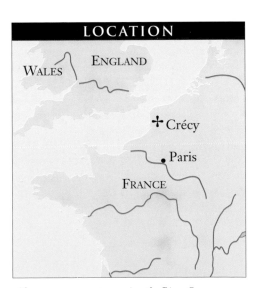

GENOESE CROSSBOWMAN (C.1340)

Professional soldiers fighting for pay, the Genoese mercenary crossbowmen at Crécy were well equipped and experienced, but very badly handled by their French paymasters. Although they were armoured and armed for close-quarters combat, the mercenaries specialized in delivering concentrated heavy firepower from their crossbows. The large and heavy shield could be emplaced to provide cover while the crossbowman reloaded his weapon and moved as he advanced upon the enemy. Cocked with a lever device, the heavy crossbow actually outranged the English longbow but could not shoot anything like as quickly. The crossbowmen's slow and deliberate style of warfare was not acceptable to the impetuous French nobility, and at Crécy they were pushed aside before achieving anything.

élite, the possibility of revolt was reduced and social control made more effective.

Commoners were despised for other reasons too. An element of chivalry existed between the bitterest of foes, especially where the custom of ransom was concerned. A captured nobleman could be ransomed back to his lord for a tidy sum, and was thus a valuable asset. Surrendering needlessly was a personal disgrace, and there were rules of etiquette concerning who was worthy to accept the surrender of whom, but in the last resort a wounded or desperately outnumbered warrior had a good chance of mercy, if only because his captors stood to make a profit from sparing him. However, ransom was of interest primarily to other nobles. Common footsoldiers were as likely to finish off a downed man-at-arms by inserting a knife through the joints in his armour as they were to try to claim a ransom. No lord would pay ransom to mere commoners anyway, so the only chance of profit was to turn over the captive to a noble and hope he remembered to be generous when the ransom was paid. Commoners, with no ransom worth having, were likely to be butchered if they surrendered. This at

LOCATION

WALES   ENGLAND

✝ Crécy

• Paris

FRANCE

After a narrow escape crossing the River Somme, Edward III grasped the nettle and offered battle on ground of his choosing rather than risk being overwhelmed on the march.

CRÉCY

THE OPPOSED FORCES

ENGLISH (estimated)
Archers:	5500
Welsh spearmen:	1000
Men-at-arms:	2500
Others: A small number of primitive cannon	
Total:	**9000**

FRENCH (estimated)
Genoese crossbowmen:	6000
Men-at-arms:	10,000
Feudal militia	14,000
Total:	**30,000**

times led to bitter acts of revenge between common soldiers and enemy noblemen.

These major social differences were very apparent in the forces that came to the battlefield that day in August 1346. On the English side, a small force of men-at-arms was supported by a larger number of free men. These men were properly trained and equipped, respected by their commanders and fighting not for pay, pardon or duty but out of choice. Most importantly, their leaders had a clear idea of how they were to be used in battle and there was a mutual trust between the different groups. Each soldier knew his part, and previous events had shown that if he played it well, victory would result.

English longbowmen fire volleys at the Battle of Crécy. The longbow was a tremendous weapon. The archers could loose a third arrow before the first struck. They often fought barefoot to improve grip. It took regular practice to keep the strength needed to pull the bow. This was its flaw, though, as firearms, which were easier to use, became more widely available from the mid-fifteenth century.

On the French side there was no such cohesion. The 14,000 or so feudal militia brought to the field were forced to be there by their commanders. They had no training, scant equipment and no real motivation to fight well. No plan existed for how they were to be used, other, perhaps, than to absorb arrows. The mercenary infantry component were more useful but were not trusted or really valued by their commanders. Even the men-at-arms, excellent individual fighters as they might be, were not used to operating together as a coherent force. The custom of the time was to seek out social equals and engage them in combat. Feats of arms against mere peasants were nothing. Any knight or man-at-arms seeking to make a name for himself needed to fight someone 'of name' if he wanted to be taken seriously. Rivalries between individuals, questions of rank and precedence and the tendency of individuals to want to perform great deeds interfered with the command structure.

Thus where the English came to the field with a trained army, the French brought a large number of individual

warriors under the loose control of their social superiors, plus an even larger swarm of virtually useless rabble. The coming battle would pit courage against discipline; martial prowess against planning and tactical skill.

THE CAMPAIGN

The battle of Crécy was part of the so-called Hundred Years War between England and France, which actually lasted from 1337 to 1453. The period was not one of constant fighting, of course, but was characterized by sporadic French attempts to oust the English from their holdings in France, and English attacks (mostly large-scale raids) against the French.

In 1346, the English king, Edward III, was on campaign in France. With him was his 16-year-old son, also named Edward (1330–76). Having scored some successes and penetrated from Cherbourg almost to Paris, the English army had got into trouble. Tired and short of supplies, with many men-at-arms riding captured farm horses after losing their own mounts, the English force dragged itself eastwards to link up with its Flemish allies.

Things looked bleak for Edward III. The French advance guard was pressing at his heels as he sought a place to cross the River Somme. With dysentery rampant in the ranks and boots falling apart on the men's feet, the army made slow progress.

The supply wagons and the new cannon, dragged halfway across France and back again, were an added encumbrance. Intended for siege warfare, the cannon were little more than crude iron tubes firing a small stone or iron ball massing perhaps 1–2kg (2.2–4.4lb). They might give good service in a siege but cannon had never yet been used in open battle.

Finding a ford just in time, King Edward sent his men across the wide Somme in the hope of reaching safety. Disaster threatened as a blocking force including Genoese crossbowmen attempted to bar the crossing. A hail of arrows from the longbowmen in the vanguard gave the blocking force pause, and the English men-at-arms advanced. Together, the armoured warriors and the disciplined longbowmen were able to force the passage and drive the French into retreat. The far bank was cleared just in time, for at this point the French advance guard caught up, bringing on a sharp fight at the tail of the column. Although some supply wagons were lost, the English army was able to make the crossing and push on.

The following day the English army took up positions near the village of Crécy-en-Ponthieu. It was an excellent spot, with

Edward, Prince of Wales, as depicted in St Stephen's Chapel, Westminster. One of England's great warriors, the 'Black Prince' as he became known, won his first laurels at the Battle of Crécy.

Aueques trouuaft on/les dolereus marcies eruelllleres fendues/coutiaus agus brifies

A fourteenth-century depiction of crossbow drill. The figure on the right has placed his foot in a stirrup on the front of his weapon to provide leverage as he pulls back the string.

French cavalry attempt to prees home a charge against English archers. Note the crossbow and helmet of a hapless Genoese mercenary in the foreground. It is unlikely that the French got this close to the English line in such good order.

the army's flanks protected by the River Maye and the village of Crécy on the right-hand side, and a small hamlet named Wadicourt on the left. There was sloping ground in front of the English – a perfect killing ground for the massed archers with their mighty longbows. In the afternoon, the French army arrived and went immediately into the attack.

DISPOSITIONS

Edward III deployed his force defensively, with two main bodies of Welsh spearmen and dismounted men-at-arms under the Earl of Northampton and Prince Edward. Each of these bodies was flanked by a force of archers. The latter were drawn up in 'herces', roughly triangular formations that allowed the archers to sweep their front and flanks with a hail of arrows, bringing intense missile fire to bear at any point on the field. The king himself took position with a reserve of men-at-arms and more archers at

the top of the slope. This tactic of breaking an army into three divisions or 'battles' was standard at the time. In fact in many armies it represented not only the pinnacle but also the sum total of tactics.

However, Edward III was a seasoned campaigner and a shrewd tactician who was willing to embrace new ideas if they might bring him victory. Dismounting men-at-arms ran contrary to the practice of the time, and treating mere infantrymen as the main striking force was positively heretical. Nevertheless, Edward had great faith in his archers. They were well trained and supplied with large numbers of arrows. About half of them had received additional training in a technique of getting off as many arrows as possible in a short time – perhaps 20 in a minute. Knowing they would soon be attacked by cavalry, the archers dug small pits in the ground in front of their position to impede the charge. Once this was done there was nothing for it

FRENCH KNIGHT

The large amount of warfare taking place in the fourteenth and fifteenth centuries (the last two centuries of the Middle Ages) led to some dramatic military technological changes. By the time of the Battle of Crécy cavalry had begun wearing a more solid and independent breastplate made from a single piece of metal fashioned to cover the chest and sides. By the end of the century this had been joined to metallic plates covering the back, neck, legs, arms and feet, and was topped by a helmet that most often fitted tightly around the head and was equipped with a visor. Over this, the soldier usually wore a surcoat, which added no extra protection, but did serve heraldic purposes. The offensive weapons remained the same as earlier, a lance and sword, although in order to better face changes in armour, the former had increased in length and the latter had become shorter and stiffer, often with reinforced, sharp points.

but to wait. Protecting their precious bowstrings from a sudden downpour, the English archers stood around in small groups and awaited the French onslaught.

The French, on the other hand, entered the field in some disorder. Marching in three battles, they came up the road from Marcheville. The army overall was commanded by King Philip himself. The first division, forming an advance guard, consisted of 6000 Genoese mercenary crossbowmen who had already been bloodied by the English archers. The second division was led by King Philip's brother, the Count d'Alencon, and consisted of a mix of militia and men-at-arms. Among the noble leaders of subdivisions under d'Alencon's command were the Kings of Majorca and Bohemia, and of the Romans. The third division of the army, consisting of more militia and men-at-arms, was commanded by Codemar de Faye.

OPENING MOVES

The French force sighted the English at about 4.00 p.m. At this point the French were in considerable disarray, with elements of the three divisions intermixed in places and out of contact with their commanders. It might have been advisable to wait until the following day to make the attack, or at

least to form up properly. In fact, King Philip ordered the army to halt. However, the men-at-arms in the vanguard had other ideas. Before them lay a pitiful force that had narrowly escaped the day before, foolishly drawn up for battle and inviting a smashing blow.

It is likely that the hot-blooded men-at-arms thought that there was but little chance for glory before them, for surely the English force would be swiftly swept aside by their charge. The idea that infantry might put up a decent fight – let alone emerge victorious – probably did not occur to them. The miserable peasant rabble milling around nearby would have reinforced this image. Thus the men-at-arms of the vanguard, knowing that their reputations depended

upon their deeds this day, were impatient to launch their attack. Any knight who showed hesitation in the face of the foe, especially a foe so obviously inferior, would lose all honour. The charge must be launched swiftly before someone robbed the vanguard of what little glory was to be had.

Bertrand du Guesclin (c.1320–80), Constable of France. In addition to holding rank, some nobles had specific appointments. The Constable of France was responsible for the defence of the realm and commanded the field army if the king was not present.

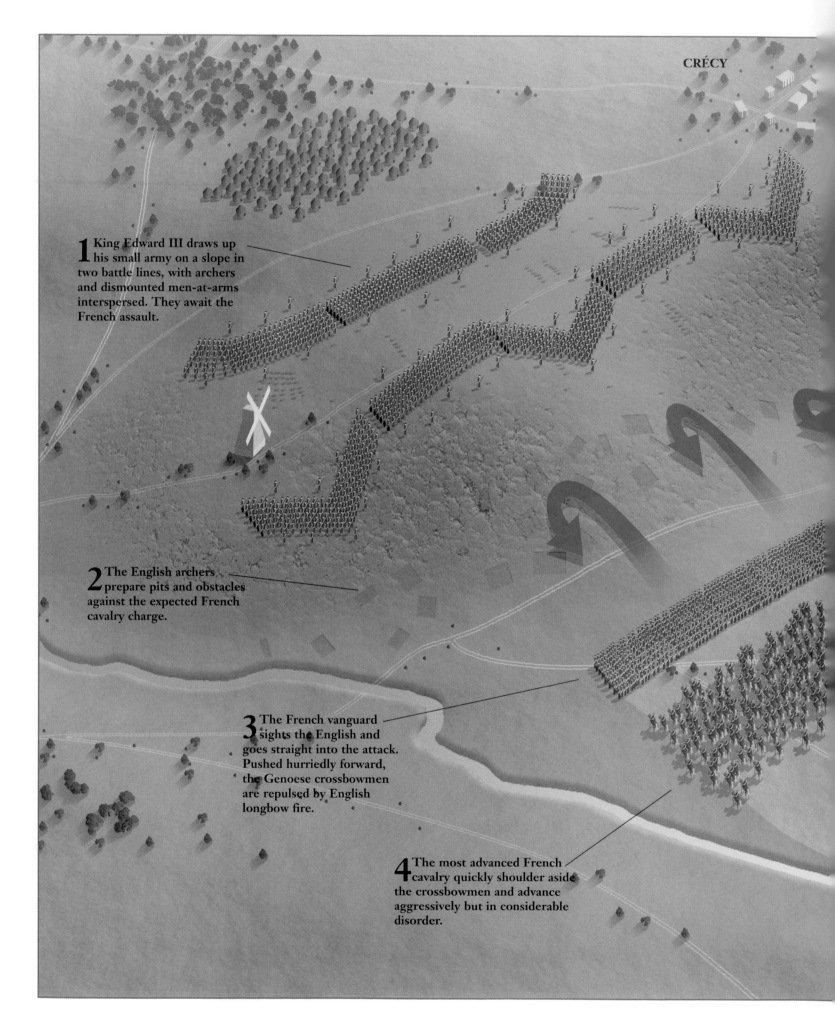

CRÉCY

1 King Edward III draws up his small army on a slope in two battle lines, with archers and dismounted men-at-arms interspersed. They await the French assault.

2 The English archers prepare pits and obstacles against the expected French cavalry charge.

3 The French vanguard sights the English and goes straight into the attack. Pushed hurriedly forward, the Genoese crossbowmen are repulsed by English longbow fire.

4 The most advanced French cavalry quickly shoulder aside the crossbowmen and advance aggressively but in considerable disorder.

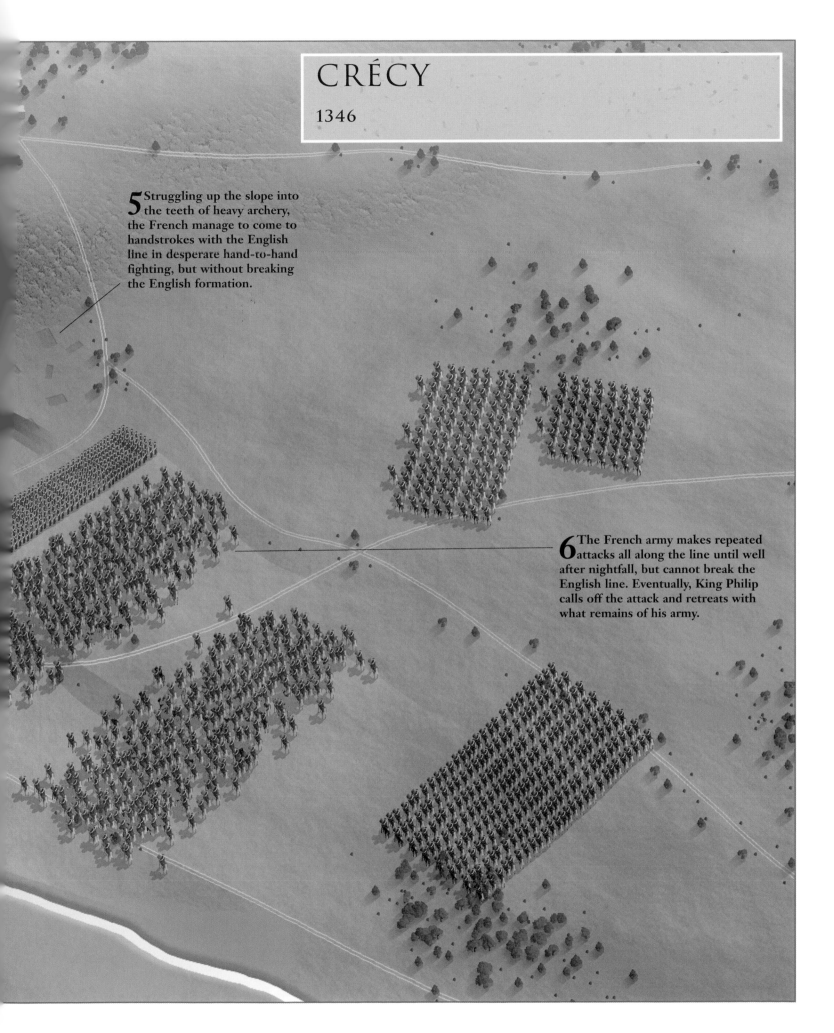

CRÉCY

1346

5 Struggling up the slope into the teeth of heavy archery, the French manage to come to handstrokes with the English line in desperate hand-to-hand fighting, but without breaking the English formation.

6 The French army makes repeated attacks all along the line until well after nightfall, but cannot break the English line. Eventually, King Philip calls off the attack and retreats with what remains of his army.

143

CRÉCY

Impatiently the men-at-arms jostled forward, driving before them the 6000 or so Genoese crossbowmen of the advance guard. The Genoese were reluctant to attack. Their weapons had been affected by the rainstorm, they were tired and disordered from the march, and they had already experienced the shooting of the English archers waiting calmly for them to come into range. They were also without their pavises – large shields behind which they could take cover while reloading – which were stuck with the baggage train. However, their protests were angrily brushed aside and the order to attack was given. Not all the French host had arrived on the battlefield when the Genoese wearily began their advance.

THE FIRST ATTACK

As the Genoese crossbowmen struggled forward, trying to sort out their ranks into some kind of fighting order, they came under murderous fire from up the slope. Their weapons normally outranged the English longbow, but a combination of damp, higher ground and the sun, which came out from the clouds directly behind the archers, gave the English the advantage. It was exploited to good effect. When the Genoese had closed to 150m (164 yards), fairly short range for a longbow, the English opened fire. They poured in several shots in the time it took the Genoese to reload their powerful crossbows, and their aim was good. The ragged line wavered under the onslaught. Blasts of smoke and flame from the English line signalled that the age of gunpowder warfare had arrived. Edward's cannon had joined the action – but it was the archers who slaughtered the enemy before them.

Behind the Genoese, the men-at-arms of the French vanguard were impatient and angry at having the honour of opening the action stolen from them. When the Genoese began falling back, it was too much for the hot-blooded knights. They began to advance, using the weight of their horses and even their weapons to force a passage through the crossbowmen. Assailed both from in front and behind, the Genoese broke. Some shot at the men-at-arms in self-defence, and vicious little fights broke

The archers who played such an important role in the action are conspicuously absent from this contemporary depiction of close-quarters fighting at the Battle of Crécy (taken from Les Chroniques de France*). The French banner is trampled into the ground while that of the English flies proudly.*

out on the slope even as the main body of knights thundered raggedly up the hill towards the real enemy.

Partly from contempt for mere archers, partly due to the pits dug in front of the archers' positions, and partly due to the 'channelling' effect of flanking fire, the French charge was directed at the dismounted men-at-arms and Welsh spearmen that awaited them. The standard broadhead arrow was not particularly effective against plate armour, but it could bring down a horse or drive it mad with pain. The English also had 'bodkin' arrows available, with long, sharp points capable of punching through plate. Volley after volley

smashed into the flanks of the knights as they pressed home their ragged charge.

Relatively few Frenchmen reached the English line, but those who got there assailed their opponents vigorously. The charge became a confused series of mêlées as small bodies of men-at-arms advanced to contact and others were thrown back to rally and come forward again. The English line stood unwaveringly, spearmen and men-at-arms fighting to repulse the French.

Philip of France knew he was committed now. He could not let his vanguard fight on unsupported. As the rest of the army hastily deployed it was sent forward at the English in a series of uncoordinated charges.

CRISIS POINT

The French attacks were disorganized due to command and control problems and the difficulty of launching an assault straight from the march. They were, however, carried out with great vigour and gallantry. Such were the numbers and determination of the French that for hours the assaults kept coming. The hand-to-hand fighting became increasingly intense, and Godfrey Harcourt, charged with the safety of Prince Edward, became gravely concerned for the young man's life.

Harcourt ran to the nearest English unit of the left wing and asked its commander, the Earl of Arundel, to carry out a counter-attack and relieve the pressure on the young prince's wing of the army. He also sent a runner to Edward III to ask for reinforcements. Seeing that Arundel was already charging to the prince's rescue, King Edward declined to commit his reserve. Instead he made the courageous – and correct – decision to 'let the boy win his spurs'.

Arundel's men tore into the flank of the French assaulting the prince's division, and together the two forces beat off the attack with heavy casualties. By the time reinforcements from the reserve could have arrived, it was all over and the prince's men were resting after their feat of arms. It was here that Edward, Prince of Wales, began to earn his fearsome reputation. He is better known to history as 'the Black Prince' for the colour of his armour – though some have suggested that the title had more to do with his temperament.

THE ASSAULT CONTINUES

Still the French came on. Inspired by the example of their leaders including blind King John of Bohemia (1296–1346), whose horse was led into battle by two knights, the ragged charges continued. Again and again the exhausted horses thundered up the slope into the teeth of longbow volleys. It is difficult to determine exactly how many charges took place. Most accounts settle on 15 or 16 distinct charges, but this does not take into account local attacks made by groups that were driven off but rallied and plunged back into the fray.

The persistence of the French force is remarkable for both the courage and the apparent lack of good sense involved. Why did the French keep up their costly and ineffective attacks? Perhaps the answer lies in the social structure of the French army. The man-at-arms was trained from birth to fight. He was confident and aggressive, and

either desired to make a reputation for himself or had many successful encounters behind him. He was accustomed to expect victory, and was not in the habit of accepting defeat. He was part of an élite force, and he had to be able to hold up his head among his fellows. Each man-at-arms was aware that his personal honour, and therefore his status in society, was at stake. To be defeated by peasant infantry or to quit the field before the battle was done would be a lifelong stigma. So, as long as others fought on, he must do the same or be forever shamed.

There is also the example of the French commanders to consider. The custom of the time was to lead from the front. The duty of the commanders was to keep attacking until they won, or until the king ordered them to desist. The duty of the lesser-ranked knights and men-at-arms was to follow their

Philip VI of France. In a society where social status was tied to prowess in war, it is hardly surprising that courage and aggression rather than tactical acumen dominated in Philip's army.

Opposite: However important the longbowman might be in actual battle, it was the armoured nobility that were enshrined in tapestry and – as in this series from Tewkesbury Abbey shows – in stained glass windows. This practice tended to conceal the importance of the common infantryman.

leaders' example. Thus, with a clear enemy in front of them and held fast by the bonds of duty and honour, the French had no choice but to continue their attacks.

Besides, the battle may not have looked hopeless to the French. Only a fragment of the field could be seen through the constricted field of view of a visored helm. With no real idea what was going on, each man-at-arms could only follow the rallying shouts of his leaders and go forward with the banners or whatever force he found himself among. The picture probably looked little different to the leaders. All was chaos and disorder, but that was not unusual in a battle of this period. In the gathering darkness it probably seemed that the mighty French host truly could overpower the ragged English. Just one more push, just one more charge, and surely French courage would prove the match for English archery. But it was not to be.

Around midnight, as King Philip was collecting whatever men he could for yet another attack, he was dissuaded by Sir John of Heynault. Reluctantly, Philip called off the attack and what remained of the French army drew off under cover of darkness. There was no pursuit. The weary English slept where they had fought. They had defeated a force three times their size, and without ever being even pushed back from their starting positions. The reserve had not even been committed.

AFTERMATH

The English suffered about 100 casualties at Crécy. French losses numbered about 1500 men-at-arms, including most of the commanders. Blind King John was found dead on the battlefield, well forward in the thick of the action and accompanied by his faithful knights. Around 10,000 footsoldiers were also killed. The French army was effectively destroyed as a fighting force. Even though there was no pursuit, the army

scattered during the night and Edward was able to resume his march. He laid siege to Calais, which fell the following year.

The Battle of Crécy was a total victory for the English, but it was more than that. Not only did it establish the English as one of the great warrior peoples; not only did it prove the effectiveness of the longbowman and establish the reputation of Edward, the Black Prince – it also proved the effectiveness of tactics that would bring many future victories.

The French seem to have learned little from their costly defeat and for many years repeated the pattern of disorganized 'chivalrous' attacks against archer-heavy English armies deployed on good defensive terrain. The result was an unbroken string of English victories that in turn led to a strategic situation whereby the French tended to give up the initiative and barricade themselves in their castles when the English were abroad.

This situation had major long-term strategic effects, in that the great strength of the French – the mobility and striking power of their armoured cavalry – was nullified, permitting the English to range

more freely in enemy territory and undertake sieges with less chance of being challenged by a relieving army.

Crécy was not the end for 'chivalrous' warfare and the mounted man-at-arms, though it was the end of his period of total dominance. Armoured cavalry would continue to be useful for centuries more. Five hundred years later they would still crash into the enemy line and emerge victorious – though less and less often. But now everything was different. It had been proven that massed projectiles could sweep the enemy, however courageous or well protected, from the battlefield before he could come to handstrokes.

In 1346, those projectiles were arrows launched from bows drawn by strong men. Later they would be bullets sent on their way by the combustion of gunpowder. And gunpowder, too, made its debut on the battlefield at Crécy.

The siege of Calais (from Froissart's Chronicles*). As a result of his tremendous victory at Crécy, Edward III was able to successfully besiege Calais, making it a possession of the English throne.*

NAJERA
1367

HAVING PROVED HIMSELF ON THE FIELD OF POITIERS IN NORTHERN FRANCE IN 1356, EDWARD THE BLACK PRINCE FURTHER DEMONSTRATED HIS GRASP OF STRATEGY IN THE CAMPAIGN LEADING TO NAJERA IN NORTHERN SPAIN, A BATTLE WHERE THE ENGLISH LONGBOW AGAIN SHOWED ITS SUPERIORITY.

WHY DID IT HAPPEN?

WHO A Spanish army of French mercenaries under King Henry II of Castile (1333–79), opposed an army of mainly English mercenaries under Edward the Black Prince (1330–76).

WHAT Henry's skirmishers distracted the English archers from the advancing French mercenaries and his knights charged the supporting English division but to little avail. Hand-to-hand fighting ensued between the men-at-arms.

WHERE Najera, northern Spain.

WHEN 3 April 1367.

WHY Pedro the Cruel (1334–69) had requested help from the Black Prince in regaining the throne of Castile from his half-brother Henry of Trastamara.

OUTCOME Although the largely French vanguard fought well they were no match for the combination of men-at-arms and longbowmen. They were cut down and the Spanish part of the army routed.

One of the perennial problems with the system of monarchy is the ease with which a potential heir to the throne can be persuaded to dispute the inheritance. After all there is much to gain. (This problem was frequently solved in the Middle East by the murder of all other candidates upon the death of the incumbent.) In Castile in the fourteenth century, the legitimate but unpopular King Pedro the Cruel was challenged by his illegitimate and popular half-brother Henry of Trastamara. Pedro's

To have had the sobriquet 'the Cruel' suffixed to his name speaks volumes for Pedro's character. However, he could also have added 'persuasive, untrustworthy, and shortsighted'.

PETRVS CRVDELIS

Multa, inauditæque cædes à PETRO Alphonsi XI. filio patratæ fuere siue malorum ut quidam ferunt, Procerum culpa, seu potius Regis sævitia, unde CRVDELIS cogno= men éidem factum, Semel cum Granatæ Rege, sæpe cum Aragonÿs bellum gessit interneci= num. Hi tandem spurium fratrem Henricum Transtamaræ Comitem suffultum Gallorum auxilÿs in eius exitium concitarunt, cuius armis PETRVS ciuium, et uicinorum præsi= dÿs destitutus acie uincitur; et in Montieli Castro obsessus, dum clam fugere tentat, ab

queen had suddenly and inexplicably died and she happened to be the sister-in-law of King Charles V of France (1338–80). Thus it was natural that Henry should appeal to Charles and an army was raised from the many mercenary bands then in France as a consequence of the Hundred Years War. In short order Pedro lost his throne and escaped via Seville to the court of the Black Prince in Aquitaine.

Edward had several motives for agreeing to Pedro's request for support: whichever candidate was successful would be indebted to their supporters, and better to make Castile an English ally than a French one; killing Frenchmen in Spain was as good as killing Frenchmen in France; and he would also be paid.

THE CAMPAIGN

Meanwhile, the first campaign being over, Henry dismissed the great bulk of his mercenary army, retaining a core of French veterans under their leader Bertrand du Guesclin. Edward, however, now had need of an army and recruited those very same, recently redundant, mercenaries and headed south. Once these had joined his payroll, Edward was compelled to move immediately to shorten the duration of their hire. Thus he found himself crossing the mountains in February, the most difficult time of year. He had to pay Charles II of Navarre (1332–87) for passage. (Charles had already been paid by Henry to block those same passes.)

Once through the Pyrenean pass at Roncesvalles, Edward and Pedro struck out for Burgos, the capital of Castile. Henry camped at Anastro on the border of Navarre and Aragon, while Edward and Pedro set up their base near Vittoria and sent Sir William Felton and his brother Thomas to scout the enemy's position. His party unknowingly passed a much larger band, 6000 strong, of Henry's army on a mission to raid the English camp.

This raid, lead by Henry's brother Tello, was highly successful. It attacked the camp of the English vanguard causing much damage and making off before the troops could be mustered to fight back. On their return Tello's much larger force encountered the Feltons' band of a mere

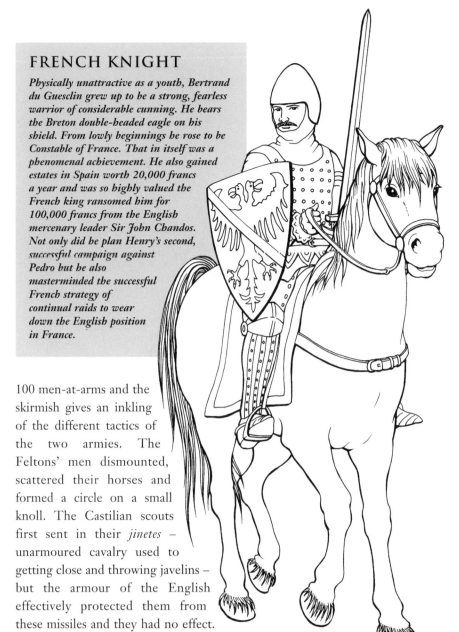

FRENCH KNIGHT

Physically unattractive as a youth, Bertrand du Guesclin grew up to be a strong, fearless warrior of considerable cunning. He bears the Breton double-headed eagle on his shield. From lowly beginnings he rose to be Constable of France. That in itself was a phenomenal achievement. He also gained estates in Spain worth 20,000 francs a year and was so highly valued the French king ransomed him for 100,000 francs from the English mercenary leader Sir John Chandos. Not only did he plan Henry's second, successful campaign against Pedro but he also masterminded the successful French strategy of continual raids to wear down the English position in France.

100 men-at-arms and the skirmish gives an inkling of the different tactics of the two armies. The Feltons' men dismounted, scattered their horses and formed a circle on a small knoll. The Castilian scouts first sent in their *jinetes* – unarmoured cavalry used to getting close and throwing javelins – but the armour of the English effectively protected them from these missiles and they had no effect. But the *jinetes* were supported by a substantial number of French and Spanish men-at-arms. The Spanish charged on horseback but were beaten off. The French knew better, they closed in on foot and massacred the English force.

For about a week the two main armies glared at each other waiting for someone to make the first move. Both suffered from the rain, which soaked men and tents and extinguished cooking fires, while the cold, biting winds chilled men to the bone. Edward and Pedro broke the stalemate. They struck camp in the night and moved southeast. Traversing the Cantabrian hills they crossed the Ebro close to Viana after two days' hard marching. From here they hoped to bypass Henry's position and resume their advance on Burgos.

Meanwhile Henry had not been idle. Having discovered his brother Pedro's army

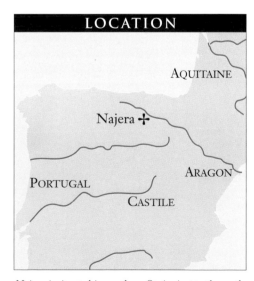

LOCATION

Najera is situated in northern Spain, just to the south of the town of Logrono in the Ebro valley. The battle was fought on a broad open plain – ideal for the two armies to test their mettle.

NAJERA

A fourteenth-century manuscript showing two crossbowmen and a longbowman (centre). The strange loop on the crossbow is in fact a foot stirrup used to hold the bow down while the string is hauled back by a hook on the loader's belt, thus cocking the weapon.

gone, he rapidly moved his own force almost due east to bar the route to Burgos just north of the little village of Najera on a broad open plain.

DISPOSITIONS

This time there was to be no stalemate. Both sides deployed for battle in remarkably similar formations. The English army all dismounted. Their vanguard, commanded by John of Gaunt, Duke of Lancaster (1340–94), with Sir John Chandos (d. 1370), consisted of 3000 men-at-arms supported by 3000 archers deployed equally on either flank. They faced 2500 dismounted French under du Guesclin and Spanish men-at-arms under Marshal d'Audreham. The latter force included several of the Spanish Holy Orders, equivalents of the Templars. These were supported by an assortment of skirmishing infantry, such as slingers, javelinmen and crossbowmen.

The main battles of both armies deployed in three divisions. The English divisions each comprised roughly equal numbers of men-at-arms and longbowmen. The division on the English left was commanded by Henry de Percy, Earl of Northumberland (1341–1408), and Olivier de Clisson. The centre was under the control of Edward and Pedro, the right under de Buch, Arnaud d'Albert and

Enriquez. The Spanish flanking divisions were the *jinetes*, plus some crossbowmen and more supporting men-at-arms. The Spanish centre consisted of 1500 mounted élite men-at-arms. Their left was ordered by Henry's brother Tello and the Grand Prior of the Order of the Hospital. The centre was under Henry and the right under his High Chamberlain, the Count of Denia and Master of the Order of Calatrava.

The English rearguard was made up of 3000 Gascon and mercenary men-at-arms plus a nearly equal number of archers, commanded by James, King of Mallorca, the Count of Armagnac, Sir Hugh Calveley and Perducas d'Albert. The huge Spanish rearguard was formed from fairly unenthusiastic town militia: infantry with an assortment of weapons. No leaders are recorded for this force.

By contemporary standards this was a huge battle. Even the English side with its 28,000 men represented a large army. But neither belligerent's forces should be thought of as a national army. Henry's army was based on his feudal levies of men-at-arms and town militias from his kingdom of Castile plus the Spanish Holy Orders, such as the Order of the Sash and the Order of Calatrava, a force of Knights Hospitaller and the veteran French mercenaries under Bertrand du Guesclin. The 'English' army was even less homogeneous. Only 400

THE OPPOSED FORCES

PEDRO'S ARMY (estimated)
Men-at-arms:	*14,000
Longbowmen:	12,000
Spearmen:	2000
Total:	**28,000**

HENRY'S ARMY (estimated)
Men-at-arms:	**6000
Jinetes:	4000
Crossbowmen:	6000
Slingers:	4000
Spearmen:	40,000
Total:	**60,000**
* All fought dismounted
** 2500 fought dismounted

men-at-arms and 600 archers led by John of Gaunt had come over from England for the campaign. The leaders of Pedro's force included English, French and Spanish nobility and even the King of Mallorca. The soldiers included many from the English territories in France, Normandy and Aquitaine as well as English soldiers already serving in France plus many, many fighting for pay in companies of the original 'free lances'.

TACTICS

Najera brought together three very different tactical traditions: the Spanish were used to fighting against the Moors of southern Spain and against each other. Here open countryside led to strong skirmishing cavalry wings where the ideal weapon in a loose mêlée was a hurled javelin. Many of their conflicts were based around fast-riding cavalry raids and more or less formal sieges. Consequently armour was comparatively lighter than that of their English and French counterparts. There were also relatively few stand-up battles.

The French had long experience of rushing headlong into the English arrow storm in an attempt to make contact. They had come to realize that wildly thrashing wounded horses caused massive disruption to their own lines and their corpses created

A rather romanticized print shows England's Black Prince persuading Pedro the Cruel to grant an amnesty to his half-brother. Pedro is on the right in the foreground listening to an unidentified herald while the Black Prince stands bareheaded to the left. His arms are mirrored on the standard flying overhead. The figure to the right rear of Pedro represents one of the Holy Orders in his army.

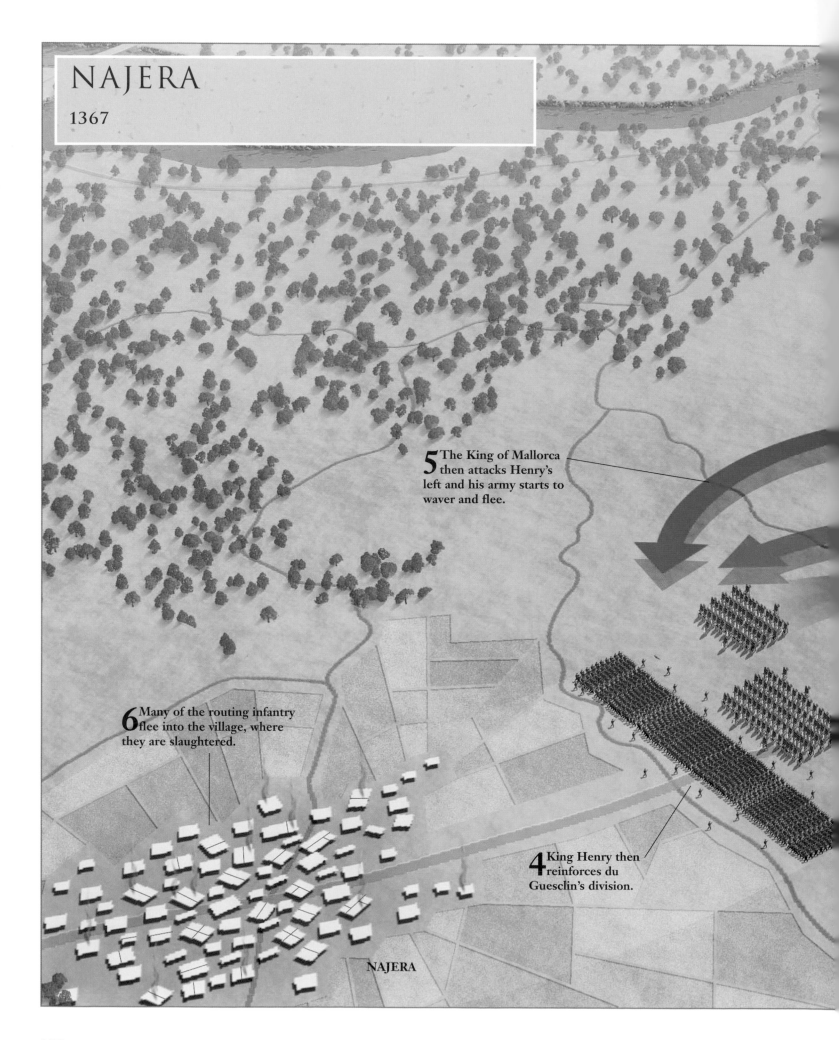

NAJERA

1367

5 The King of Mallorca then attacks Henry's left and his army starts to waver and flee.

6 Many of the routing infantry flee into the village, where they are slaughtered.

4 King Henry then reinforces du Guesclin's division.

NAJERA

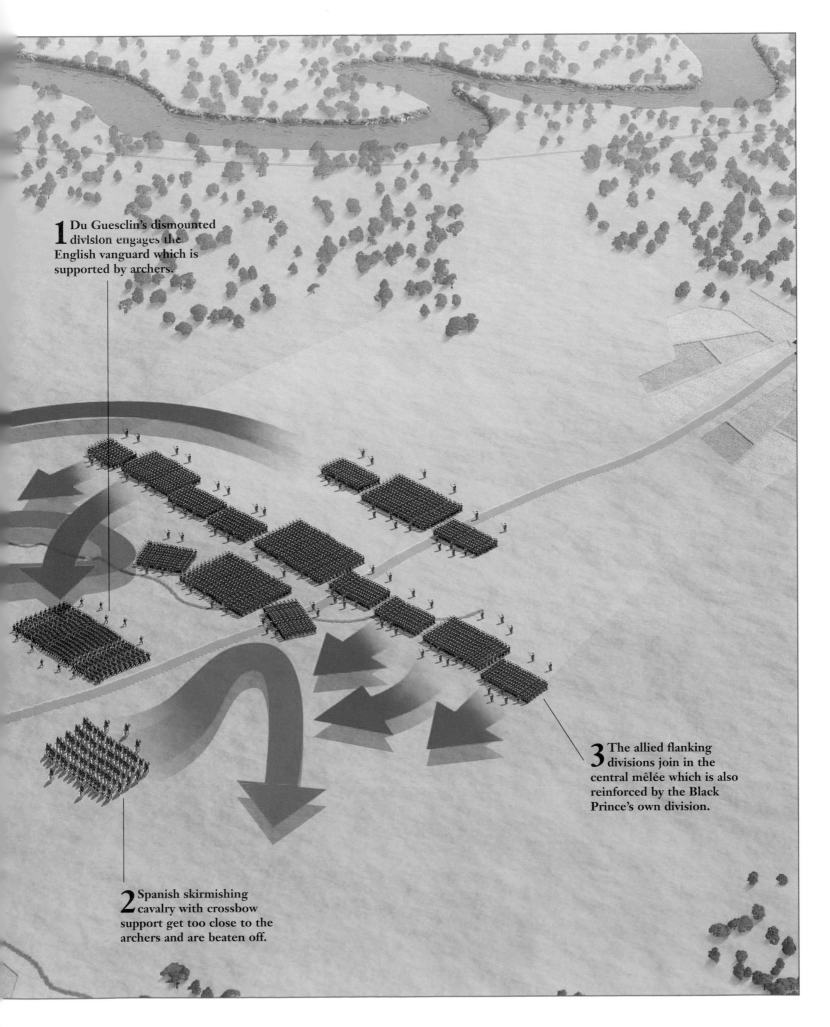

1 Du Guesclin's dismounted division engages the English vanguard which is supported by archers.

3 The allied flanking divisions join in the central mêlée which is also reinforced by the Black Prince's own division.

2 Spanish skirmishing cavalry with crossbow support get too close to the archers and are beaten off.

Pedro the Cruel of Castile is defeated at Montiel (1369) by his half-brother, Henry of Trastamara, with the aid of the French under Bertrand du Guesclin (from Froissart's Chronicles*). Although this illustration gives a good impression of the awful nature of injuries inflicted in a medieval battle it does not reflect the polyglot nature of Pedro's army, which included Moorish cavalry and infantry from Granada and Jewish infantry as well as Spanish troops.*

an obstacle that took time to cross, giving the enemy archers the chance to loose more arrows, making the situation even worse. As a result, they had evolved the tactic of advancing on foot, each soldier presenting a smaller target or obstacle if wounded. The English tactics had not changed, after all they worked time and again. However, their arrowheads had.

The weight and velocity of an English longbow arrow caused an impact greater than a prize fighter's punch even if it didn't penetrate. But usually it did, with devastating results. Against an unarmoured target you could use a broad 'V' head which cut through cloth, flesh and sinew to the vital organs and arteries beneath. Removing the arrow caused further damage. Most arrows were of this type. For use against mail they developed a long – 100–150mm (4–6in) – wire-thin, arrowhead. The point would slip past the mail and as the arrow

slowed in the target's body the momentum would be absorbed by the wire shank, deforming it into a sort of corkscrew – inside the body. As plate armour became more prevalent from the start of the fourteenth century a further refinement was added: an arrowhead we would all recognize as conical or bullet-shaped in form. A blob of beeswax on the tip would make the point stick on all but the most steeply angled plate long enough for the point to penetrate.

Once it was inside, flesh and bone presented little resistance. Of course, you had to take the armour off before you could extract the arrow and there were no anaesthetics.

The English still formed their archers on the flanks and bided their time while the bowmen laid the enemy low. Those enemy troops that got through to the English lines could then be dealt with by the waiting men-at-arms. This battle, however, was to be different.

THE BATTLE

The French men-at-arms came forward in a rush. The skirmishing infantry and *jinetes* from the main battle distracted the English archers long enough for the men-at-arms to contact their English counterparts in good order. This clash hurled the English back about 4m (5 yards). Each side came to a halt and then drew together for desperate hand-to-hand fighting. Meanwhile the flanking *jinetes* could not sustain the heavy casualties they were receiving from the longer-ranged archers and soon fled the field.

The two vanguards were evenly matched in terms of men-at-arms. The flight of the *jinetes* alone would have been enough to turn the tide against the French but now the flank divisions of the central English battle were able to close on the beleaguered enemy, outnumbering them 2:1. This left the mounted Spanish from the main battle to try and break the bloody stalemate in the centre. They charged three times but must have been facing up to 7000 archers supported by leading men-at-arms from the flank divisions of the centre battle. Inevitably they had no success and they too routed from the field as had so many French armies before them.

Edward meanwhile led his 4000-strong main battle to bolster the duke's men to the further discomfort of the French. There can have been scarcely enough Frenchmen to go round. They were now outnumbered more than 4:1, not counting the archers. Routing is infectious and at this stage the Spanish infantry in the

This footsoldier carries the banner of Castile and Leon. His shield is a distinctive shape thought to provide good protection while not impeding the movement of the left leg.

Although Edward, the Black Prince, is revered in English legend, his Spanish jaunt cost the English cause dear in both cash and fiefdoms. This effigy in Canterbury Cathedral gives an excellent likeness of the armour of the time.

rearguard caught the drift of the moment and they too started to leave the field. Vast numbers were subsequently caught and killed by the pursuers and even more drowned in the swollen river which ran through the village. Not to be left out, the final part of Edward's army came up and joined in the fight. The remaining French, having fought bravely and lost nearly one-third of their number, now surrendered to the English.

AFTERMATH

Pedro refused to pay the Black Prince for the mercenary army he had raised and then had to defend his throne a second time. King Henry had escaped to fight another day. He raised another force in Aragon and the southern French provinces. He took Leon and besieged Toledo. A further battle ensued, with Pedro this time employing the Moors from the south of Spain as well as Jews and Portuguese. Pedro's army was surprised in the early hours before it had assembled properly. His vanguard broke and ran but the main battle, mainly consisting of the Moorish troops, fought valiantly before routing.

Pedro, however, lost his nerve and fled to the nearby castle of Montiel. Besieged there by his half-brother he was captured attempting to escape and brought before Henry. An unseemly brawl developed between the two rivals and Pedro was killed less than two years after having been restored to the throne of Castile.

Bertrand du Guesclin was captured by Sir John Chandos and taken back to England, from where he was ransomed by the French king for 100,000 francs, an enormous sum. He returned to Spain in 1368 and again helped Henry to overthrow Pedro. He conducted the battle of Montiel, receiving estates worth a further 20,000 francs a year. He was recalled to France in 1370 and promoted to Constable of France, second in power only to the king himself. He masterminded the French policy of continuous harassing raids and avoiding pitched battle.

Despite his record he lost the king's trust when his native province of Brittany rebelled against the monarch. He died, in his late fifties, in 1380.

The great mercenary leader Sir John Chandos continued his trade and paid for it in the traditional way. In 1370 he slipped on the wet grass during a grubby, insignificant skirmish with the French, was stabbed in the face and later died.

Edward had to disband the mercenary army and returned to Aquitaine and empty coffers. Reputedly 2000 leaders of value were captured and they were ransomed as quickly as was prudent. But despite this he was forced to raise taxes to replenish his funds. However, the new taxes were disputed by the Gascon lords and many moved their allegiance to the French court. He was unable to counter the new French strategy and by the time he died in 1376 the French had recovered Aunis, Normandy, Poitou, Saintonge and much of Aquitaine. To add to this insult the Castilian fleet of King Henry beat the English fleet off La Rochelle in 1372 (capturing the £12,000 pay chest in the process). Although Edward had won the glory of victory, the Spanish jaunt cost him dearly financially and he left the English cause much poorer than he found it.

Gold dobla de cabez *coin of Pedro the Cruel. Having one's face and name on coins, however small, was the ultimate statement of power from earliest times. The coat-of-arms depicted on the reverse (right) is the forerunner of the modern Spanish coat-of-arms.*

NICOPOLIS
1396

THE BATTLE OF NICOPOLIS WAS THE FIRST COMBINED MILITARY EFFORT BY WESTERN EUROPEAN FORCES AGAINST THE OTTOMAN TURKS. 'CRUSADERS' FROM NUMEROUS WESTERN PRINCIPALITIES UNITED WITH MORE PROXIMATE HUNGARIAN, WALLACHIAN AND TRANSYLVANIAN FORCES TO HALT THE EXPANSION OF THE OTTOMAN EMPIRE.

WHY DID IT HAPPEN?

WHO A mixed European army of about 12,000 led by John the Fearless of Burgundy (1371–1419), opposed an Ottoman Turkish force under Sultan Báyezîd I (1354–1403) which numbered around 15,000.

WHAT The Crusaders' mounted men-at-arms charged without order into the solid infantry lines of the Turks, were halted and beaten by counter-attacking cavalry.

WHERE On the plains south of the Bulgarian city of Nicopolis.

WHEN 25 September 1396.

WHY In the late 1300s the Ottoman Turks began their conquest of southeastern Europe. As Turkish armies began to threaten the kingdom of Hungary, a Crusade was called.

OUTCOME The first encounter of the Crusaders with an Ottoman army led to a devastating defeat. The Turks built on this victory to complete their conquest of southeastern Europe.

The Christian forces sought to bring a stop to rapid Ottoman expansion in southeastern Europe and to recapture Christian lands previously lost to Ottoman conquests. But they were quickly defeated, suffering many thousands dead, both during and after the battle.

Already propagandized by the late fourteenth century, it is difficult to accurately know the origin of the Ottoman Turks. By 1400, with the Ottomans already in control of a large amount of territory in the eastern Mediterranean, the story of 'Osmán, their founder, had taken on mythic qualities. In fact, their birth as a world power (and one which would last until the twentieth century) began quite humbly at the end of the thirteenth century as one of many states that arose in Asia Minor as the Seljuk Turks began to lose power and the Byzantine Empire was too weak to fill the vacuum that was created. One local

Báyezîd I became Sultan of the Ottoman Empire in 1389 following the death of his father, Murád I. Immediately after securing the throne, he continued his father's acquisition of Balkan lands. In 1396 he defeated a large Crusader army of Western European and Hungarian soldiers at a battle fought to raise their siege of Nicopolis.

chieftain, Ertughrul, successfully led his small army in a conquest over the land around Sögüt, between Ankara and Constantinople. In 1285, he was succeeded by his son, Gházi 'Osmán (d. 1326), who would build on this small state until in 1301 he defeated a much larger Byzantine army at the battle of Baphaeum.

RISING POWER

From that time on, the armies of the fledgling Ottoman Empire seemed unstoppable. In 1304, 'Osmán captured Nicaea and almost took Philadelphia (modern-day Amman, in Jordan); the Ottoman siege of the latter was raised only when the Latin Grand Company in Greece came to the aid of the Byzantine defenders. In 1329, 'Osmán's successor, Orkhán (d. 1362), beat a Byzantine army led by Emperor Andronicus III Palaeologus (1296–1341) at the battle of Pelekanon, and in 1337 he conquered Nicomedia; on these victories he established the first Ottoman state, west of Constantinople, in Western Anatolia and Thrace. But it was his son, Murád I (d. 1369), and grandson, Báyezîd I, who are credited with adding the largest amount of land and making the Ottoman Turks a military power to rival any in the world at the time. They added Seres and Demotika in 1361, Macedonia in 1371, Armenia in 1375, Sofia in 1385, Nis in 1386, the rest of Bulgaria in 1393, Salonika and Rum in 1394, and Dobrudja in 1395. They also defeated the Serbian army in one major battle, at Kosovo in 1389, killing Prince Lazar of Serbia. Only at Rovine in 1395 did the Ottoman Turks lose a significant military engagement, and the defeat seems hardly to have slowed their progress.

Initially, Western European princes did not pay much attention to this new power in the East. After the shock of the final loss of the Holy Land in 1291, calls to fight a Crusade there were made continually, but they attracted no participants, even among those making the calls. No doubt the expense and time that such an endeavour required were the primary reasons for this, but the increase of inter-European conflict must also be taken into account, especially the Hundred Years War which began in

earnest in 1337. This war, fought on and off for 116 years, involved all principalities of Western Europe, although primarily France, England, and, after 1367, Burgundy.

From the very beginning of the Hundred Years War, the papacy tried to use the call to Crusade to bring peace between these warring states. In 1345, Pope Clement VI wrote separate letters to King Philip VI of France (1293–1350) and

to Edward III of England (1312–77) asking them to stop their conflict and unite to go on Crusade. 'Oh, how much better to fight against the Turkish enemies of our faith, than the present fratricidal strife,' the pontiff wrote to the English king. But in the following year, the battle of Crécy and the siege of Calais proved that distant Turkish incursions were unimportant. In 1370, a new pope, Urban V, repeated a call to Crusade to the Kings of France and England, hoping that the peace brought about by the Treaty of Brétigny, signed 10 years previously, might encourage them to unite against the Turks. But, in this the pope's timing was poor, as the Hundred Years War had just begun to heat up again.

LOCATION

HUNGARY

SERBIA

Nicopolis ✝

Constantinople ●

OTTOMAN EMPIRE

Attempting to raise the Crusader siege of Nicopolis, Ottoman Turkish troops, led by Emperor Báyezîd I, fought a battle against the Christian forces on the plains outside the town.

159

NICOPOLIS

A tournament scene at the time of Charles V, who ruled France from 1364 to 1380 (from the Grandes Chroniques de Saint Denis). *Tournaments, which began taking place sometime in the eleventh or twelfth century, were used as a means of preparing a Western cavalryman for combat. In a tournament he could practise charging on horseback and couching his lance.*

THE OPPOSED FORCES

OTTOMANS (estimated)
Cavalry: 10,000
Infantry: 5,000
Total: **15,000**

CRUSADERS (estimated)
Mounted men-at-arms: 6000
Infantry: 10,000
Total: **16,000**

At the same time, it became apparent that the enemy such a Crusade would fight was not that encountered in previous Middle Eastern engagements between Muslims and Christians. It would be the Ottoman Turks. As early as the 1340s, French 'travel writer' Burcard warned Philip VI that the Ottomans were so powerful that should there not be a peaceful, unified effort by all Western nations against them, a Crusade would fail. His worry was echoed by many other voices, and by the second half of the fourteenth century, it was recognized by all in Europe that should there not be assistance provided to those then fighting against the Ottoman Turks, there was little to stop their onslaught against Christianity.

But who was there to answer the call? The various German, Italian and Spanish princes had neither the strength nor the inclination to fight a Crusade against Islam, while the English, French and Burgundians seemed to have no mind to end the warfare against each other. Only the Hungarians, primarily because of the proximity of the early Ottoman conflicts, began to prepare both an offensive and a defensive military response to these Turkish enemies.

THE CAMPAIGN

However, in 1396 a 28-year truce was arranged in Paris in an attempt to halt the Hundred Years War. It was dependent on the marriage of the still-young English monarch, Richard II (1367–99), to Isabella, a daughter of the current French king, Charles VI (1368–1422), and a co-equal Anglo-French participation in a Crusade against the Ottoman Turks.

It was expected that the kings of both France and England would lead the

The Ottoman Turks used a variety of infantry soldiers including spearmen, spear or javelin throwers, and archers. All played a role at the Battle of Nicopolis in stopping the charges of the Crusaders cavalry.

Crusade, but before long they had passed this responsibility on to their relatives, Louis, Duke of Orléans, Philip the Good, Count of Burgundy, and John of Gaunt, Duke of Lancaster. Not long afterwards, however, they too had sidestepped this onerous duty, and leadership of the Crusade fell to Philip the Good's militarily inexperienced son, John the Fearless, and a group of French military leaders.

The English, French and Burgundian Crusaders gathered at Dijon on 20 April 1396, from where they marched quickly and without difficulty through Central Europe arriving at Buda, in Hungary, at the end of June. Along the way, more had joined – Hungarians, Wallachians, Transylvanians, Germans and Knights Hospitalar swelled the ranks, although the largest contingent remained that from Western Europe. At Buda, John the Fearless listened to those who had witnessed Ottoman warfare first-hand, and he discussed strategy and tactics with his generals and with Sigismund I (1368–1437), King of Hungary.

Although Sigismund argued against the strategy, it was decided that the army should march directly against the nearest Ottoman holdings, fortresses and towns which lay south of the Danube River. The King of Hungary recommended taking up a defensive posture: let the Crusaders help to defend his land against the Ottoman invasion that he felt was imminent. But he was overruled by John the Fearless and the

Sigismund I had become King of Hungary in 1387 and immediately faced the threat from the Ottoman Turks against his borders. In 1396 he was encouraged by the appearance of a Crusader army from Western Europe, only to see his experienced and sound advice on campaigning against the Ottomans ignored by the Crusader leaders. At Nicopolis the battle was finished before he could lead his armies into action. They would escape on boats down the Danube River.

other leaders, who believed that no one could withstand their military strength. The initial progress of the campaign seemed to confirm this belief. Early attacks against Turkish fortresses were quite successful, with Vidin and Rahova (Oryakhovitsa) surrendering after strong Crusader attacks. They moved on to besiege Nicopolis.

The Crusaders had yet to meet the main Ottoman army, however. Báyezîd, then attacking the remnants of Byzantium, soon heard of their victories and marched quickly to Serbia to counter them. Yet, John the Fearless seems not to have known of Báyezîd's plans or progress. In fact, it was not until the day prior to the battle of Nicopolis, when the Ottomans were less than 6.4km (4 miles) away, that the Crusader leaders learned that a large enemy army led by the sultan himself was approaching and seeking battle.

The Crusaders broke off their siege of Nicopolis and prepared for a battle outside its walls. This was precisely why they had come east, and they felt that a great victory was in the offing.

THE OPPOSING FORCES

Báyezîd led a force of troops from his homeland, Asia Minor, and from his vassal countries, including Serbs, Bulgarians, Bosnians and Albanians. Fighting with them were the Janissaries, élite footsoldiers raised from young Christian tribute-children and prisoners of war, converted to Islam and dedicated to the defeat of their former co-religionists. Contemporary chroniclers estimate the size of the Turkish army at more than 100,000, which is undoubtedly an exaggeration. It was probably closer to 15,000. From the sources, it cannot be determined how many of these were cavalry and how many infantry, although as will be seen, both worked well together to defeat their opponents.

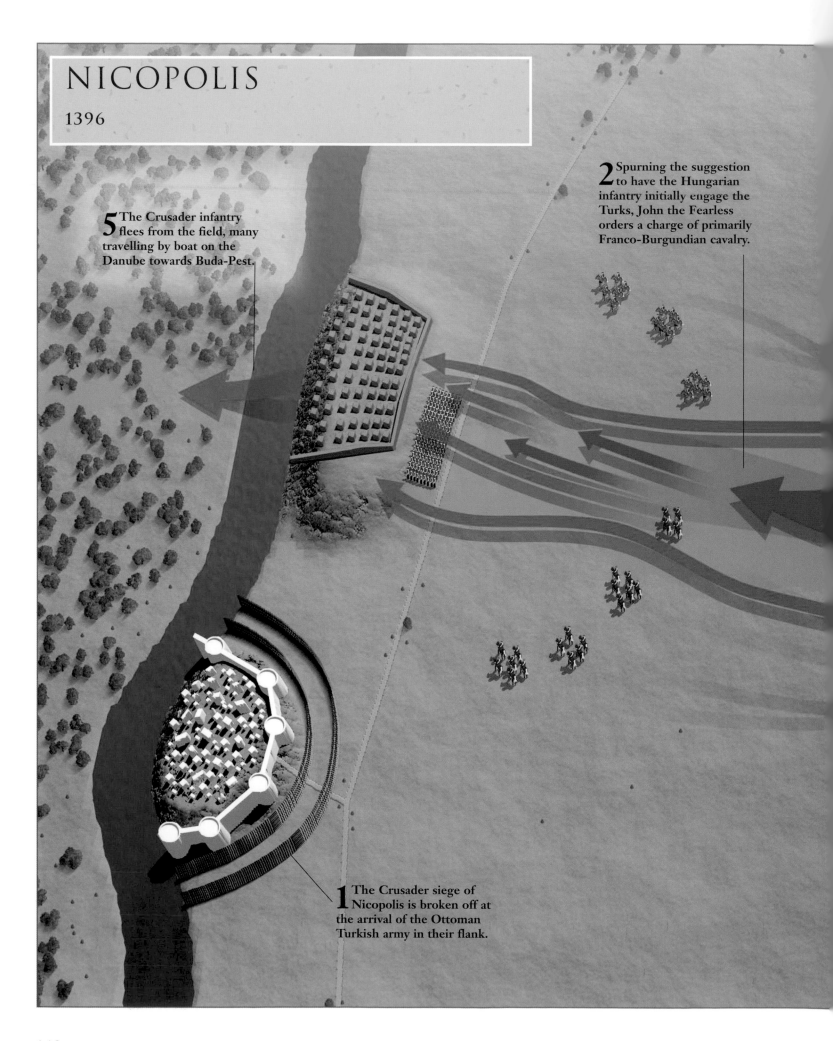

NICOPOLIS

1396

5 The Crusader infantry flees from the field, many travelling by boat on the Danube towards Buda-Pest.

2 Spurning the suggestion to have the Hungarian infantry initially engage the Turks, John the Fearless orders a charge of primarily Franco-Burgundian cavalry.

1 The Crusader siege of Nicopolis is broken off at the arrival of the Ottoman Turkish army in their flank.

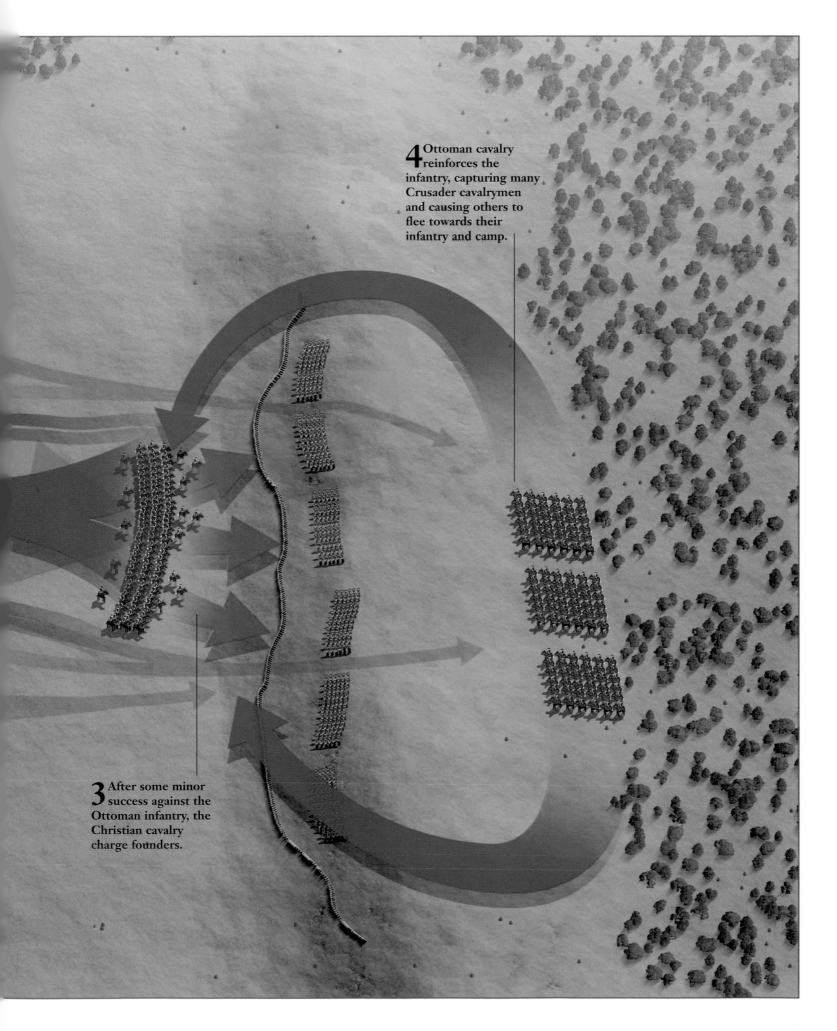

4 Ottoman cavalry reinforces the infantry, capturing many Crusader cavalrymen and causing others to flee towards their infantry and camp.

3 After some minor success against the Ottoman infantry, the Christian cavalry charge founders.

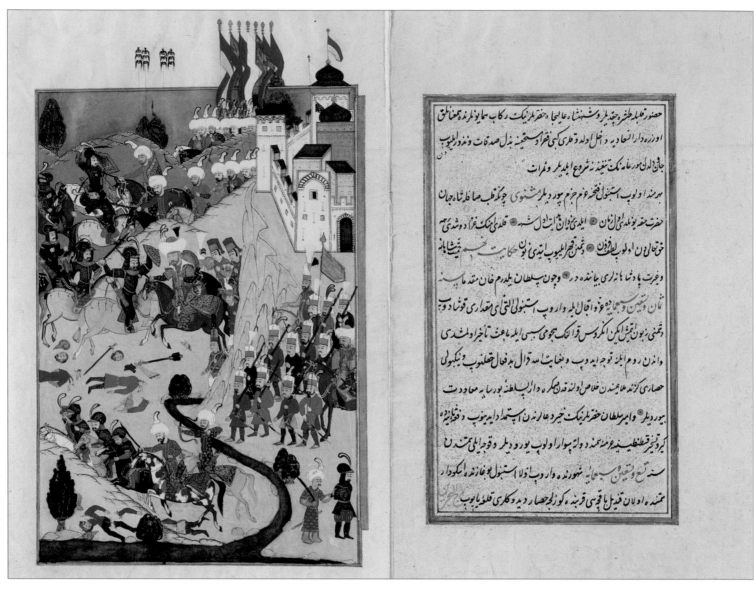

The defeat of the Crusader armies at Nicopolis brought great renown to Sultan Báyezîd I, and the victory was frequently depicted in Ottoman artworks, such as this illumination from a sixteenth-century manuscript of the 'Hunernama' school.

The Crusaders were a truly diverse force of allied troops drawn from throughout Western and Central Europe. Fewer in number than the Turks, although closer to a total of 12,000 than to the 100,000 found in contemporary sources, this army was controlled by the Franco-Burgundian mounted men-at-arms and their leaders. Among these were highly experienced Franco-Burgundian generals, such as Philip of Artois, the Constable of France, Jean II le Meingre dit Boucicault, the Marshal of France, Jean de Vienne, the Admiral of France, Guillaume de la Trémoille, the Marshal of Burgundy, and Sir Enguerrand de Coucy VII.

Footsoldiers, many from Hungary, greatly outnumbered the cavalry, but they were kept out of the battle, and this may well have been a central factor in the Crusaders' defeat.

DISPOSITIONS

Realizing that the Ottomans were approaching Nicopolis, John the Fearless called a council of war with all his various generals. King Sigismund recommended that the Hungarians and other Central European troops, almost entirely infantry, should be in the front of the Crusader forces, the vanguard. He suggested that they would meet what – based on previous experience – would be the irregular infantry of the Turks, who were always in front of their own army. He would take a defensive stance to try and provoke the Ottomans into a charge that might be defeated by the contact of the two infantry forces or reinforced by the strong Franco-Burgundian cavalry in the second rank. But, as with the strategic decision, he was again overruled by most of the Franco-Burgundian leaders. The chronicles blame

Philip of Artois, who used his constabulary office and influence to argue against Sigismund's counsel. He believed that the mounted charge of the armoured knights would bring resounding success on the battlefield. According to one prominent Western writer, Jean Froissart, he used these egotistical words:

'Yes, yes, the king of Hungary wishes to gain all the honour of the day. He has given us the vanguard, and now he wishes to take it away, that he may have the first blow. Let those who will believe what he sends to us, but for my part I never will.... In the name of God and Saint George, you shall see me this day prove myself a good knight.'

THE BATTLE

This decision was met with great enthusiasm among the Franco-Burgundian knights and mounted sergeants. They took to their horses and without much delay proudly charged headlong into the vanguard of the Turks. This was the very infantry that Sigismund said would be there, safely protected behind a line of stakes. Initially, the shock of this mounted charge brought some success, breaking through the stakes and pushing the Turkish irregular infantry back. However, unfortunately for the Crusaders, these Ottoman troops, obviously more disciplined than had been

reckoned, did not break, but instead quickly re-formed in the lull before a second cavalry attack could be mounted.

That second Crusader charge also pushed the Ottoman vanguard back, but again they did not flee, and when a counter-attack came from Báyezîd's regular troops – cavalry, infantry and archers – the impetus of the Crusader horsemen had been spent. Although some German and Hungarian infantry rushed to reinforce their cavalry, all were quickly defeated.

The Battle of Nicopolis had lasted only a very short time, no more than an hour. Those who could, tried to flee from the battlefield, but the Danube River blocked their path and few were actually able to escape what had become a massacre. Among those did manage to get away were the Wallachians and Transylvanians. King Sigismund of Hungary and his army, which had never actually taken part in the battle because it had been so short, retreated to the Danube, boarded boats and sailed back to Buda. To his disappointment, he had proved to be a prophet of Crusader doom.

A MASSACRE

Those Franco-Burgundian soldiers who were left on the battlefield were cut down without mercy, not granted the option of ransom traditional in Western warfare.

Only after the Crusaders' leader, John the Fearless, was recognized by Báyezîd were prisoners accepted by the Ottomans, and even then several hundred more Christian troops were summarily executed at the sultan's order. John the Fearless convinced Báyezîd to ransom some of the more important prisoners.

No more than 300, from a total of perhaps as many as 6000 who had been involved in the fighting, were spared. They did not return to their homes for nine months, and only after their noble relatives paid a huge ransom of more than 200,000 ducats. The Turks, too, had suffered heavy losses, perhaps giving them a rationale for the execution of so many prisoners, but far fewer had died than on the Crusader side.

THE AFTERMATH

It took time for the news of this defeat to reach France and Burgundy. The great Crusader propagandist, Philippe de Mézières, whose speeches and writings had helped encourage the Crusade that had ended at the battle of Nicopolis, criticized those who had been defeated. In his *Épistre lamentable et consolatoire* (Lamentable and Consolatory Letter), written soon after he learned of their defeat, he accuses the Crusaders of following the 'three daughters of Lucifer' – 'pride, cupidity, and luxury' – instead of the four virtues of good governance – 'order, the discipline of chivalry, obedience, and justice'.

Others, like French poet Eustace Deschamps, honoured those who had fallen. In a poem entitled '*Pour les Français morts à Nicopolis*' ('For the French who Died at Nicopolis'), he praises the Crusaders for 'they carried the banner of Our Lady against the Turks; but these devoted men were slain

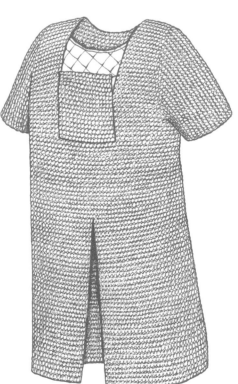

Early medieval suits of armour were most often made of chain links or metal scales. Chain armour (favoured in Western Europe) consisted of thousands of round metal rings, the ring ends welded or riveted together. Chain coverings for the head, legs, feet, arms and hands later added extra protection for both cavalry and infantry soldiers. Scale armour (favoured in Byzantium) was made of a large number of metallic scales attached to each other by wire or leather laces and affixed to a linen undergarment by linen cord.

NICOPOLIS

by the lance. May God have mercy on each of their souls.' However, most received the news only with sadness. Marshal Boucicault's biographer writes:

'When the reports [of defeat] were made known and published, nobody could describe the great grief which they caused in France, both on the part of the duke of Burgundy, who doubted whether he would be able to get his son back for money, and [thought] that he would be put to death, and on that of the fathers, mothers, wives, and male and female relatives of the other lords, knights and squires who were dead. A great mourning began throughout the kingdom of France by those whom it concerned; and more generally, everybody lamented the noble knights who had fallen there, who represented the flowers of France ... All our lords had solemn masses for the dead sung in their chapels for the good lords, knights and squires, and all the Christians who had died ... But it may be well that we had more need of their prayers on our behalf, since they, God willing, are saints in Paradise.'

Opposite: In this illustration from Froissart's Chronicles, *Sultan Báyezîd I accepts ransom money for the Comte de Nevers and other French knights captured during the Battle of Nicopolis.*

For a long time after this battle there were to be very few more Western European 'saints in Paradise' at the hands of the Ottoman Turks. Nicopolis was to be the last engagement between a large number of Western European troops and the Turks for more than 140 years.

The fall of Constantinople to the Ottoman Sultan Mehmed II (1432–81) in 1453 did not even inspire a Western European military response, despite many calls to Crusade from the papacy and others. It was only after the Battle of Mohács – fought in 1526 and a defeat for Christian forces – and the unsuccessful Turkish attack on Vienna in 1529 that another large Western European army would oppose Ottoman invasions into southeastern and Central Europe.

Entitled The rescue of King Sigismund of Hungary, *this wood engraving from a painting by Hermann Knackfuss (1848–1915) shows the Hungarian king fleeing with his troops to boats on the Danube after the crushing defeat at Nicopolis.*

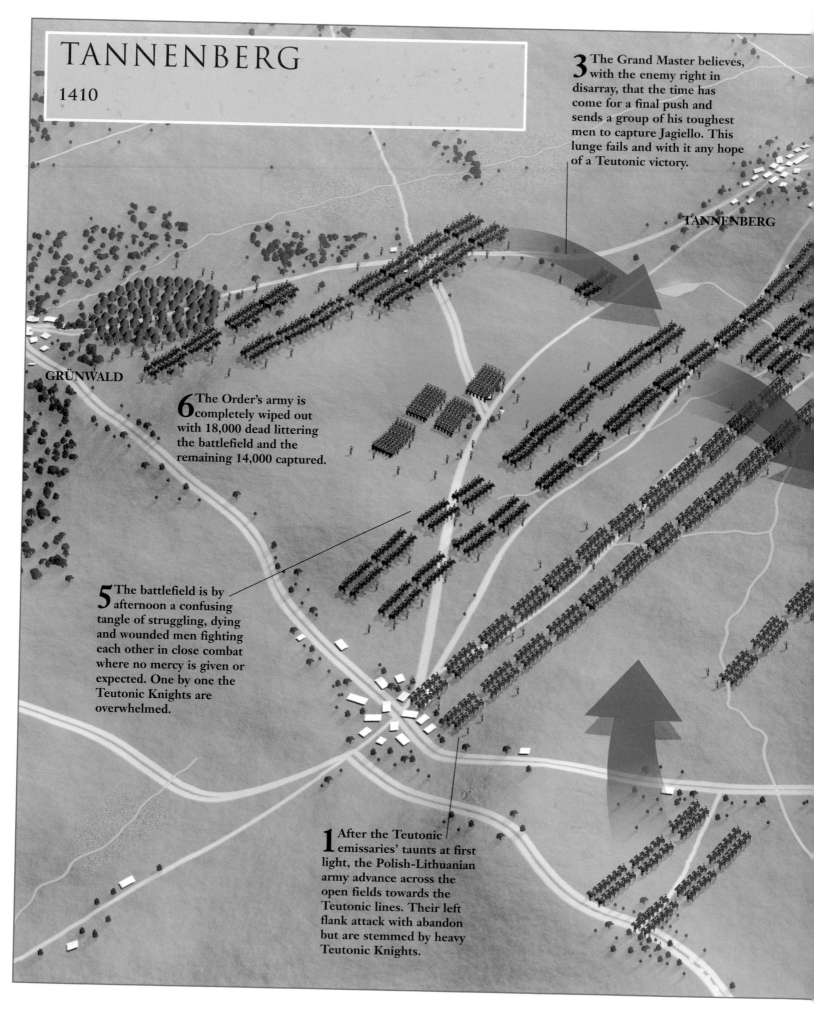

TANNENBERG

1410

3 The Grand Master believes, with the enemy right in disarray, that the time has come for a final push and sends a group of his toughest men to capture Jagiello. This lunge fails and with it any hope of a Teutonic victory.

TANNENBERG

GRÜNWALD

6 The Order's army is completely wiped out with 18,000 dead littering the battlefield and the remaining 14,000 captured.

5 The battlefield is by afternoon a confusing tangle of struggling, dying and wounded men fighting each other in close combat where no mercy is given or expected. One by one the Teutonic Knights are overwhelmed.

1 After the Teutonic emissaries' taunts at first light, the Polish-Lithuanian army advance across the open fields towards the Teutonic lines. Their left flank attack with abandon but are stemmed by heavy Teutonic Knights.

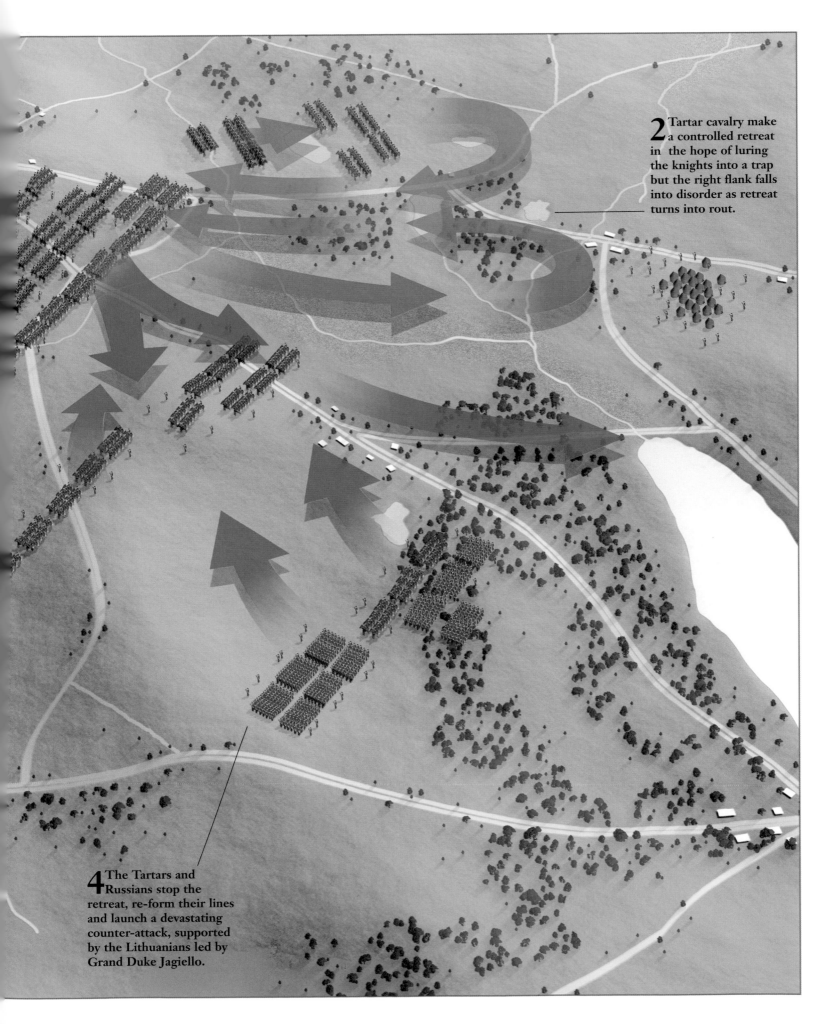

2 Tartar cavalry make a controlled retreat in the hope of luring the knights into a trap but the right flank falls into disorder as retreat turns into rout.

4 The Tartars and Russians stop the retreat, re-form their lines and launch a devastating counter-attack, supported by the Lithuanians led by Grand Duke Jagiello.

TANNENBERG

In this painting by Jan Matejko (1838–93), the Polish-Lithuanian army is at the point of crushing the reeling and bleeding troops of the order, with a triumphant Jagiello in the centre of the action.

then he would have to be goaded by an appropriately insulting gesture.

The Grand Master sent out his two highest-ranking knights to provoke the 'slow-witted' Jagiello into attacking. One was the Imperial German herald, whose shield displayed the Black Eagle (symbol of the emperor) on a gold background, and the other – with a red griffon on a white background – was Duke Kasimir of Stettin. They rode forth across the fields under a white flag of truce and were politely received by Jagiello – who had hoped the Teutons might be willing to negotiate instead of fighting.

Instead the two knights, rudely and arrogantly, rebuked Jagiello and the Polish-Lithuanian army for 'cowardice'. They should come out, said the knights, on the open field and fight like real men. Not surprisingly Jagiello lost his monumental patience, told the Teutonic Knights that they would regret their insolence, told them to return and gave Witold, the actual commander of the army, the signal to commence battle.

The Poles advanced in good order with lances and spears at the ready. On their right the Lithuanians, with their Russian and Tartar auxiliaries, could not be restrained any longer. With an almighty battle cry they crashed into the Teutonic lines, sweeping all before them until the Grand Master committed his knights. These heavily armoured troops fought the Lithuanians to a standstill. The Tartars tried to spring their trap of the controlled retreat to lure the Teutonic Knights into a trap but the plan backfired. Their own troops thought the Tartars were fleeing and began to flee themselves. The knights moved forward methodically, coldly butchering the fleeing Tartars, Lithuanians and Russians. Only three squadrons of Lithuanians and Russians held the line as Witold cut his way through the confusion to beg Jagiello to swing the Poles around and save the right flank from total collapse.

Jagiello could not have made out what was going as the whole battlefield was enveloped in thick dust stirred up by the hooves and feet of thousands of horses and

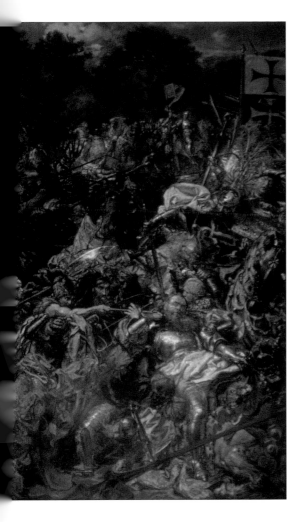

them with their bows, while the Lithuanians and Russians used their swords and battle-axes to good effect.

The Poles had in the meantime held more than half of the order's army at bay and had forced them back in close combat. As the Lithuanian army streamed back to the fight the Teutonic army began to give way, some even fled while others died where they stood. As the Teutons began to give way they were surrounded on all sides by the enemy. To their credit the Order did not capitulate or flee in wild disorder – most of them, including the Grand Master himself, fought to the death. Others who had been able to disengage from the advancing enemy continued to fight on the road that led to Grünwald. It was in this village that the Teutonic army made its last stand and fought to the death with the Poles and Lithuanians. By 7.00 p.m. the battle was finally won.

The Teutonic Order had ceased to exist as a proper military force. The number of Teutonic dead was 18,000 and 14,000 had been taken prisoner. The Grand Master, his deputies and most of his district commanders (komturs) lay dead on the battlefield. Only two senior knights had survived: Prince Conrad the White of Silesia and Duke Kasimir of Stettin – the same man, presumably, who had taunted Jagiello for his 'cowardice' at the outset of the battle.

AFTERMATH

Instead of marching on the Teutonic Order's capital of Marienburg to the west the Polish-Lithuanian army – utterly exhausted – remained on the battlefield to divide the loot, rest and recuperate. When it was ready to march on Marienburg – held by Count Heinrich von Plauen and 3000 troops – it was too late. This immense fortress complex with stone walls 8.2m (27ft) high and 2.1m (7ft) thick and ample supplies of food and water proved impregnable. Jagiello's victorious army arrived on 25 July but failed to make any headway during the two-month-long siege. The war would continue for years and the Order would recover. For the Prussians this defeat left a permanent, humiliating scar that never healed, and in 1914, General Paul von Hindenburg – a Prussian – named his epic World War I victory over the Imperial Russian army in the same region after the village of Tannenberg.

This manuscript illustration by Stanisław Durink from 1448 shows the colours and heraldry found on captured Teutonic standards seized at Tannenberg (from Bibliotheka Jagiellonka, *Cracow).*

men. A sudden downpour settled the dust and finally the two sides could make out what was going on and who was fighting whom. Witold called up his last remaining reserves to stem the Teutonic attack that had seemed unstoppable only half an hour before. But the enemy had clear visibility. Jagiello was only protected by a small guard and Grand Master Ulrich ordered an attack upon the Weissberg by some of his best knights. One of these, clad in white, rushed forward but was stopped by the king's secretary, Count Zbigniew of Olesnica, who thrust a broken lance into the German's side. The white knight fell to the ground where he was bludgeoned and stabbed to death by Polish infantrymen.

THE TIDE TURNS

Meanwhile the fleeing Lithuanians, Tartars and Russians had been prevailed upon to halt and now streamed back as fast as they had fled before. They rode at the enemy with their customary courage and élan. A rain of arrows fell on the Teutonic troops as the Tartars, riding at full gallop, shot at

AGINCOURT
1415

THE BATTLE OF AGINCOURT PITTED A TIRED AND DISEASED ENGLISH ARMY AGAINST A FRENCH HOST ALMOST FIVE TIMES ITS SIZE. THE FRENCH WERE DETERMINED TO BREAK THE CHAIN OF ENGLISH VICTORIES AND TO PREVENT KING HENRY V FROM REACHING CALAIS WITH HIS ARMY.

WHY DID IT HAPPEN?

WHO An English army numbering 5700 under King Henry V (1388–1422), opposed by 25,000 French under Charles d'Albret (1369?–1415), Constable of France.

WHAT The main action took place between French men-at-arms (mounted and dismounted) and a combined force of English archers and dismounted men-at-arms.

WHERE East of the village of Agincourt, between Abbeville and Calais.

WHEN 25 October 1415.

WHY Marching to winter in Calais, Henry's tired and sick army was brought to battle by a vastly superior French force.

OUTCOME The French initially intended to fight a defensive action, but instead attacked down a narrow frontage between two woods. The result was a shattering defeat for the French.

The English system of making war was by this time well established. The firepower of longbow-armed archers combined with the staying power of dismounted men-at-arms was a potent force in a defensive battle.

The English longbowman in 1415 was little different than his predecessor who fought at Crécy or Halidon Hill. His main weapon had a combat range of 250m (273 yards) and could shoot perhaps 100m (109 yards) further. The plate armour of the time

King Henry V, a portrait by Benjamin Burnell (1790–1828). One of England's great captains, Henry's real-life deeds at Agincourt and Harfleur would grant him a place in heroic legend, even if he had never been immortalized in Shakespeare's plays.

was difficult to penetrate but the longbow was sufficiently powerful to drive an armour-piercing bodkin arrow through it into the man beneath at up to 50m (55 yards). Conventional broadhead arrows would bring down an unarmoured man or a horse at greater distances. Most archers carried a back-up weapon. In some cases this was a sword; more often a hatchet, dagger or a maul – a huge mace-like weapon that could be deadly in the hands of a strong man. Few archers wore armour of any sort. What there was included quilted or leather jerkins and a very basic helmet made of *cuir boulli* – leather boiled in oil or wax to make it almost as hard as metal. Many of King Henry's troops were suffering from dysentery contracted during the recent siege of Harfleur. Thus when some men went into action stripped to the waist, others chose to remove their hose for convenience instead.

All archers were professionals, recruited and paid for the campaign. They were well supplied with arrows and, more importantly, could shoot fast and accurately. At longer ranges a cloud of arrows could be arched into any target, falling directly downwards to wound the horses' backs and make looking up hazardous despite a visored helm. At close ranges hitting a moving target such as a mounted man was an easy shot for any archer competent enough to be able to hold up his head among his fellows. Most archers were good enough to shoot for the head, resulting in large numbers of men shot through their visors.

ENGLISH MEN-AT-ARMS

The 750 or so English men-at-arms that accompanied King Henry were equipped in a full-body suit of plate armour and armed with the knightly sidearm – a long sword. The sword was merely a back-up in most cases, however. To get through an enemy's armour something more substantial was necessary. Thus a mix of axes and maces was also borne, along with pole-axes and similarly lethal instruments. Henry's men-at-arms were accustomed to fighting on foot alongside the archers, though of course they were also skilled with the lance and in horsed combat.

The English army was wracked with disease, half-starved and tired from its long march. It was not in good shape for a battle even without the immense advantage in numbers of the French. However, the army did have great confidence in King Henry V, who had shown his courage and warrior skills at the recent (victorious) siege of Harfleur.

FRENCH KNIGHTS

On the French side, the main striking force was, as usual, men-at-arms encased from head to foot in steel. Improvements in armour meant that the shield had largely been abandoned, permitting knights to fight with two-handed weapons on foot and to have recourse to the sword only when disarmed. Specialist armour-piercing weapons such as military picks were much in evidence.

Although the French had lost some of their reluctance to fight on foot, the massed charge of lance-armed chivalry was still their ideal of warfare. Despite a string of humiliating defeats at the hands of the English, the French seemed determined to disprove the old adage that 'defeat breeds innovation'. This was, as much as anything, for social reasons.

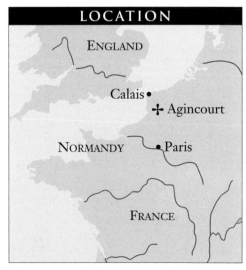

ENGLISH ARCHER AND MAN-AT-ARMS (1415)

The English men-at-arms (a term which embraced knights, squires and some non-noble warriors) were always prepared to dismount to fight alongside the archers, who were their social inferiors. These longbowmen usually deployed on the flanks or in broken ground to give them protection against more heavily armed opponents should it come to hand-to-hand fighting. At Agincourt, King Henry V ordered that every archer should cut himself a stake to provide portable protection against cavalry charges. This worked to great effect in defeating the French. The miserable state of the English army, starving and living on filthy water, is shown in the archer's need to let down his breeches, due to diarrhoea.

LOCATION

ENGLAND

Calais

✟ Agincourt

NORMANDY

Paris

FRANCE

The village of Agincourt lay on the Calais road 50km (32 miles) south of the port. The battle was fought in a narrow gap between two woods, which still survive to this day.

AGINCOURT

Henry V (centre, with crowned helm) was a fearsome warrior who personally saved the life of the Duke of Gloucester during the battle. More than great speeches, such deeds inspired his followers to fight on when things looked bleak.

footsoldiers from, and no desire to create one. The idea of arming peasants made French noblemen uneasy, and rightly so. What good was victory over the English if the way of life of the French rulers was swept away in the process?

And so, as always, it was the upper echelons of society who came to the field of Agincourt with banners flying, their numbers filled out by professional men-at-arms who might aspire to winning a knighthood on the field. The rivalry between these noble warriors, whose status in society depended upon what they did on the field of battle, made them impetuous and unreliable. Their charge would be furious, but it was also uncontrolled. One concession to the dominance of the English archer was to provide many of the knights' horses with barding – horse armour – to give them a measure of protection. In earlier battles the charge of the knights had foundered as their mounts were shot down. The French hoped that even if barding slowed their mounts it would enable more of them to reach the enemy line. The French also brought a force of about 3000 crossbowmen and some early cannon to the field, but they played little part in the battle.

THE CAMPAIGN

The Battle of Agincourt was part of the so-called Hundred Years War (actually 1337–1453) between England and France. The war was not continuous, and at times subsided into an uneasy peace of sorts.

In 1415, France was weakened by civil war, and Henry V of England decided that the time was right to resume hostilities. In mid-1415, his army landed in France and laid siege to the fortress of Harfleur. Five weeks later, despite dysentery and all the other hardships of siege, Henry had captured the fortress. He then set off with what remained of his army to march to Calais, intending to winter there.

The French, intimidated by their string of defeats, tended to adopt a very defensive stance when the English attacked. In practice this meant withdrawing into fortresses and surrendering the initiative to the English. However, with a clearly far superior force at hand, the Constable of France, Charles d'Albret, decided to bring

The feudal system in France included a sharp divide between the ruling class, whose right and responsibility was to bear arms, and the peasantry, who were generally ground underfoot and had to be kept disarmed to reduce the chances of a rebellion. The miserable performance of peasant levies whenever they were taken to the battlefield had served to further convince the French nobility of the futility of arming the lower orders. There was therefore no proud yeoman class to recruit the English to battle. His men placed stakes and broke down the banks at river crossings, making the English march a lengthy and dangerous one.

Henry's army was already short of provisions as it set out for Calais. Struggling to find a usable river crossing wasted more time, but at length the army managed to cross the Somme at St Quentin. Struggling onward, the sick and weary English then found d'Albret's powerful host camped across its line of march. With his men starving and soaked by a downpour during the night, Henry nevertheless resolved to fight his way through to safety.

DISPOSITIONS

Knowing very well that the English were short of food – and wishing to avoid a repeat of previous defeats, where French charges had battered themselves to pieces on a static English line – d'Albret was determined to force the outnumbered English to come to him. By refusing to attack he would force the English into moving forward. His enemy was constrained by his lack of supplies, while d'Albret had all the advantages – numbers, mobility and position. He could wait; Henry could not.

D'Albret's force was drawn up in three battles, as was usual. The front and second

THE OPPOSED FORCES

ENGLISH (estimated)
Men-at-arms:	750
Archers:	4950
Total:	**5700**

FRENCH (estimated)
Men-at-arms (mounted):	7000
Men-at-arms (dismounted):	15,000
Crossbowmen:	3000
Others: Some primitive cannon	
Total:	**25,000**

Charles, Duke of Orléans. One of the French commanders at Agincourt, Duke Charles was captured and spent 25 years imprisoned in the Tower of London. He spent much of his time there writing poetry.

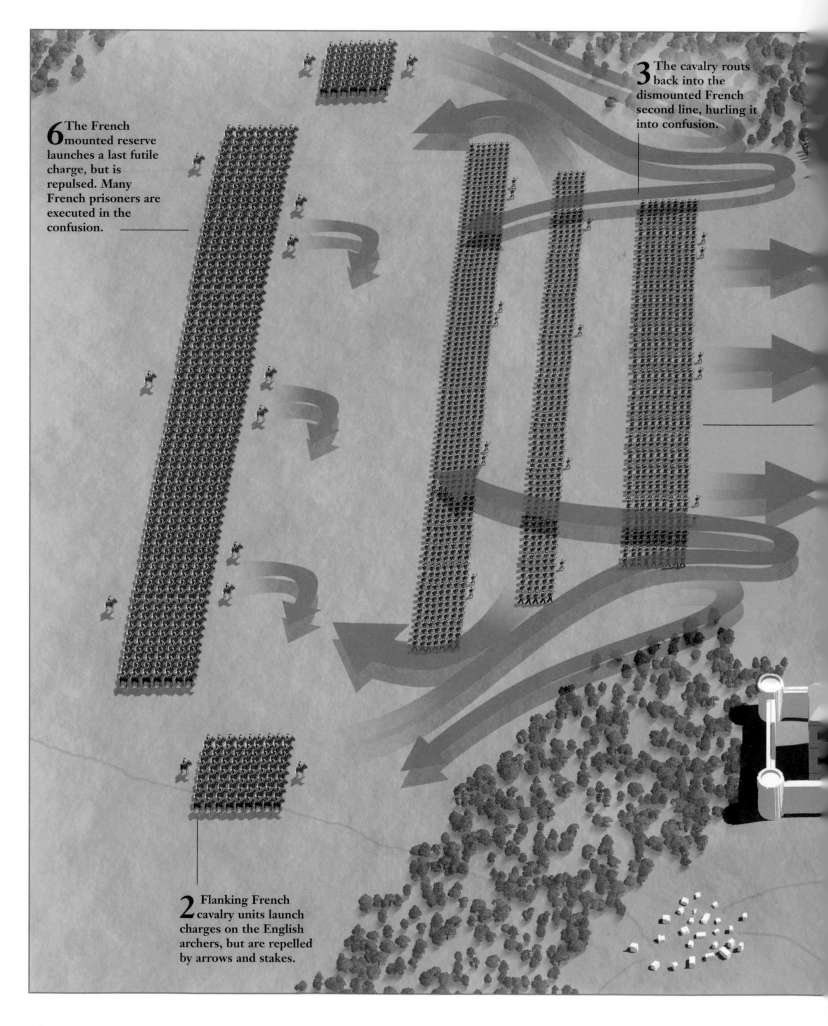

3 The cavalry routs back into the dismounted French second line, hurling it into confusion.

6 The French mounted reserve launches a last futile charge, but is repulsed. Many French prisoners are executed in the confusion.

2 Flanking French cavalry units launch charges on the English archers, but are repelled by arrows and stakes.

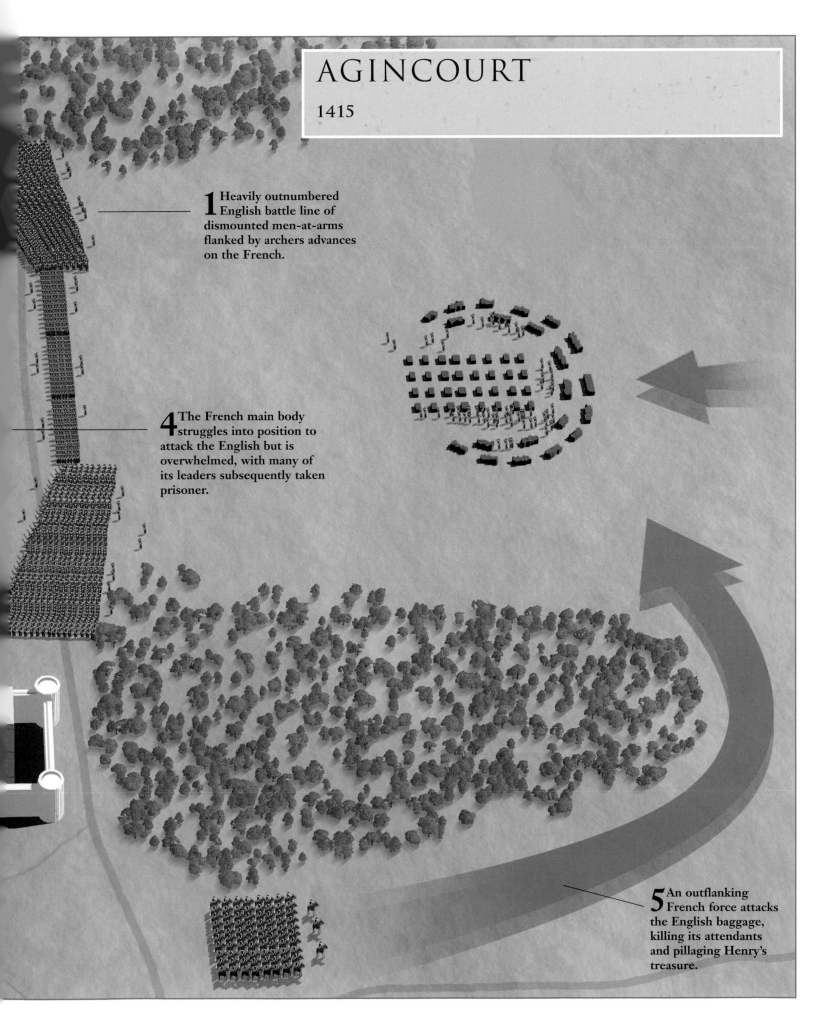

AGINCOURT

1415

1 Heavily outnumbered English battle line of dismounted men-at-arms flanked by archers advances on the French.

4 The French main body struggles into position to attack the English but is overwhelmed, with many of its leaders subsequently taken prisoner.

5 An outflanking French force attacks the English baggage, killing its attendants and pillaging Henry's treasure.

AGINCOURT

At Agincourt King Henry fought on foot, but the horse was a powerful status symbol. Thus in this manuscript illustration showing the seal of the king he is depicted as a mounted warrior bearing a sword, another symbol of power and rank.

lines were mostly dismounted, while the third was composed of mounted men. The 3000 crossbowmen attached to the French force were also in the rear where they could achieve little.

Given what had happened to the Genoese at Crécy, the crossbowmen were probably grateful that at least they would not be ridden down by their own side. D'Albret also positioned two forces of mounted men-at-arms, each numbering about 600 men, on the flanks. He hoped to be able to launch a mounted charge directly at the English archers and either scatter

them or at least distract them from shooting into the main attack. The force assigned to make this assault included many knights mounted on barded horses. He was sure that Henry could be induced to attack, which would in turn lead to the ruin of the English army.

DEPLOYMENT

The English deployed in what had become the conventional manner, with three blocks of men-at-arms flanked by triangular formations of archers. The centre block was commanded by Henry himself, with the right commanded by Edward, Duke of York, and the left by Lord Camoys. Henry knew of the French plan to destroy his archers, and came up with a counter to it. During the march, the archers were commanded to furnish themselves with long stakes, sharpened at both ends. These were rammed into the ground in front of and among the archer formations, pointing forward and offering a measure of protection against an enemy charge. The archers were easily able to step around the stakes and move within their protective hedge, but to a horseman approaching at speed the chances of being impaled were considerable. Some of the men were charged with uprooting the stakes and moving them if the archers were ordered to change position.

Henry's flanks were protected by woods. On the right lay Tramcourt woods and on the left were Agincourt woods. To the rear lay the English baggage camp, virtually undefended. Some accounts claim that Henry placed archers and men-at-arms in the woods, but this is unlikely. The English scarcely had enough men to form a line and could not afford a reserve, let alone a flanking force.

While the English nobles and men-at-arms knew that they might expect some degree of mercy from their enemies, there was no such hope for the common soldiery. So hated were the infamous longbowmen that 300 had been hanged after the fall of Soissons to the French. Indeed, one reason for the provision of stakes to the archers was the rumour that the French intended to 'make a dead-set' against the archers and massacre them at the first opportunity.

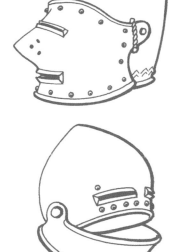

Late medieval cavalry helmets varied in style with the wearer's preference. They generally fitted more tightly to the face and neck. Still, some soldiers and leaders felt that they limited vision and communication too much. Therefore, they chose to raise their visors or fight without them.

Their preparations made, the two armies faced one another across the sodden ground. Each waited for the other to attack. For four hours the stand-off continued.

Eventually, Henry was forced to act. If the French would not attack, he had to advance against them. It seemed that the enemy had learned from their previous headlong attacks. There was little chance for the tiny English army to make a successful assault, but there was no alternative. At the command to advance, the English crossed themselves, the archers pulled up their stakes, and the whole force slowly moved forward. Eventually, having paused more than once to allow the men-at-arms to rest and maintain their formation, the English reached longbow range. The archers re-emplaced their stakes in the wet ground and began to shoot.

THE FRENCH ATTACK

The English halted at bow range and opened a steady fire on the front battle of the French army, which had no means of reply. The only troops able to match the

In this nineteenth-century illustration of Agincourt, it is the mounted knight that takes centre stage. Even today, it is widely (and erroneously) believed that medieval warfare was the exclusive province of the armoured nobleman.

AGINCOURT

AGAINST THE ODDS

Given the disparity in numbers and sheer fighting power of the two armies deployed at Agincourt, it is obvious that the odds were heavily in the French favour. Yet the English won. The main reason was the tactics employed by both sides. Outnumbered by foes with superior mobility, Henry could not afford to be flanked. He thus carefully chose ground where his flanks were covered. Meanwhile the French threw away their main advantages – mobility and numbers – by attacking on a narrow frontage over muddy ground that slowed their assault and gave the English archers more time to barrage the attacking force. The French did employ some basic good practice, such as the flanking forces and dismounting the first line of attackers, but overall they gave the advantage to Henry's tiny army and suffered terribly for it.

Longbowmen depicted in a fifteenth-century manuscript. Their only armour is a helmet of metal or more likely leather. The bowmen are shown with a sheaf of arrows stuck in their belts; at Agincourt many archers stuck arrows in the ground in front of them for convenience.

archers at that range, the French crossbowmen, were far to the rear and unable to contribute to the action. The French were forced to take the offensive after all, or else stand under fire all day. First the cavalry of the flanking forces advanced against the archers on the English flanks. The flanking forces were smaller than they should have been due to command and control issues that resulted in many knights being out of position or deployed in the wrong units.

Despite this, the flanking cavalry make a brave attempt. On the English left flank, the charge was broken up by archery and the majority of the force turned back. Three knights pressed the attack but were soon brought down. On the right, the assault fared a little better. Part of the force managed to come to handstrokes despite the re-emplaced stakes and intense archery. The attack was quickly repulsed, however.

Meanwhile the lead battle, under d'Albret and the Duke of Orléans, began to advance. The going was slow, through ankle-deep mud churned up by the cavalry

Opposite: King Henry V makes a rallying speech to his troops on St Crispin's Day, inspiring his men for the desperate battle ahead. By nightfall the English had won one of the greatest victories of all time.

and weighed down by armour. Even for the mounted men the pace was not fast. This was no headlong charge but a steady advance coming forward at a slow walk, and it offered a perfect target for the English longbowmen. As d'Albret's force pushed laboriously forward, it was disrupted by the routing cavalry and riderless horses of the initial attack.

The formation was also compressed onto a smaller frontage by the woods, which acted as a funnel. The French force was bunched together as it approached the shorter English line. So tightly compressed were the French that some men struggled to find room to wield their weapons. Two-handed swords, then just entering service, were useless in the press.

The lead French battle finally came into contact with the English line and a fierce

mêlée developed. Unable to shoot, the archers took to their hand weapons and assailed the French alongside their armoured companions. Although the French had the advantage of numbers they were exhausted by their laborious advance and, jammed together, could not fight effectively. Many were killed or taken prisoner in the fighting. Offensive weapons were not the only killers in that desperate struggle. A man-at-arms who slipped or fell wounded into the thick mud had little

chance of rising easily, even if he was not trampled down by others.

Men died of drowning in the mud or suffocated under the weight of their armour and that of others. This fate befell the Duke of York. Still others were slain by the vengeful longbowmen, who dispatched downed noblemen with a knife through the joints in their armour or beat them to death with mauls.

The second French battle came up to support the first, and the battle intensified.

The Count d'Alencon and a party of knights, sworn to kill King Henry or die trying, cut their way through to the English monarch, who was fighting heroically in the front rank. Henry covered himself with glory once more, coming to the rescue of the Duke of Gloucester who was in serious trouble at d'Alencon's hands.

Although part of the crown that surrounded his helm was cut away, Henry emerged victorious from the combat. Eventually, d'Alencon's assault was beaten off and his band of knights were dispatched. The French assault gradually ebbed and the English eyed the third French battle, as yet uncommitted, across the corpse-strewn and sodden ground.

A LATE REVERSE

King Henry boldly – some might say cheekily – sent a herald to the remaining French battle saying that that it must leave the field immediately or receive no quarter.

Having seen what had happened to the other two-thirds of their army, the men of the third battle began to comply.

Even as the French third battle was retreating, one of its leaders, de Fauquemberg, scraped together a force and made a minor, though determined, attack through the knee-deep mud and the carnage of previous assaults. At much the same time, the local lord, Isembert d'Azincourt, made an attack into the English rear with his own forces.

The English were at this time occupied with the removal of prisoners to the rear and reorganizing their weary army. Then came word that the French had attacked the baggage camp. This meant that a French force of unknown size was in the English rear area and might at any moment fall upon Henry's battered force. Worse, the French third battle

French crossbowmen of the late fifteenth century are depicted in a nineteenth-century engraving based on a medieval manuscript. Here they demonstrate the importance of the large pavise, often carried by an accompanying pavisier, to the slow-loading missilemen.

had returned to the field and begun to slowly advance.

Henry did not have enough men to guard the prisoners, repulse the force in his rear and face the remainder of the French army. The order was given to put the prisoners to the sword, since they posed a severe threat if they obtained weapons. However, although the baggage was pillaged, the threat posed by d'Azincourt's force proved to be fairly minor and it was soon driven off, at which point the remaining prisoners were spared.

The rallied French forces, even though they still outnumbered Henry's entire force, thought better of pressing their attack against the English line. They drew off, leaving the field in English hands and the road to Calais open.

AFTERMATH

King Henry was able to gain Calais with what remained of his army, though he was not in a position to pursue the beaten French and make more of his victory.

Agincourt was the third of a trio of great English victories – after Crécy and Poitiers – won by English archers over heavily armoured French men-at-arms. The battle cost France half of its nobility, including three dukes, 90 other nobles and about 1560 men-at-arms. About 200 more were captured. The English lost about 400 men.

However, the total dominance of the English archer was drawing to an end by 1415, with the emergence of gunpowder and the increasing use of firearms. The pattern of victories of steady English troops over aggressively advancing Frenchmen would continue for many years, however. Four centuries later, during the Napoleonic Wars, the Duke of Wellington observed that the French continued to come on in the old manner, and that the English continued to defeat them in the old manner.

The Battle of Poitiers, fought on 19 September 1356, was the second great battlefield defeat of the French by the English during the Hundred Years War. Using a combination of longbow archers, infantry and dismounted cavalry, the English Black Prince led a force that withstood charges from both French cavalry and infantry to capture the opposing general, France's King John II. This defeat forced the French to agree to the Treaty of Brétigny, which ceded large amounts of land to the English.

VITKOV
1420

EVERY PROBLEM HAS ITS SOLUTION: HOW COULD PEASANTS ARMED WITH AGRICULTURAL IMPLEMENTS HOPE TO CONTEND WITH WELL-ARMOURED AND SUPREMELY CONFIDENT KNIGHTS WIELDING MODERN WEAPONS? WHETHER IT WAS LATERAL THINKING, DIVINE INSPIRATION OR PREVIOUS EXPERIENCE, JAN ZIZKA FOUND THE ANSWER IN THE USE OF WAGONS.

WHY DID IT HAPPEN?

WHO A Hussite force numbering approximately 9000 under Jan Zizka (1360–1424), opposed an army of the Holy Roman Empire numbering 80,000, led by the Emperor Sigismund (reigned 1410–37).

WHAT Troops of the Holy Roman Empire suffered a devastating flank attack whilst assaulting an outpost of besieged Prague.

WHERE The hill of Vitkov, now known as Ziscaberg, to the east of Prague in the modern Czech Republic.

WHEN 14 July 1420.

WHY The population had risen against the Catholic Church's attempt to suppress the Hussite heresy and held the city of Prague.

OUTCOME The rout carried away the greater part of the main Imperial army and although casualties were less than 1000 they lifted the siege and the mostly mercenary army partially dispersed.

God loomed large in the mind of medieval man, who was surrounded by phenomena like birth, plague and the Mongol invasions for which he had no other explanation than 'God wills it'. But he could see the enormous gulf between what was said by the clergy, 'poverty and chastity', and what they did, 'profligacy and licentiousness'. Consequently, in several places in Europe a counter-movement sprang up. In Bohemia Jan Hus, a rector at Prague University, preached against the behaviour of the clergy. His words were warmly received by his congregation, but not by the church, which began to feel threatened. Under a guarantee of safe conduct from the Holy Roman Emperor

Sigismund, also King of Hungary, and at the request of the pope he travelled to Rome in 1415 to address the Council of Constance. Here he was imprisoned, tried and burnt as a heretic.

THE HUSSITE MOVEMENT
Outraged by this duplicity, numerous small groups of dissidents joined under the name of their martyr and the Hussite movement was formed. In 1417 the church declared all of Jan Hus's followers to be heretics and sent in an army raised by the Holy Roman Emperor. The situation went from arrests, trials and burnings to open rebellion following an incident in 1419 when some of the king's councillors were thrown from an

'Jan Hus Burned at the Stake' from the sixteenth-century The Chronicle of Ulrich of Reichental. *Jan Hus was invited by the pope to go to Rome and given safe passage by the Holy Roman Emperor. When he arrived he was tried, condemned and burnt at the stake, thus becoming a martyr for his cause.*

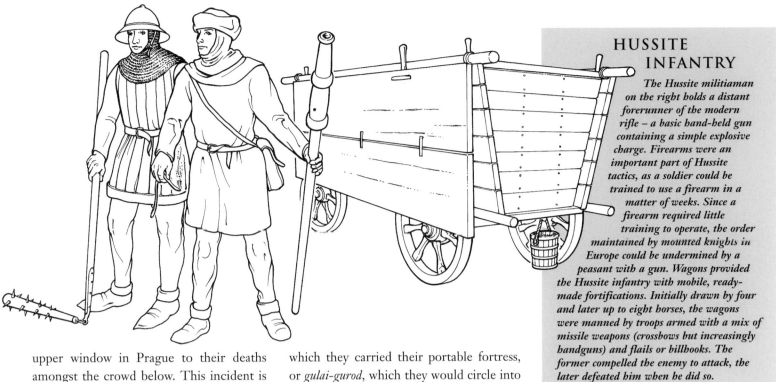

HUSSITE INFANTRY

The Hussite militiaman on the right holds a distant forerunner of the modern rifle – a basic hand-held gun containing a simple explosive charge. Firearms were an important part of Hussite tactics, as a soldier could be trained to use a firearm in a matter of weeks. Since a firearm required little training to operate, the order maintained by mounted knights in Europe could be undermined by a peasant with a gun. Wagons provided the Hussite infantry with mobile, ready-made fortifications. Initially drawn by four and later up to eight horses, the wagons were manned by troops armed with a mix of missile weapons (crossbows but increasingly handguns) and flails or billhooks. The former compelled the enemy to attack, the later defeated him when he did so.

upper window in Prague to their deaths amongst the crowd below. This incident is now known to history as the first defenestration of Prague.

On 1 March 1420 the pope declared a Crusade against the heretics. Newly crowned Sigismund of Hungary raised an army in neighbouring Saxony and invaded. The Hussites elected four military commanders, one of whom was a half-blind but sharp-minded former royal gamekeeper called Jan Zizka. He had already been successful in December the previous year when he mounted small cannons on seven wagons to repel an attack by 2000 royalist troops at the siege of Nekmer. Zizka had got his first taste of military life in the war between King Wenceslas IV of Bohemia (now the Czech Republic) and his nobles. He later led his own band of soldiers at the behest of the king in alliance with the southern Poles against the formidable Teutonic Knights. His band was probably present at the battle of Grünwald, otherwise known as Tannenberg, an infamous defeat for the Teutonic Order.

It was his experiences in this campaign that shaped his tactics when he came to lead the Hussite army. He had witnessed the power of the mounted knight at first hand and seen how militia infantry could not stand against them in the open. He must also have been aware of tales from the East, of how the Tartars of the steppes lived and fought from horseback and followed their flocks and herds in their wagon homes on which they carried their portable fortress, or *gulai-gurod*, which they would circle into a defensive formation when trouble threatened. He would bring these together into the unique Hussite way of warfare.

THE CAMPAIGN

When the religious dissidents first drew together as the Hussites they formed a tented encampment – calling it Tabor after Mount Tabor in the Bible – in the countryside 80.5km (50 miles) south of Prague. Zizka, however, was still in the city with a strong following of Prague militia. After a few days of streetfighting he had eliminated all of the royal garrison and Prague was in the hands of the Hussites. Leaving the city in safe hands, he set out for the west, intent on attracting more recruits to the cause.

Meanwhile German Catholics in the eastern city of Kutna Hora massacred the local Hussites, indicating that this was going to be a long, bitter struggle. Zizka became trapped in the western city of Plzen by a force of local Catholics. Unable to risk the arrival of Sigismund and his much larger army he signed a truce with his besiegers and left for Tabor with only 400 men and a train of just 12 supply wagons. The Catholics broke the truce and 2000 men-at-arms attacked him on the march at Sudomer. He drew his small force up with the earthbanks of some fishponds on one flank and secured his other flank with the wagons. Although the Catholic men-at-

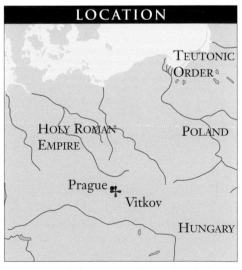

Prague, capital of Bohemia and situated at the heart of the Holy Roman Empire, became a hot spot of religious dispute and a focal point of resistance for the Hussite movement.

A sixteenth-century facsimile engraving of Jan Hus, who had started by preaching against the hypocrisy of the Catholic Church. In life he was an annoyance, in death he became an unassailable enemy.

equipped with agricultural tools such as flails, billhooks and axes used as weapons with little modification. They also had one other weapon vital in time of war – grim determination. Convinced of their cause and having seen friends or family burnt for their beliefs, Zizka's troops would always be formidable opponents. Flight or surrender were never a real option, because they knew they would be massacred.

DISPOSITIONS

In the nick of time Zizka moved the army into Prague (although the castle of Hradcany on the west bank and Vysehrad had been earlier recaptured by royal troops). Medieval Prague lay astride the River Vltava and was dominated on the eastern bank by the hill of Vitkov on which stood an old watchtower. The slopes of the ridge were cleared of any form of cover and the watchtower was reinforced by a strong palisade backing a ditch across the 100m (328ft) wide ridge and flanked by a tower at each end. Its garrison was formed from the Taborites, the most fanatic sect of the Hussite movement.

The inevitable arrived in midsummer; the Emperor Sigismund, at the head of an army of perhaps 80,000 men. The army comprised troops from all over the Holy Roman Empire: there were Bohemians from Sigismund's feudal lands, plus Germans, Hungarians and others, mostly mercenaries. They made camp on the higher north bank around the village of Bubny. The knights were so well armoured by this time that the shield was becoming obsolete. The feudal contingents were overconfident and arrogant, while the mercenaries, of which there were many, were better trained but more cautious – they wanted to win the battle and return home with their pay. In addition there were mounted crossbowmen and Hungarian cavalry who fought as skirmishers with the bow – a vital and often overlooked role.

This plethora of mounted men was further augmented by feudal infantry with a mixture of mêlée and missile weapons. The reliance of the Holy Roman Emperor on the Diet, or parliament, to provide money for troops and their unwillingness to ever provide enough, except for his coronation

arms dismounted and pressed their attacks until nightfall, they failed and quit the field. Both sides had suffered heavy casualties.

Back at Tabor he set about acquiring weapons in raids on noble residences and building an organized army from the men available. It was here that he started building more of the famous war wagons by converting peasant wagons and crewing them with 16 men and a pair of armoured drivers. Zizka's army was an army of the people. True, there were a few nobles mounted and armed with lance and shield just like other knights, but these were few in number. More numerous cavalry were provided by the lesser gentry, some armed with lances, some with missile weapons and a few armoured with breast and back plate. The great majority, however, were infantry

procession to Rome, meant that this army was largely mercenary and paid for with the money provided by the Diet for a lavish coronation by the pope.

Prague could not be safely assaulted with the Vitkov ridge in enemy hands. So Sigismund deployed his bombards at Bubny to the north beyond the river and on the Sickhouse Field, giving them a converging field of fire onto the northern section of wall or onto the position on the ridge, albeit at extreme range.

Zizka knew this was dangerous but could see from the walls that the guns were not closely supported and gambled on a sortie from the Porici Gate, which drove the crews back north over the river and captured a couple of the bombards. This was the first hint of the lax command and control within the army of the Holy Roman Empire. If the guns had been properly supported this sortie could have been disastrous for the Hussites.

DIVERSIONARY TACTICS

For the empire this was just the opening move. The next day Sigismund planned two diversionary attacks, one from Hradcany on the east bank of the city, the other from Vysehrad to the south. Meanwhile, a thousand or more Saxon cavalry under the command of Henry of Isenburg were to launch themselves at the improvised fortifications on the ridge. These were to be followed by an assault by German and Hungarian knights across the Sickhouse Field to storm the gates in the city wall. A good strategic plan – drawing Zizka's reserves away from the main point of the attack, which was to be delivered with overwhelming force. Unfortunately Zizka wasn't going to be drawn by the diversions and the poor tactics of the Imperialists in front of the Vitkov palisade fell far short of what was needed.

THE BATTLE

Zizka had foreseen that the Imperialists would attack the palisade on Vitkov first and positioned his first line of reserves between the ridge and the city walls. Since the ridge effectively channelled the Imperialist army to one side or the other this was the ideal spot to cover any eventuality. A second force, led by Jan Zelivsky, was waiting, unseen by the Imperialists, behind the

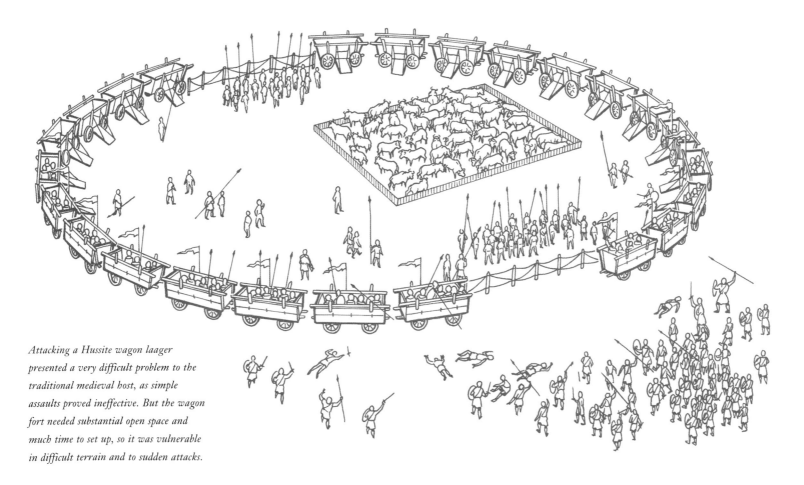

Attacking a Hussite wagon laager presented a very difficult problem to the traditional medieval host, as simple assaults proved ineffective. But the wagon fort needed substantial open space and much time to set up, so it was vulnerable in difficult terrain and to sudden attacks.

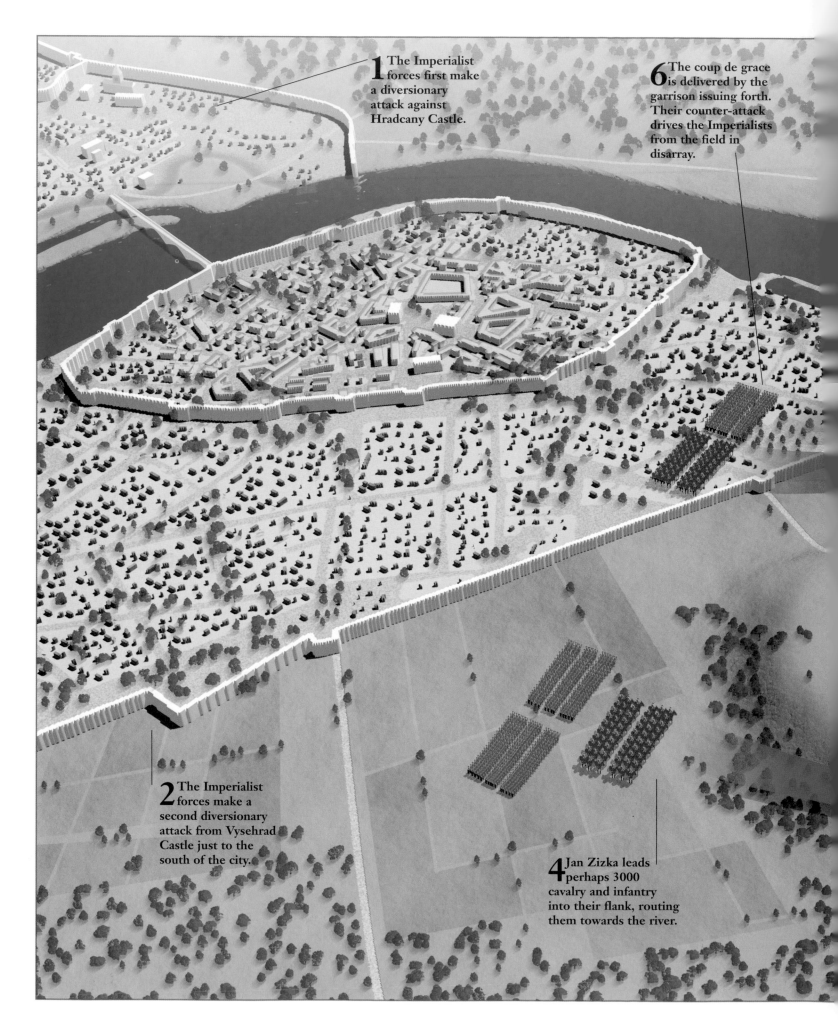

1 The Imperialist forces first make a diversionary attack against Hradcany Castle.

6 The coup de grace is delivered by the garrison issuing forth. Their counter-attack drives the Imperialists from the field in disarray.

2 The Imperialist forces make a second diversionary attack from Vysehrad Castle just to the south of the city.

4 Jan Zizka leads perhaps 3000 cavalry and infantry into their flank, routing them towards the river.

VITKOV
1420

5 The Imperialists by the river bank are thrown into severe disorder by their routing allies coming down the hill.

3 16,000 mounted knights squeeze onto the ridge to assault the Hussite palisade, but fail to make significant progress.

Siege cannons were developed from the 1300s and became increasingly efficient and important through the later Middle Ages. A typical bombard (right) was made of iron and bound with iron hoops. An ordinary bombard could fire a shot weighing 136kg (300lb).

Porici Gate. The ridge assault went in with the men-at-arms dismounting as they got close. Fighting here was fierce, the noise was deafening and confusion was inevitable with too many men and horses trying to assault the palisade. The advancing column must have been 100 men deep while they were mounted, each mounted man requiring a 1m (3ft) frontage. As they dismounted they would have required more space, both to the side to stand and behind for the horse. Ranks behind the first 10 or so would not have known what was happening, or when they were to stop, retreat or go forward. As the front ranks dismounted, those behind had to pass an ever-increasing herd of horses before they could join the fight. However, they did capture the old watchtower, most of the palisade and one of the small forts. The other, garrisoned by a mere 26 men and three women, held out.

COUNTER-ATTACK

Zizka headed out in support at the head of his bodyguard and the rest of the reserves followed. They surged up the southern slope and caught the dismounted and preoccupied men-at-arms in the flank. It is an oft-observed phenomenon that troops engaged in an assault or mêlée become so focused on their immediate objective that they notice nothing else around them. The inadequate Imperial command and control meant there was no one to warn them or respond to this recent development. The Hussite counter-attack would have taken them completely by surprise.

Opposite: A nineteenth century illustration of Jan Zizka's attack on the flank of the Imperialist forces at Vitkov. Modern research has somewhat superseded this image: the palisade and towers were wooden, temporary structures, and the attack was made at the opposite end of the palisade.

The men-at-arms, doubtless mingled with many riderless horses, broke and fled down the steep northern slope leaving several hundred casualties behind them. As they came careering down the slope the hidden Hussite reserves sortied from the Porici Gate and attacked the men on the Sickhouse Field. Taking stock of their situation – routing friends and riderless

horses coming downhill into their flank and now the enemy uphill besides – these troops too turned and fled in disorder. They were pursued by the reserves under Jan Zelivsky as far as Liben on the banks of the River Vltava. The diversionary attacks were never expected to achieve much and this part of the scheme went exactly according to plan!

THE SIEGE IS LIFTED

Sigismund's best effort had come to nothing. While he now hesitated, the climate came to the Hussites' aid. As the Imperial troops sweltered in the hot central European summer with the river at its

Hus, the Czech religious leader, is taken to be burnt at the stake for heresy (from a contemporary manuscript held in the University of Prague).

Early arquebus, c.1450. By this time handguns were becoming lighter, more portable and more accurate. This is the type of simple handgun the Hussites were able to manufacture after the capture of Prague.

lowest, disease broke out amongst them. Money was also running out and bickering over the defeat amongst the leading noblemen did not help. Many mercenaries left the army at this point. Sigismund decided to lift the siege of Prague at the end of July, intending instead to relieve the siege of Wyschrad with just 18,000 men – only to suffer another bloody defeat.

AFTERMATH

Securing the area around Prague meant that the Hussites now had access to one of the most industrially productive areas in Europe. Silver and gold were mined near Kutna Hora; iron and quicksilver near Prague. Zizka took full advantage of this mineral and fiscal wealth and began equipping large numbers of his men with handguns. From the safety of their wagons these wreaked havoc time and again on the Imperialist horsemen. In the end, after nearly a dozen significant battles and despite the urgings of their

commanders, the Imperialist troops just would not engage the Hussites again.

The following year, 1421, Jan Zizka was wounded in his good eye during a siege and was blinded. He died aged 64 in 1424. The seeds of the doom of the Hussite rebellion were sown right back at the beginning. From the moment of their triumph over the armies of Sigismund the different factions started to squabble and then split. Five separate parties grouped and split, each with its own aims and agenda. The Taborites accepted only what was stated in the Bible and nothing else. The Orebites or Utraquists – a sect founded by Zizka before his death – lived a more communal life, sharing booty and everything else. They started calling themselves Orphans following his death. The Praguers were held in contempt by the first two for their wealth and worldliness, and they in turn resented the growing independence of the Taborites and Orphans. The rebellion broke into civil war as the factions fought each other.

Eventually, the moderate alliance faced the extremists in battle on 30 May 1434 at Lipany. The extremists were vanquished following a feigned retreat and peace was concluded with the Imperial states. There was another anti-Hussite Crusade from 1464 to 1471. Again the Hussite armies made use of wagons but by then much bigger ones crewed by 18–20 mercenaries each. This last phase was more a campaign of territorial acquisition by the son-in-law of the Bohemian King Georg.

Having lost every battle against the Hussites, Emperor Sigismund went on to be beaten by the Ottoman Turks at Golubac in 1428. Thereafter he left campaigning to his subordinates and died in 1437.

The illustrations below show various pole-arms popular amongst peasant militias in the fifteenth century. From left to right: two 'bearded' axes; a glaive with a hook to pull horsemen to the ground; a Flemish goedendag, combining a spear point with an iron-rimmed club; a flail, based on an agricultural instrument, but turned into a deadly spiked club which could be swung at a distance; and two weapons that are an early and later form of the halberd.

Opposite: Painted in an era of Czech nationalism, this painting by Alphonse Marie Mucha (1860–1939) depicts the Hussite meeting at Krizky from the series Slav Epic (1916).

CONSTANTINOPLE
1453

THE OTTOMAN TURKISH SIEGE OF CONSTANTINOPLE IN 1453 WAS ONE OF THE GREATEST SIEGES OF ALL TIME. IT SAW THE TURKS USE – FOR THE VERY FIRST TIME – HEAVY SIEGE ARTILLERY TO BREAK THROUGH THE ENORMOUS THEODOSIAN WALLS THAT HAD HELD OFF ATTACKERS FOR MORE THAN A MILLENNIUM.

WHY DID IT HAPPEN?

WHO Ottoman Sultan Mehmed II (1432–81, reigned 1444–46 and 1451–81) besieged the city with 120,000 troops, opposed by some 8–10,000 Christian defenders under Emperor Constantine XI Palaeologus (1405–53, reigned 1449–53).

WHAT The Turks used Urban's massive cannon against the finest fortification works in Europe.

WHERE Siege of the Imperial Byzantine capital of Constantinople (Byzantium) on the Bosporus and Sea of Marmara. The city is better known today by its Turkish name of Istanbul.

WHEN 5 April–29 May 1453

WHY Mehmed II wished to eliminate this tiny Christian stronghold deep behind the Turkish frontier and make it the new capital of his growing empire.

OUTCOME The fall of Byzantine Constantinople to Mehmed's expanding Ottoman Empire.

The fall of the capital of the Byzantine Empire, Constantinople, to the Muslim Turks in May 1453 was a disastrous event for the Christian world, especially for Orthodox Christians, who viewed it as the beginning of the end for their faith. That Constantinople was going to fall to the Ottoman Turks was a foregone conclusion. The beginning of the end for the Byzantine Empire had been the disastrous defeat of their once-victorious army at the hands of the Seljuk Turks at the battle of Manzikert in 1071. During the following centuries the Turks conquered the whole of Anatolia and

A medieval illustrated map from British Library showing in the centre the formidable walls of Constantinople. Across the waters of the Golden Horn is the fortified suburb of Galata (Pera) held by the neutral Genoese.

were united under the Ottoman dynasty into one single sultanate. The Catholic West, instead of aiding the hard-pressed Byzantines, stabbed them in the back. In 1204 'Crusaders', paid by Venice, sacked Constantinople, and the city itself, like the rest of the empire, began a long, sad decline.

The Western invaders were eventually expelled but the Ottoman Turks, taking advantage of the ravages of the Black Death, crossed into the Balkans in 1356, seizing Byzantine lands there. By 1396 the whole of Bulgaria was in Ottoman hands, and Constantinople itself – practically all that was left of the empire – was surrounded by Turkish-occupied territory and cut off from the West.

The city was a mere shadow of its former self and its disastrous decline was reflected in the city's population – an impressive one million in the twelfth century had been reduced by the 1450s to a mere 100,000. Constantinople, however, continued to trade both with the West and the East, while the Theodosian Walls – built in the fifth century in the reign of Emperor Theodosius II (401–450) – remained intact and protected the city from enemy attack with their 5.7km (3.5-mile) long moats and triple line of walls and fortified towers which stretched from the Sea of Marmara to the Golden Horn.

Constantinople was given a respite when a most unlikely saviour appeared in the East in the shape of the savage but brilliant Mongol warlord Timur Lenk, or Tamerlane (1336–1405), who defeated the Ottomans at the battle of Ankara in 1402. This gave the city a reprieve for half a century mainly due to Ottoman civil wars and the fact that after a failed siege in 1422 Sultan Murád II (1404–51) chose to live in peace with the Byzantines. He argued, sensibly, that Constantinople posed no threat in the hands of the feeble Byzantines and that an Ottoman attack upon the city might unite the divided and decadent Christians against the Muslim menace.

MEHMED II

Unfortunately Murád II – admired and respected by Ottomans and Byzantines alike – died in February 1451 and his place as sultan was taken by a callow, arrogant,

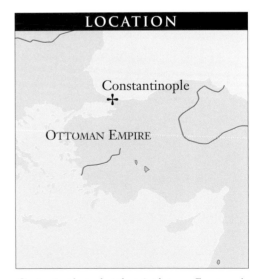

TURKISH JANISSARY (c.1450)

Founded in 1330, these Turkish slave-soldiers, drawn from converted Christian tribute-children and prisoners of war, were essential to the military success of the Ottoman state and went on to become the model for discipline in the Western armies of the sixteenth century. This infantryman is armed with the standard curved scimitar of the period and a short bow. Janissary bowmen first proved their worth at the Battle of Nicopolis (1396), where they were deployed against cavalry to great effect behind stakes in a skirmishing formation. By the time of the siege of Constantinople, they were an essential part of the Ottoman Turkish army.

drunken and aggressive youth of 19, Mehmed II, who was to rule and make war on his neighbours until his death from overindulgence at the age of 49. Mehmed II had many bad qualities but he was determined and was to prove, with time, a good military leader. His one overriding, indeed consuming, passion was to take Constantinople and make it the capital of an Ottoman Empire that would straddle the world. He had the temerity to call himself the 'Shadow of God upon Earth' and with the fall of the Byzantine capital that seemed justified. After all, walls that had stood for a thousand years had been breached and stormed by his Ottoman troops.

In the summer of 1452 Mehmed II had recruited and paid a Hungarian gunmaker, Urban, a huge sum to build him a monstrous gun that would be able to breach the walls of Constantinople. By January 1453 Urban's gun was ready for inspection at Adrianople (the Ottoman capital to the west of Constantinople): its barrel measured 8.1m (26ft 8in) in length, had a calibre of 20.3cm (8in) and required a crew of 700, but could lob a cannonball weighing a tonne (1 ton) over 1.6km (1 mile).

Obviously Mehmed II had the hardware for a successful siege and during the spring he called up men from across his vast empire that stretched from the Balkans in the west to Anatolia in the east. He had a huge army concentrated at Adrianople

LOCATION

Constantinople

✝

OTTOMAN EMPIRE

Constantinople stood at the point between Europe and Asia Minor and also between the Mediterranean and the Black Sea. In 1453 it remained the last vestige of ancient Byzantium not yet conquored by the Turks.

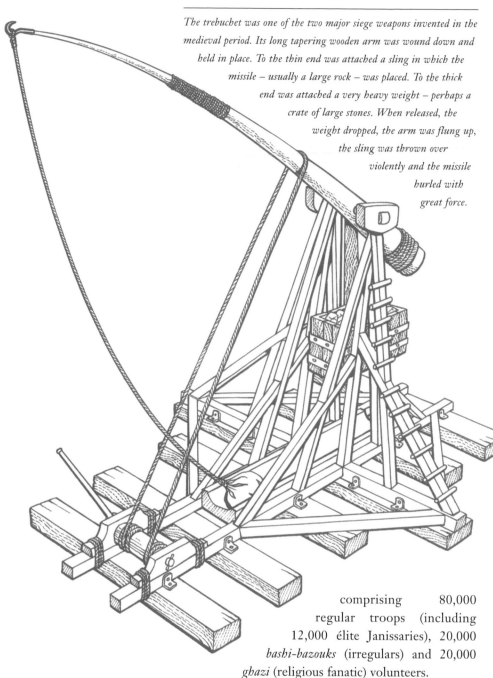

The trebuchet was one of the two major siege weapons invented in the medieval period. Its long tapering wooden arm was wound down and held in place. To the thin end was attached a sling in which the missile – usually a large rock – was placed. To the thick end was attached a very heavy weight – perhaps a crate of large stones. When released, the weight dropped, the arm was flung up, the sling was thrown over violently and the missile hurled with great force.

comprising 80,000 regular troops (including 12,000 élite Janissaries), 20,000 *bashi-bazouks* (irregulars) and 20,000 *ghazi* (religious fanatic) volunteers.

THE SIEGE BEGINS

The first step in Mehmed's relentless assault upon Constantinople began a year before he commenced the formal siege of the city. First and foremost Constantinople's access to grain from the Black Sea had to be cut. Mehmed, no respecter of Christians or the niceties of diplomacy, broke all his father's agreements with the Emperor Constantine XI – who had ascended the throne in 1449 – and sent his army to occupy Byzantine territory along the Bosporous.

The Ottomans, partly using Christian slave labour, began to construct a fortress at the shoreline. In only five months, between 14 April and 31 August 1452, the Turks had

constructed a fort named, in appropriately grisly fashion, Boghaz-Kesen, or the 'Throat Cutter', by Mehmed. The fort soon lived up to its name. In November 1452 a Venetian ship – ignoring the Turkish blockade of Constantinople – was hit with a single shot and sunk. The crew were slaughtered and the captain, Antonio Rizzo, was impaled. His body was left to rot as a warning for others that they ignored the fort's guns at their peril.

None of the Italian states, except for the pope, lifted a finger to aid Constantinople and in the doomed city the population realized that the hapless Venetian captain's gruesome fate was only a foretaste of what the barbaric Turks would do to them. For once all the disparate elements of the city's population – Greeks, Balkan Slavs, Italians and others – united in a desperate resolve to fight to the bitter end. One man had more reason that any other to fear Turkish atrocities. He was in fact an Ottoman Turk and a distant relative of Mehmed: Prince Orhan. He and his men would fight with more desperation and courage than the Byzantines.

Mehmed II spent the following winter making elaborate and meticulous preparations to attack Constantinople by the following spring. An unpleasant surprise in March 1453 was the appearance of the Ottoman fleet under Suleyman Baltoghlu in the Marmara. Thus Constantinople's seaborne lines of communication were cut.

DISPOSITIONS

The first Ottoman detachments arrived beneath the walls of Constantinople on 1 April and were met by Byzantine skirmishers. As more Turks arrived Constantine XI, who took an active part in the defence, ordered the bridges across the outer moat burnt and the gates shut and bolted; meanwhile the walls were manned. It was a valiant effort but he had only 7000 Byzantines and 5000 foreigners (mainly Italians) facing over 100,000 Turks.

On 6 April Mehmed moved his main camp closer to the walls. He faced an unenviable task, despite his enormous numerical preponderance, since the walls were in good repair. Where should he attack? The Marmara Sea Wall was strong

THE OPPOSED FORCES

OTTOMAN TURKS (estimated)

Regular infantry:	68,000
Janissary infantry:	12,000
Bashi-bazouks militia:	20,000
Ghazis (Islamic volunteers):	20,000
Total	**120,000**

CHRISTIAN DEFENDERS (estimated)

Byzantine Greeks:	7000
'Foreigners or Latins' (Italians, Catalans & other European volunteers):	5000
Total	**12,000**

and was protected by a strong current and underwater reefs. The Golden Horn Wall was also strong. So the assault had to be made against the massive Land Wall. A logical place would be to attack the Blachernae district that protruded northwards from the wall. But the Byzantines – brilliant fortifiers – had reinforced its defences. The actual Theodosian Walls consisted of three separate but parallel lines of walls fronted by a 18.2m (60ft) moat that could be flooded in an emergency. The Outer Wall – which lay behind this moat and a low crenellated breastwork – was 7.6m (25ft) high and had a strong square tower every 46–56m (50–60 yards). Facing a powerful enemy with few troops the emperor decided to man the Outer Wall with Byzantines and his Italian allies. Prince Orhan's Turks held the harbour while Don Péré Julia's Catalans held the Hippodrome. The Sea Walls were thinly held as the Byzantines, rightly, expected Mehmed to launch his main attack against the Land Wall. The defenders' artillery was unusable due to the shortage of saltpetre in the besieged city but the troops had good armour, far superior to that of the lightly armoured Turks.

Mehmed placed the Rumelian army under Karadja Pasha from the Golden Horn to the Lycus Valley and from there to the Marmara, Ishak Pasha's Anatolian army. Mehmed pitched his red and gold silk tent about 400m (440 yards) from the Land Wall with his best troops and Urban's monstrous gun around him.

THE ATTACK BEGINS

On 9 April the Ottoman admiral Baltoghlu Pasha made an unsuccessful attempt to break through the boom erected by the defenders across the Golden Horn. That same day the Turks began to attack two forts, Therapia and Studius, to the west of the Land Wall. The castles held out until 11 April when both capitulated. The brave defenders, some 76 men, were impaled on Mehmed's express orders in front of the Land Wall to show what happened to those that resisted his will. A third fort, on the island of Prinkipo, held out and the garrison chose to burn itself to death rather than fall into the hands of the Turks.

On 12 April the Turks began bombarding the Theodosian Walls and the artillery fire would continue without interruption for six weeks. The Ottoman guns were heavy and unwieldy with a tendency to slide off their mud and wood firing platforms. Urban's giant gun only fired seven times a day, so complex and time-consuming was the process of loading and firing it, but it had a deafening roar and did great damage to the wall and the defenders' nerves.

By 18 April the wall across the Lycus Valley – the weakest section of the

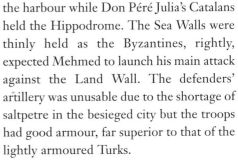

An illustrated 'map' from a medieval document that shows in high colour and fascinating detail the camp of the besieging Ottomans east of Constantinople's Theodosian Walls (bottom of picture).

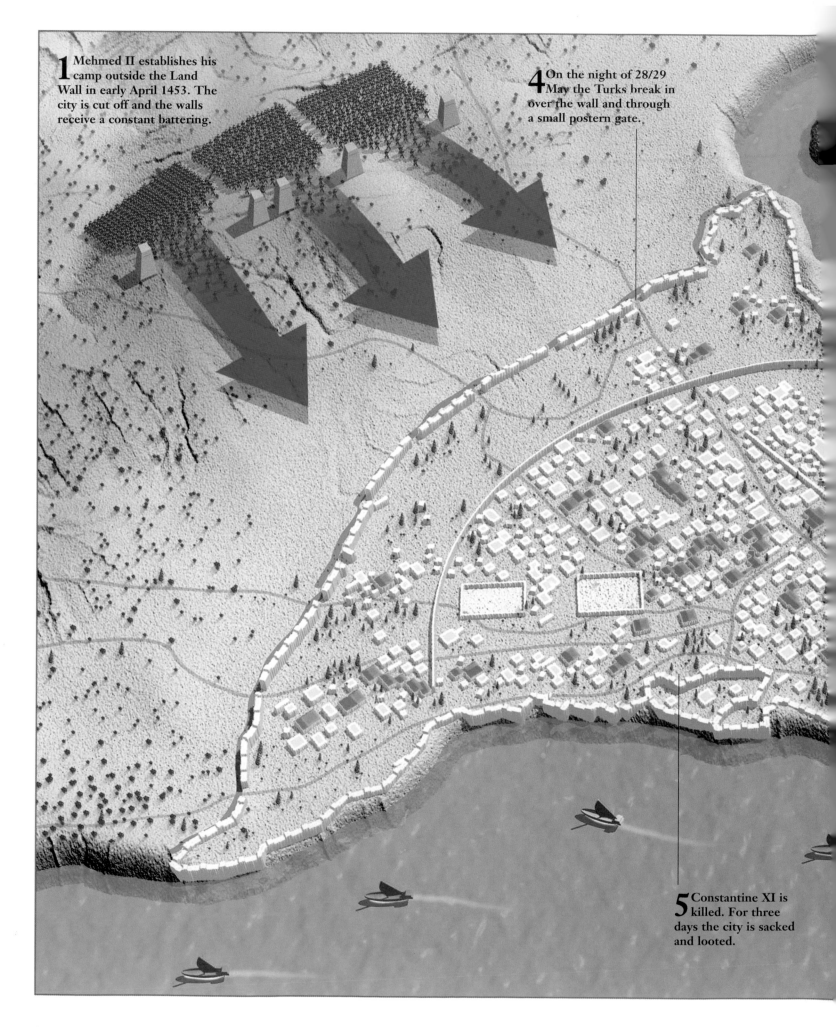

1 Mehmed II establishes his camp outside the Land Wall in early April 1453. The city is cut off and the walls receive a constant battering.

4 On the night of 28/29 May the Turks break in over the wall and through a small postern gate.

5 Constantine XI is killed. For three days the city is sacked and looted.

CONSTANTINOPLE
1453

3 Mehmed sends Turkish ships overland round Pera on rollers and into the Golden Horn. Constantinople is now fully blockaded.

2 A small Italian fleet breaks through and is let into the Golden Horn, giving temporary relief.

Theodosian Walls – had been completely destroyed but General Giustiani Longo (the emperor's field commander) had it repaired by Byzantine volunteers. That same day, two hours after sunset, Mehmed launched his first attack against this area, known as the Mesoteichion. The Turks had filled in the moat and rushed the wall but were thrown back by heavily armoured Byzantines and Italians led by Longo. The fighting lasted for four hours with the Turks losing 400 men to no loss for the Christians. Morale among the defenders soared.

NO RELIEF

Two days later came an even greater success when Baltoghlu Pasha tried and failed to defeat a fleet of Italian ships that were sailing to Constantinople with badly needed

Opposite: The Turks entered Constantinople on 29 May 1453. The Byzantine Emperor, Constantine XI, was killed. The sultan, Mehmed II, gave the city up to his troops to destroy and loot for three days.

This restored section of the Theodosian Walls shows their formidable strength, with three parallel lines of towers and thick crenellated walls. Breaching such defences proved near impossible for many centuries.

supplies of grain. The Turkish galleys were no match for the heavy Italian ships which blasted their way through with cannon and Greek Fire. The enraged Mehmed – who had seen the defeat unfold before his eyes – dismissed the hapless admiral.

Mehmed took charge and managed to move part of his fleet overland to the Golden Horn without the Byzantines being able to stop it. Now Constantinople was threatened from the north and a bravely led night attack, on 28 April, to launch fire

ships against the flotilla failed due to spies in Pera. The Venetians and Genoese, sworn enemies, began to fight amongst themselves prompting Constantine XI to tell them: 'The war outside our gates is enough for us. For the pity of God do not start a war between yourselves.' Thus admonished, the squabbling Italians buried the hatchet – but only temporarily.

On 7 May the Turks made a night attack against the Mesoteichion section of the

The Cannon of Mehmed II (below) was cast in 1464 and used by the Turks to protect the Bosporus strait. The gun was divided into two parts for ease of transportation. It weighed 18.2 tonnes (18 tons) and was 5.25m (17ft) long.

This highly romanticized and propagandistic illustration from 1832 shows Mehmed II Fatih leading his men over the walls of Constantinople while (at the bottom of the picture) the Byzantine Emperor Constantine XI is killed.

saw their massive siege tower opposite the Mesoteichion go up in flames after the Byzantines made a night raid and blew it up with a powder keg. By 23 May further tunnels had been eliminated after the Byzantines captured the Serb mining engineer in the sultan's service. After refined torture he revealed everything he knew and Grant's anti-mining unit set to work. But that very same day a lone Venetian vessel sailed into the harbour with the devastating news that there would be no Western fleet to save Constantinople. Morale began to slide.

On 24 and 25 May morale collapsed. In an age of deep religious fervour and belief in omens or signs, the events of these two days could only have a catastrophic impact. The first day during a procession, the Holy Icon of the Mother of God was dropped and the whole proceedings were interrupted by a thunderstorm that flooded the street. The following day, the city was blanketed in a thick fog that was unusual for the time of year. The populace, remembering the ancient prophesy that Constantinople would fall when the emperor had the same name as the founder, Constantine the Great, was convinced the fog hid God's departure from the Holy City.

What the defenders did not know was that morale among the besiegers was also low. After a seven-month-long siege with an army that now numbered 150,000, only setbacks and humiliations had been experienced. The sultan's ministers – all Murád II's men – and especially the Grand Vizier, Halil Pasha, were unimpressed with the boasts and arrogance of the 21-year-old ruler. Mehmed wanted a grand assault during the night of 28/29 May and agreed to withdraw if that failed.

THE GRAND ASSAULT

Medieval armies besieging a stubborn enemy would offer terms. If these were rejected then the city would, if stormed, be shown no mercy. This was the fate that would now befall Constantinople. By 28 May all the preparations had been completed on both sides. Across the doomed city the Christian populace, knowing that the last battle was upon them, assured each other that they would fight. In

Theodosian Walls that ended with the sultan's standard bearer, Amir Bey, being killed by the Byzantine knight Rhangabe. Five days later another night assault ended in defeat. Turkish attempts to build underground tunnels for mining were discovered. The Scottish mercenary knight, John Grant, in Byzantine service, led the defenders in counter-mining and flooding the Turkish tunnels. On 18 May the Turks

the evening, everyone, including the emperor, attended mass where both Orthodox and Catholic prayed to God for deliverance. Catalans, Castilians, Venetians and Genoese as well as the Byzantine Greeks stood shoulder to shoulder and took Holy Communion together from their respective clergy.

At 1.30 a.m. Mehmed signalled for the huge horde of poorly disciplined and lightly armed *bashi-bazouks* to attack in the Lycus Valley. During two hours of fighting the Christian defenders stood their ground, leaving hundreds of enemy dead. But Mehmed was only wearing down the defenders in preparation for further assaults. The Anatolian army attacked – in wave upon wave – but each successive surge of men was halted, cut to pieces and sent reeling back in retreat. Similar attacks against the Sea Walls failed equally miserably and even Mehmed began to lose faith in a Turkish victory. There were now only the Janissaries – some 12,000 of them – left for a final, desperate attack.

At that moment, as the Janissaries, accompanied by the Ottoman musical corps, attacked, two disasters befell the defenders. Firstly the Turks discovered that someone had left a small gate (Kerkaporta) open between the Blachernae and the Theodosian Walls. The attackers wasted no time in rushing the open gate. The Byzantines hurried to defend it but were simply swamped by sheer numbers. At the same time Giustiani Longo was wounded and despite Emperor Constantine XI pleading with him to stay he was taken aboard a Genoese ship which sailed to Chios where he died two days later. The Genoese fled in panic down to the harbour or to Pera. The Venetians claimed betrayal while the Byzantines fought on in sheer desperation; the emperor died fighting. The Turks opened the gates, more of their troops poured in and they penetrated the city. Orhan's Turks fought to the death, knowing they would die slowly at the hands of the bloodthirsty Mehmed, and the Catalans fought to the last man defending the

Hippodrome and Old Palace. The Turks ran amok in the city, looting, killing and raping, until even Mehmed had had enough and by evening imposed some order. Some 50,000 Byzantines were enslaved while 4000 were killed in the battle. The greatest siege of all time was over.

AFTERMATH

The fall of Constantinople was a high point in the relentless and ruthless expansion of the Ottoman Empire. Mehmed II became known by his honorific title, *Fatih*, or 'Conqueror'. During the next three centuries, until an equally famous siege and battle beneath the walls of Vienna in 1683, the Turks remained the scourge of Christian Europe.

Crossbowman were more effective in a siege situation, and a number of Aragonese and Genoese crossbowmen mercenaries were employed to defend Constantinople. By this time Western plate armour had become so heavy that knights ceased using a shield, freeing them to use heavy two-handed weapons.

BRUNKEBERG
1471

THE BATTLE OF BRUNKEBERG NOT ONLY SAVED THE NASCENT SWEDISH NATION STATE FROM BEING SUBMERGED IN A DANISH-DOMINATED SCANDINAVIAN UNION BUT SAW A MODERN, PROFESSIONAL ARMY DEFEATED AND ROUTED BY A COMMITTED AND WELL-ORGANIZED PEASANT MILITIA.

WHY DID IT HAPPEN?

WHO A royal army of 6000 Danish regulars and German mercenaries led by King Christian I Oldenburg of Denmark, opposed an army of 10,000 Swedish peasant levies led by Sten Sture.

WHAT Professional troops, including heavily armoured knights, were defeated by lightly armed but numerous peasant troops.

WHEN 10 October 1471

WHY As part of a long-standing conflict, the rebellious Swedes, seeking full independence, clashed with the Danish king, seeking to restore royal (Danish) control over Sweden by seizing the capital, Stockholm.

OUTCOME The Danes overconfidently charged the Swedes, who, using superior numbers and knowledge of the local terrain, encircled and defeated their foe.

In 1397 the three kingdoms of Denmark, Norway and Sweden – with the Grand Duchy of Finland – created a union, with Queen Margaret of Denmark (1353–1412) as head of state. Due to the mutual suspicion and antagonism of the Danes and Swedes the union functioned poorly and when Margaret died in 1412 the Swedes broke away. They chose their own ruler, Charles VIII (Karl) Knutsson Bonde (1408–70), as their king, but when in May 1470 he died after a series of disjointed reigns, King Christian I of Denmark (1426–81), the legitimate ruler of Sweden, saw his chance to wrest back his throne.

In Stockholm, however, King Charles VIII's nephew, Sten Gustavsson Sture (1440–1503), was elected by the Swedish grandees as *Riksföreståndare* (Lord Protector or Regent); he was supported by the old king's followers and his relatives, such as Nils Sture (1426–94). But Christian I was determined to assert his legitimate claim and during the early summer of 1471 set about mobilizing his army. He secured shipping to transport his force to Stockholm by making a deal with the Hanseatic League, which was granted a monopoly on trade with Sweden once it had been forced back into the union with Denmark.

The two armies were fundamentally different. Both militarily and economically, the Danes were the stronger of the two peoples, coming from a more prosperous, populous and fertile country. The king's army consisted of 3000 Danish troops that

The political make-up of the Baltic region in 1471. The United Kingdom of Scandinavia, as ruled from Copenhagen by the Danish kings since the Union of Kalmar in 1397, consisted of Denmark, Norway and Sweden (including the Grand Duchy of Finland). In reality Sweden-Finland was independent. The arrow shows the route of the Danish invasion fleet in 1471.

BRUNKEBERG

varied from mounted knights to regular infantry and armed peasant levies – the latter contained a small Swedish contingent loyal to their legitimate ruler. In addition there were 2000 or so German infantry – hardened professional mercenaries. The Danish army liked to fight regular battles in the open field where their material preponderance, military experience and superior discipline could be used to best effect. If the Swedes faced the Danes and Germans in the open they would be, or so the Danes believed, cut to pieces and slaughtered wholesale.

By contrast Sten Sture's Swedish army consisted of lightly armed yet mobile peasants in arms, some tough professionals, and a handful of mounted knights (about 400). The core of the army, nine-tenths of it, would be made up of peasant levies armed with swords, pikes, axes, crossbows and longbows. The favourite tactic among the Swedish peasants – put to good use in the wooded, hilly Swedish countryside – was the ambush, and at Brunkeberg, Sten Sture would use that peasant tactic, but on a far greater scale, to good effect.

THE CAMPAIGN

In late July 1471 the Danish fleet of 76 ships with the army on board set sail from Copenhagen harbour heading east towards Stockholm. To reach the city the Danish fleet would have to navigate through the treacherous, shallow waters of the vast archipelago that blocked the entrance to the Swedish capital. The archipelago consisted of literally hundreds of low-lying islands

and underwater rocks sitting just beneath the surface. This made the Stockholm archipelago a navigator's nightmare but it says something for the Danish admiral's skills that the entire fleet sailed safely into the harbour of Stockholm without losing a single ship. No doubt a well-paid Swedish pilot had been recruited!

The Danish fleet anchored between the islands of Käpplingeholm and the larger, wooded island of Vargö (Wolf's Island), just across the water from Stockholm Castle. The city, located on an island, could not be stormed by a conventional army nor assaulted properly by a fleet. Its approaches from the easterly side, facing the Baltic, were protected by a strong wooden palisade that protruded out of the water and blocked off Stockholm from a naval assault. It could only be attacked by an invader on the landward side from either the north or south. Both approaches were blocked by powerful turreted drawbridges and fortified gates. In the north Stockholm Castle gave added protection should the Danes attack.

But Christian had no intention of subjecting this formidable fortress city to a regular siege. He wanted his enemy, Sten Sture, to come to the relief of Stockholm, where the king hoped to defeat the 'rebel' Swedes in a regular battle he was sure his

modern and well-equipped army would easily win. The Danes began to land their troops on Käpplingeholm on 18 August and immediately began to build a fortified camp atop the southern end of Brunkeberg. They built earthen ramparts topped by earth-filled wicker baskets, wooden palisades and a strong stockade. The Swedes were shocked at the speed of construction and the

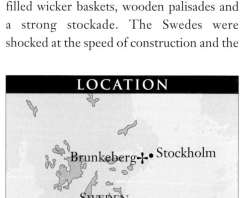

LOCATION

Brunkeberg ✝ • Stockholm

SWEDEN

DENMARK

Stockholm lay at the centre of the kingdom of Sweden, close to Finland, and the major shipping lanes of the Baltic. If Christian I managed to capture Stockholm, then he would control whole north-central Baltic.

BRUNKEBERG

This detailed manuscript illustration shows King Christian I with Queen Dorothy. Underneath the figures are their respective coat-of-arms. Christian was not able to return and avenge his defeat of 1471. It was his grandson King Christian II (1481–1559) who would exact a revenge suitable for Brunkeberg – in 1520 he arrested and executed the entire élite of Sweden during the infamous 'Bloodbath of Stockholm'.

Brunkeberg, knights in armour, artillery and regular infantry would not be in their element. Swedish chances of winning were heightened by Christian I's dispositions. In the face of an enemy of unknown strength an army should be kept together and not divided up.

The king, however, split his far smaller army into three parts to defend vital strategic points on the battlefield. Should things go badly wrong for the Danish side then their retreat back to the fleet had to be secured by a detachment of cavalry and some infantry. Furthermore the Stockholm garrison had to be prevented from joining up with the Swedish field army – so Christian placed another detachment to defend the pivotal position around the convent of St Klara. The main part of his army remained in the Brunkeberg camp.

The Swedes and Danes agreed to a truce that was to last until late September in order to make crucial preparations for a battle that could prove decisive. While Sten Sture went south to recruit more peasant troops and provincial knights, his cousin, Nils Sture, went to central Sweden for the same purpose. If Sten Sture wanted to win against King Christian then he had to secure the support of the belligerent anti-Danish population of Darlecarlia and Bergslagen. It took Sten and Nils what remained of the month of August and the whole of September to recruit the vast host of armed peasants that would make up the Swedish army at Brunkeberg. But on 9 October their contingents were finally assembled and united into a single army at Järva, north of Stockholm. In total the Swedes numbered some 10,000 men, or twice the number that Christian had at his disposal. This numerical preponderance would prove crucial and more than make up for the enemy's higher troop quality.

THE OPPOSED FORCES

SWEDISH (estimated)
Peasant levies including
some regular troops: 8–10,000
Mounted knights: 1–2000
Total: **9–12,000**

DANISH (estimated)
Regular Danish troops: 3000
German mercenaries: 3000
Total: **6000**

defences. At regular intervals were openings for cannon – a new form of weaponry that came as a unpleasant surprise to the Swedes. This Brunkeberg camp was pivotal to Danish strategy. Had King Christian kept on the defensive he might have secured a victory by attrition. Sten Sture would have had to relieve Stockholm and this would have forced him to attack if the Danes remained on the defensive.

DISPOSITIONS

Both sides were quietly confident that they would win. The Danes had skill, better weapons and a fortified camp to bolster their chances. The Swedes, however, were fighting on home ground and knew the terrain far better than their enemy. On the high, wooded and boulder-strewn ridge of

During the following day Sten Sture's army marched from Järva and took up position, under cover of darkness during the night of 9/10 October, just northwest of St Klara. On the morrow not only his but his entire country's fate would hang in the balance, but he was sure that his strategy would work. Christian's plan was to lure the Swedes into fighting in the open, to be annihilated by a modern European-style army. But Sten Sture had no intention of doing what the king wanted. Instead he would use a simple but shrewd plan to trap, overwhelm and defeat the Danes.

While his army attacked the Danes from the front against the slopes leading up to their camp and the St Klara convent, Nils Sture would take his Darlecarlians around the ridge to the north. Once they had crossed it and made their way east they would regroup on Ladugårdslandet, where the inhabitants of the capital grazed their cattle. As quickly as possible, Nils would then attack the vulnerable rear of the Danish position from the east and hopefully overcome the Danes through a combination of surprise and sheer numbers.

To make doubly sure that this strategy would work, Sten Sture had ordered Knut Posse, the Commandant of Stockholm, to put his troops and armed Stockholm burghers into boats, row across the narrow canal separating the capital from the mainland and land on the opposite shore. Posse was to attack the Danes holding St Klara in the rear and give Christian a nasty surprise. Now if everything went according to Sten Sture's plan the Danes would be attacked on three sides giving them two simple options: fight to the death where they stood or flee for their lives towards their anchored fleet. Only the unfolding battle the following day would show if Sten Sture's clever plan would work.

THE BATTLE BEGINS

By early morning the Swedes were in position. The battle began at 11.00 a.m. and would continue for four gruelling and bloody hours. The Swedes fired volley after volley of arrows at the Danish camp and positions. The Danes, better equipped and with modern weaponry, answered with cannon fire. Sten Sture launched his first attack against the Danish troops sited around St Klara. Unfortunately for him the Danes and the German mercenaries held fast – here the terrain, compared with the Brunkeberg, was relatively open and flat giving them an advantage. The attack failed miserably and Swedish morale slumped momentarily while the Danes' contempt for their enemy soared: as they had believed all along the Swedes were surely nothing but poorly armed and badly led peasants masquerading as troops. This arrogance was to cost them dear, as they underestimated their enemy. It also made them oblivious to the trap that was slowly being sprung by the shrewd and cautious Sten Sture.

Sten Sture regrouped his men, whose discipline and morale held for another

In this seventeenth-century Swedish propaganda lithograph, Sten Sture – by this time a Swedish national hero – is shown leading an army of knights in regular formation through the Danish throng, with the Swedish flag of three crowns aloft.

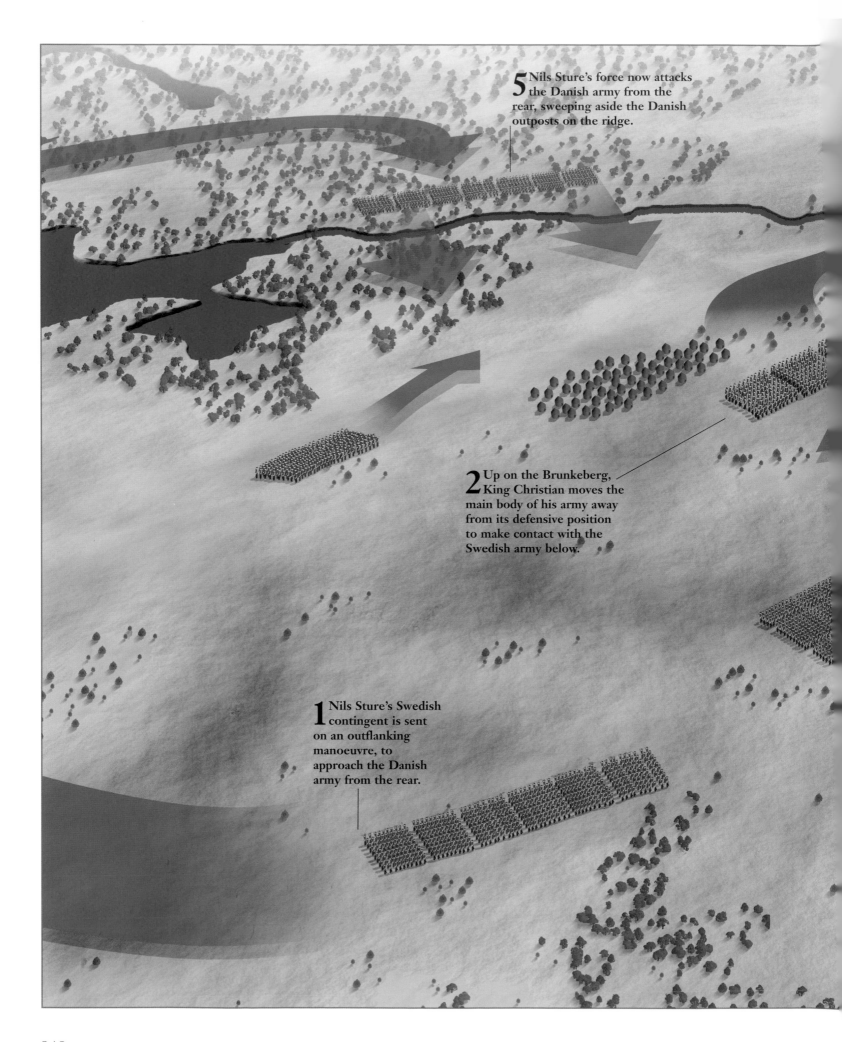

5 Nils Sture's force now attacks the Danish army from the rear, sweeping aside the Danish outposts on the ridge.

2 Up on the Brunkeberg, King Christian moves the main body of his army away from its defensive position to make contact with the Swedish army below.

1 Nils Sture's Swedish contingent is sent on an outflanking manoeuvre, to approach the Danish army from the rear.

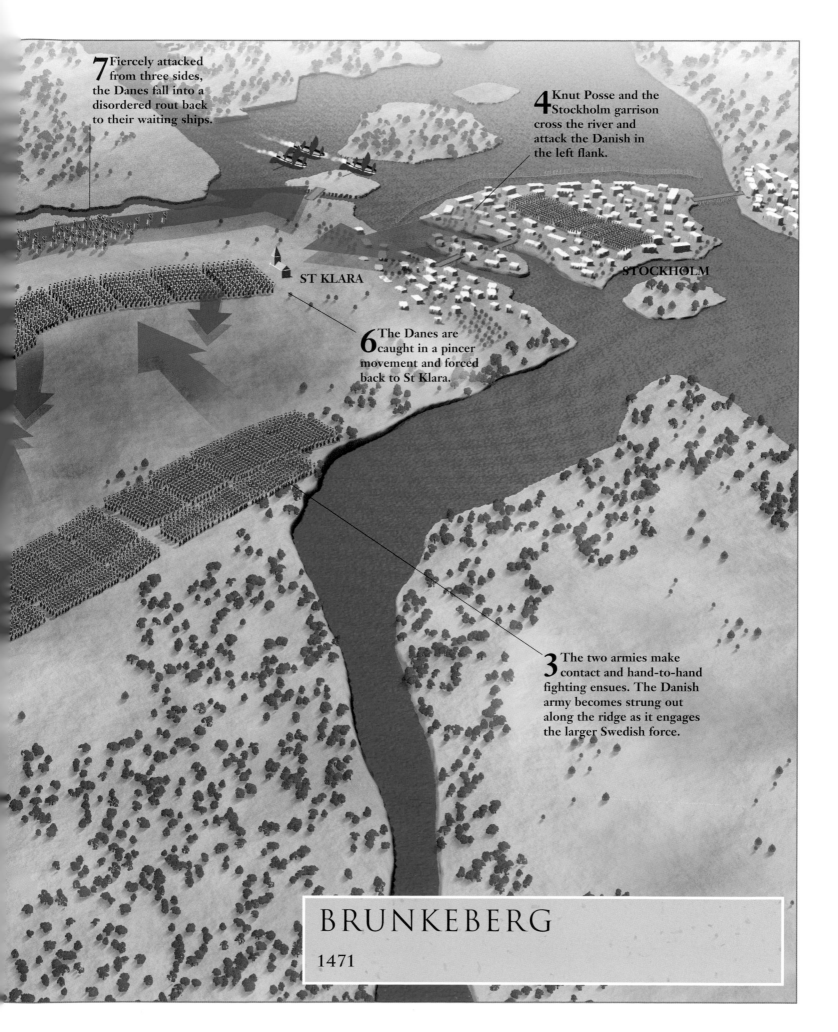

7 Fiercely attacked from three sides, the Danes fall into a disordered rout back to their waiting ships.

4 Knut Posse and the Stockholm garrison cross the river and attack the Danish in the left flank.

ST KLARA

STOCKHOLM

6 The Danes are caught in a pincer movement and forced back to St Klara.

3 The two armies make contact and hand-to-hand fighting ensues. The Danish army becomes strung out along the ridge as it engages the larger Swedish force.

BRUNKEBERG

1471

BRUNKEBERG

Sten Sture, from a sixteenth-century painting (National Museum of Stockholm). It shows him in his twilight years when the wars and struggles that followed his victory of 1471 had taken their toll.

attack that was met by the Danes. Seeing his exposed corps around St Klara threatened by this second Swedish offensive, Christian committed his troops. They left the safety of the camp and counter-attacked in the open to save the St Klara position. Danish self-confidence soared as their flanking attack against the Swedes seemed to take effect. The battlefront was now one long chain of fighting men stretching for almost a kilometre (0.6 miles) through partially open fields and rocky woodland. It was close-quarters fighting, man against man with axes, pikes, swords, spears, cudgels and daggers. The continuing battle had distracted the Danes as Sten Sture's strategy of encirclement began to take shape. Finally, by the afternoon, Nils Sture's Darlecarlians were in position to the east

while the Stockholm garrison rowed as silently as they could for the opposite shore.

SURPRISE ATTACKS

Nils Sture signalled for his men to advance. The Danish outposts were swiftly and brutally dealt with. Then, when they reached the Danish camp the Darlecarlians, the most feared of the Swedes, launched themselves at the poorly defended ramparts facing east with a roar. Meanwhile, led by Posse and Trolle, the Stockholm troops had landed on the shore and regrouped rapidly for an attack towards the convent, where they hoped to surprise and overwhelm the Danish defenders. It worked. The Danes were taken completely by surprise by Posse's attack. Here the training and superior arms of the king's troops were of little avail as wave after wave of snarling Swedes poured in on them from all sides.

The Danes were no weaklings and as professional troops fought back with controlled ferocity and great skill. But there were too many of the enemy as the infantry fought a hand-to-hand battle while the mounted Danish knights were unhorsed one by one. As they came crashing down, the knights were bludgeoned or stabbed to death by the peasant soldiers they had held in such contempt at the beginning of the battle. Christian shared his knights' contempt for the enemy and the usurper-rebel Sten Sture, and had thus expected an easy triumph once the Swedes were committed to battle. Instead it was his army that had walked blindly into a trap. Now, as the horrified king saw his men dying and his proud army buckling under the enemy's onslaught, the question was how much, if any, of his army could be saved?

The Swedes were not having everything their own way, however. Knut Posse – in contrast to Sten Sture – led his men from the front and paid a terrible price for his bravery. Danish crossbowmen hit him in the legs and then a Dane or a German infantryman hit him over the head with an axe. He was carried, dying from his wounds, back to Stockholm. Nevertheless, his demise did not dampen the resolve of the Swedes, who scented victory and redoubled their efforts to destroy the enemy. Christian had committed a series of blunders and he

may have had his faults as a commander but cowardice was not one of them. He ordered his personal guard to join him at the very centre of the fighting to drive back the Swedes and rally his faltering men. Perhaps the king was courting death, preferring to meet an honourable end in battle rather than survive a defeat. His bravado ended abruptly as he was hit by a small cannonball, leaving him badly wounded. His place was taken by one of his toughest and bravest commanders, Count Strange Nielsen, who tried to rally the troops carrying the *Dannebrog* (the white and red Royal Danish flag). He was killed outright.

The Danes and Germans began to waver and break. A handful of fleeing men became a hundred and then the flow of retreating soldiery became a torrent of panic-stricken and terrified humanity with only one thought on their mind: to flee. There was now no pretence of a well-

ordered retreat – it was a rout and it ended in tragedy as the rickety bridge between the mainland and the island of Käpplingeholm collapsed under the enormous weight of fleeing men and horses. Danish boats, sent out from the fleet, rowed up to shore and picked up survivors. Once those that could be saved had been taken aboard, the fleet sailed back to Copenhagen. King Christian had lost half his men – some 900 had drowned, another 900 had capitulated to the triumphant Swedes at the camp and the rest lay dead on the battlefield.

AFTERMATH

Sten Sture had saved Sweden's fledgling statehood and independence but it had been a dearly bought victory for the Swedes. For the next 250 years Denmark and Sweden fought a series of bloody wars against each other with all the hatred and ferocity showed at Brunkeberg.

Sweden has no contemporary artwork from 1471 depicting the Battle of Brunkeberg, but this late medieval manuscript illustration celebrates the Swedish victory over the Danes in fanciful terms.

PICTURE AND ILLUSTRATION CREDITS

All maps and black-and-white line artworks produced by **JB Illustrations**.

AKG-Images: 16 (Biblioteque Nationale), 21 (British Library), 28 (Erich Lessing), 36, 37 (Electa Fuer Italien Gesperrt), 43, 79 (Cameraphoto),
  87 (British Library), 89 (British Library), 124 (British Library), 166, 170, 175, 206
Art Archive: 49
Art-Tech/MARS: 11, 15, 18, 20, 24–25, 118, 146, 147, 177, 207
John Batchelor: 195 (t), 205 (b)
Bridgeman Art Library: 57, 86 (Biblioteque Municipale), 107 (K. Savitsky Art Museum), 156, 164 (Worcester Art Museum), 168, 174 (Museum Naradowe),
  178, 197 (Mucha Trust)
Corbis: 30, 33, 46, 47, 50, 53, 63, 68, 69, 70, 72, 92–93, 96, 97, 104, 110, 114, 128, 145, 161, 171, 183, 188, 190, 205 (t)
Mary Evans Picture Library: 26, 27, 29, 32, 40, 58, 59, 83, 100, 105, 116, 122–123, 135, 139 (r), 141, 151, 154–155, 158, 167, 176, 179, 186, 187, 194, 195 (b)
Getty Images: 39, 78, 101, 119, 125, 126, 134, 136, 140, 148, 185
Heritage Image Partnership: 62, 98, 129, 144, 157, 198
Malta Tourism Authority/visitmalta.com: 108
Nationalmuseum, Stockholm: 210, 211, 214, 215
Photos 12: 61 (ARJ), 77 (ARJ), 80 (ARJ), 82 (ARJ), 106 (Collection Cinema), 115 (Oronoz), 133 (Oasis), 201 (ARJ), 204 (ARJ)
TopFoto: 12
TRH Pictures: 52, 98, 139 (l), 150, 160, 182, 184